The
Student
Writer

The
Student
Writer

Kathryn R. Fitzgerald
Jamie McBeth Smith
The University of Utah

HarperCollins*Publishers*

Sponsoring Editor: Jane Kinney
Project Editor: Thomas R. Farrell
Art Direction/Cover Coordinator: Heather A. Ziegler
Text Design: N.S.G. Design
Cover Design: Zina Scarpulla
Cover Illustration: Thomas Thorspecken
Production: Paula Keller

For permission to use copyrighted material,
grateful acknowledgment is made to the
copyright holders on page 261, which is
hereby made part of this copyright page.

The Student Writer

Library of Congress Cataloging-in-Publication Data

Fitzgerald, Kathryn R.
    The student writer / Kathryn R. Fitzgerald, Jamie McBeth Smith.
      p.   cm.
    Includes index.
    ISBN 0-06-046323-6
    1. English language—Rhetoric.   I. McBeth Smith, Jamie.
  II. Title.
  PE1408.F464   1991
  808′.042—dc20   90-47317
                                                                    CIP

91 92 93 94   9 8 7 6 5 4 3 2 1

We dedicate this book with love to our families

Gene, Erin, and Andrew Fitzgerald
and Bill and Peg Remmele
KRF

Charles and Ian Smith
and James and Laura McBeth
JMS

Contents

C H A P T E R 3

Character Sketch   22

C H A P T E R 6

Analyzing and Classifying Product Names   76

------------------------------- ◈ ----------------------------------

C H A P T E R 7

Structural Analysis of an Advertisement   97

---◆---

C H A P T E R 8
Expository Essay   115

CHAPTER 9
Summary Writing   140

C H A P T E R   1 0

Documented Expository Essay   169

Handbook

Preface

We wrote this book to meet specific needs that we felt were not met in currently available process-oriented textbooks for beginning college writers. First, we wanted a book that *really* taught the writing process; that is, one that guided students through a series of full-length writing assignments, not one that focused on components of the process divorced from the product. Second, we wanted a text that prepared students for academic writing, and that made students aware of how the writing they were doing in our classes would directly contribute to improved writing in other college courses. Third, we wanted a text that began each writing assignment by having students explore ideas and then find the forms to fit the ideas, rather than fitting ideas to forms. Finally, we wanted our students to feel in control of their own writing processes by the time they completed our courses, so that they no longer had to rely on teachers' feedback to write and revise their own texts.

Organization

Each chapter of this text coaches students through the process of writing a full-length essay. Each chapter's assignments progress from the kinds of writing with which students tend to be familiar to the genres more specific to the college setting. The table of contents, therefore, looks familiar, moving from descriptive and narrative writing through expository essays and summary writing to a documented expository essay.

Actually, each assignment pushes students to use analytical processes by asking them to examine their subject matter to find a point of interest appropriate to a larger audience. In this way, from the beginning, students are working with a fundamental requirement of college writing, that they move beyond subject matter itself to consider it in the context of larger issues and audiences.

Chapters are sequenced in other ways. Later chapters build on the skills learned in earlier chapters. For instance, Chapter 5, on narrative, incorporates descriptive and anecdotal writing about objects, places, and people practiced in Chapters 2, 3, and 4. Chapters 6 and 7, each of which makes assignments dealing with advertising, use descriptive techniques while introducing students to the organizational structures of expository writing. The assignment in Chapter 8, an expository essay about a topic of the students' own choosing, explicitly defines expository structures and introduces various kinds of evidence students can develop to support their own points. Chapter 9 teaches summary techniques at the same time that it reviews various expository formats. Chapter 10 requires students to write an expository essay using evidence from their research and personal experience and serves as a culmination of the work of the course.

Though each chapter works with sentence and diction concerns appropriate to its assignment, we have provided a handbook as the final section of the textbook to allow teachers to offer students additional instruction in specific areas of grammar, usage, and mechanics.

Special Features

Each chapter integrates prewriting and drafting activities into its full-length writing assignment. Prewriting begins with the reading at the beginning of each chapter, which serves both as stimulus for ideas and as a model for student writing. Readings address thought-provoking topics like self-understanding, familial relationships, stereotyping, racism, advertising, and ability grouping in schools. As models, the readings demonstrate the style, structure, and format of a variety of genres (essay, newspaper story, textbook, and scholarly writing), some of which the students themselves will attempt. Authors vary from students to scholars and from frequently anthologized writers to some who, we are fairly certain, have never been anthologized.

The reading questions are designed to do more than simply help students to understand content and theme. They also address the issues of audience, point, structure (unity, cohesion, sequence), and evidence with which students will be working in their own writing. In other words, they learn about the writing concerns they must address in their own writing through discussing the reading questions.

As students discuss the reading questions, they are already moving toward the invention stage of writing. While the discussion questions and class brainstorming exercises provide a public forum for exchanging ideas, journal writing assignments encourage students to think privately about their responses to readings and their own related experiences.

The heart of each chapter is the collaborative activities that support the drafting stages of writing. Every chapter (except the first) guides students through at least two drafts before the final draft. Students' attention is focused on the development of the content and point in the first draft and on meeting the more conventional requirements for form and organization in the second. Surface error editing is reserved for the third and final draft.

All but two chapters (the introductory and summary chapters) conclude with unedited examples of our own students' final drafts of each assignment. Also, we include a set of criteria for students to use to evaluate the examples, their peers' writing, and their own drafts. Instructors can use these samples of student writing in a variety of ways, for instance, as a model for productive peer-group discussions as editing exercises.

The text includes enough material for a two-quarter or two-semester sequence of courses. If the course is only one quarter or semester, however, the wealth of material allows teachers to select and sequence the chapters to meet their own students' needs best.

The accompanying instructor's manual discusses in greater depth the purposes and rationale for each writing assignment, suggests ways of using the materials, and offers advice for handling the typical problems students encounter as they attempt to write the various assignments.

We have developed and used this manuscript over the past several years, and we are convinced that this approach helps students to understand and meet the requirements of college writing. The students will also gain confidence in their own ability to continue writing independently in other courses and no longer have to rely on the instructor's feedback to write and revise their own texts.

Acknowledgments

We wish to acknowledge the contributions of our colleagues at the University of Utah; writing teachers who have used these materials and offered their invaluable suggestions for revision: Dean Rehberger, Helen Hogan, Regina Oost, Nancy Tippets, Eric Walker, Bernie Wood, and the others such as Patricia Sullivan whose ideas have enriched these materials. We also wish to thank Paul Mogren for sharing his expertise on research technology important to the preparation of Chapter 10. As well, our heartfelt thanks goes to Wendy Fuller and Laurel Brown for their help in preparing the manuscript and to Michael Rudick, Director of the University Writing Program, for his support throughout the production of this manuscript. And finally, our deep gratitude goes to Susan Miller, without whom this project would never have been conceived, and, of course, to our students of the past ten years, whose writing development has made our efforts worthwhile.

KATHRYN R. FITZGERALD
JAMIE MCBETH SMITH

The
Student
Writer

Beginning the Process

INTRODUCTION

It is probably not much of an exaggeration to say that the process of writing is a lot like that of living—we learn about the process by doing it, and by having some fun along the way. Sometimes the process is joyful, seemingly effortless; sometimes it is worrisome and difficult; sometimes it is humdrum, its meaning elusive; sometimes it is clear and defined; sometimes we know what we want from it, and sometimes we do not.

Sometimes when writing, we have unrealistic expectations of ourselves. We expect to know exactly what we think about a topic, exactly why we think the way we do, and exactly how to convince our readers of the importance of our thoughts. We develop these expectations because of what we read. When we read published writing, it seems clear that the writers knew from the beginning their opinion about a topic and what evidence to use to convince us of its importance. We must realize, however, that we are reading the final version of the author's writing, a version that has been reached after a careful process of writing and rewriting.

To become more realistic about what to expect from ourselves as we write, we must learn what the writing process entails and how to use that process (1) to make sense of a topic for ourselves and to discover our purpose in writing and (2) to make sense of both the topic and purpose for our readers.

This book is designed to help you master the writing process by teaching you effective strategies to practice as you write college essays. The essay is a particularly useful writing form to master because it is widely used not only in colleges and universities, but also outside academia as well: many articles in magazines and some articles in newspapers are essays. Regardless of where successful essays appear—in a classroom, in a newspaper, as an editorial, in a popular magazine, or in a scholarly journal—they all have certain elements in common that can serve as guidelines for writers to follow.

Guidelines for Writing Essays

The following guidelines apply to all essays:

1. Essay writers must make a specific audience interested in their topic. For writing students this audience can include many people but must include classmates as well as the professor of the course.
2. Essay writers must state, or at least imply, their **point** of view, or opinion, about a topic either at the beginning or at the end of the essay.
3. Essay writers must supply evidence in the body of their essay to convince their audience of the value of their point of view.
4. Essay writers need to explain why their audience should care about the topic and the point of view in the essay's conclusion.

Why Write Essays?

So far you have read about what to expect from an essay and are probably asking why it is important to learn how to write one. Writing essays obligates you to find out what you think about a topic. You begin to "think" by remembering and writing down any knowledge you have about your topic. This knowledge includes personal experiences with the topic along with information learned from others—teachers, friends, parents—as well as information learned from reading and other research. Thinking also means that you analyze the information that you have remembered and written down. In other words, you ask yourself what this information means and why it is important. This analysis leads you to formulate a point of view, or point, about your topic, and you will find that you have arrived at an understanding of your topic that you did not have at the beginning of the writing process. Thus, writing educates you, and in turn, what you write may help educate others, too.

To write fine essays, you do not have to be an authority on a topic. However, you do have to acquire an interest in the topic, the energy to formulate a point of view about it, and the willingness to learn how to write clearly, concretely, and fully in support of your point. With this in mind, you are now ready to begin your first assignment, a warm-up, or introduction, to essay writing.

WRITING ASSIGNMENTS

Each chapter of this textbook helps you to work through the process of writing a full-length essay. At the beginning of each chapter is a brief description of the kind of essay you will be writing. The readings, journal assignments, questions, exercises, and group activities that follow the description will help you discover what you want to say and how to write each assignment. As you and your classmates work through the chapters, you will also be practicing the steps that are common to all writing. If you get into the habit of using these steps, you will find that they work for writing in all of your college classes.

This chapter provides an introduction to the concept of essay writing and the stages of the process. Here is the writing assignment for this chapter:

> Choose a topic; make a point (that is, express an opinion) about it; support your point with evidence; and explain why that point is important to your audience.

Don't try to do the whole assignment right now. Relax. Read the information below about the writing process. Then begin to work through the process as your teacher instructs.

THE WRITING PROCESS: INVENTION

Brainstorming

The first step of the writing process is to choose a topic that you find interesting. Do not just settle on the first topic that occurs to you. Instead, as a class, in a small group, or on your own, *create* a list of possible topics by quickly jotting down any topics that occur to you without being critical about them or discarding them no matter how difficult, common, or offbeat they may seem. This activity is called **brainstorming.** It is a technique that you will use frequently to get as many ideas as possible from which to choose. It stimulates creativity by generating numerous writing possibilities, which is important as you begin to find various topics and explore approaches to them.

Freewriting

After you have generated a number of topics, the next step is to review them and briefly list possible points (opinions you may have) and audiences for each topic. Then, pick the topic on this list that yields the most information and write down, in as much detail as you can, your answers to the following questions:

1. **What do I think about this topic?** or **What do I want to say about this topic?**

    Your answer(s) will lead you to state a variety of possible points or opinions about the topic, one of which you will choose as the major point to make and to support in your essay.

2. **Why do I think so?**

    Your answers to this question will lead you to develop evidence to support your point.

3. **Why is what I think important, and who else would think so?**

    Your answers here will force you to think about who your audience should be and thus to state the significance of your point and topic not only to yourself but to your audience as well.

Remember, your purpose in answering these questions is simply to get the ideas down. That is why this process is called **freewriting.** Do not worry yet about the order of your ideas or the correctness of your grammar, spelling, or punctuation. When you have finished your freewriting, you should be able to choose from it a major point to make about the topic; you should know toward which audience to direct your point; you should have compiled some evidence to support that point; and you should understand your purpose in writing about the topic. Examples of possible purposes you might have for writing are to clear up a common misunderstanding about the topic, to add little-known information to a familiar topic, or to offer advice about a topic with which you have had a lot of experience.

An Example of the Invention Process

Before you begin this process on your own, it will help if you follow the brainstorming and freewriting process of another class. Here is a list of topics one class brainstormed:

1. Students attitudes toward taking preparatory writing courses
2. Advantages and/or disadvantages of working part-time and going to school full-time (or vice versa)
3. Time management for new college students
4. The first day of college—expectations versus reality
5. Living on campus versus living in an apartment
6. Living at home versus living on your own
7. Differences between night classes and day classes

Obviously, and understandably, this class was preoccupied with issues affecting new college students. They all had something to say about topic 2, so they discussed possible answers to the freewriting questions. Acting as their **scribe,** a person whose job is to record, not generate ideas the group wants written, the instructor took notes on the blackboard as they dictated.

1. **What do I (we) think about having a job and going to school?**
    a. It has some *advantages*.
        (1) Working gives you the money to help pay for school and living expenses (tuition, fees, books, room and board), or maybe just gives you a little extra to go out (movies, dinner, concerts) or to buy some things you want (clothes, cosmetics, athletic equipment, music equipment).
        (2) It gives you a break from school and studying (because you often get to meet different people or at least socialize with your co-workers).
        (3) It gives you experience and makes you more responsible (because you have to learn how to work well with others and get your job done if you want to get paid).

    b. It also has some *disadvantages*.
        (1) You really do not make too much money (for example, if you make minimum wage, you cannot possibly pay for both school and living expenses) and rarely receive benefits (insurance) in the jobs available to students (salesclerks, restaurant workers, janitorial workers . . .), especially if you work only part-time.
        (2) Working cuts down on your social life (because sometimes you have to work odd hours or on holidays when nobody else wants to work).
        (3) Working can interfere with your studies (because sometimes you cut classes or miss your study time if your boss asks you to work longer hours or changes your work schedule).
        (4) The pressure of working and going to school can contribute to illness (because you sometimes skip meals and lose sleep and get rundown) and depression (because you may not have enough time to do "nothing" or be with your family and friends and still keep up with all your work as well as friends).

According to this class, the major point (or opinion) to draw from all of the freewriting to question 1 is that, in the short run, there are more disadvantages than advantages in having to work while going to school. Then the class went on to answer freewriting question 2:

2. Why do I think so?

The class pointed out that all of the advantages and disadvantages they had itemized in freewriting question 1 supplied **evidence,** that is, specific reasons and examples, to support their more general point, or opinion, that working while going to school had more disadvantages than advantages. Then they went on to discuss freewriting question 3:

3. Why is what I (we) think important, and who else would think so?

The topic is important because it affects so many students: knowing about the advantages and disadvantages of working while going to school can help them decide whether or not they want to work if they are lucky enough to have that choice. The more likely audience, however, is students who have to work. They will find this topic important because they will need to know about its positive and negative aspects before they can realistically begin to cope with the challenges of their situation.

If we review the brainstorming and freewriting process of this class, we can see that the students have discovered the main point to make about their topic, the audience to whom the point is directed, the significance of that point for their audience, and supporting evidence for the point that the audience would find convincing. Finally, although the students did not directly state their purpose for writing about their topic, it seems clear that they discovered it by the time they finished freewriting.

Exercise 1   Review the conclusions the class reached as it brainstormed and freewrote:

1. Restate their point.
2. Name their audience.
3. State the point's significance for that audience.
4. State the author's purpose for writing about their topic.

Exercise 2   As you read through the above example of brainstorming and freewriting, you may have thought of other points to make or other evidence to add. Also, you may have noticed that the topic the students chose provides background information for, and thus closely relates to, another topic on their list—the importance of effective time management for new college students. If your instructor wishes, as a class or in small groups, answer the freewriting questions about this topic, or else brainstorm for, and freewrite about, a topic of your own class's choice.

◈ Journal Assignment

In this text, you will use the journal assignments as brainstorming and free-writing tools. They will aid you in developing ideas for your essays.

On your own, brainstorm a list of topics you might write about. Then, choose one and answer the freewriting questions, pages 5–6.

THE WRITING PROCESS: DRAFTING

First-Draft Guidelines

Now you are ready to write a **draft,** or preliminary version, of your essay. This means that you order your ideas with your audience in mind; you do not just jot them down as they occur to you. To help you draft your essay, let us review what an audience expects when reading an essay. An audience expects to be able to

1. identify the topic of your paper in the introductory paragraph(s).
2. find your point in either the introductory or closing paragraph(s).
3. follow the development of the evidence that supports your point in the body of your essay.
4. read a conclusion that emphasizes the significance of the topic and your point for your particular audience.

As you write your first draft, remember that your purpose in drafting is to make your private writing public, so follow the above four steps to help you keep your audience's needs in mind.

◈ Responding to the Writing of Others

The Importance of Group Work

All writers need some response to their writing before they can revise it, and no one is in such a good position to respond to your writing as your classmates. Having gone through much the same process as you, they will empathize with your struggles; yet, having a different topic from yours, they may be able to see and point out your essay's strengths and weaknesses more objectively than you. They will also have a strong interest in reading your paper because they may pick up some ideas for revising their own papers.

Empathy with your classmates' writing processes and a strong self-interest in learning from their writing, as well as from their comments on your writing, combine to help you learn how to edit and revise your essays successfully. In addition, discussion questions for group work are offered in every chapter of this text to provide guidelines for responding to each other's essays and to help you revise your own essays.

Directions for Group Work

After you have written your first draft, make three photocopies of it so that three of your classmates can read and make comments on your draft. Meet in groups of four. Read your classmates' essays through once very carefully. Then answer the following questions on the draft itself:

1. Can you find the topic of the essay clearly stated in the opening paragraph? If so, circle it.
2. Can you find a clearly stated point within the first paragraph? If so, underline it.
3. Is the point directed toward a particular audience? If so, name the audience.
4. Examine the evidence in the body of the essay:
   a. Does the evidence support the essay's point? In other words, can you identify information in the paper that does not seem to belong there? If so, put parentheses ( ) around the questionable supporting evidence.
   b. Are there statements in the body of the paper that need more evidence to support them? That is, do some parts of the paper need more explanation to make sense? If so, put brackets [ ] around the statements that need more support and write "Evidence?" above them.
5. Does the concluding statement or paragraph convince you, or whomever you think the audience is, of the importance of the topic and of the point the author makes? Write briefly, explaining why you are or are not convinced by the essay.

After you have read and commented on your classmates' essays, return the copies to them and discuss your responses.

Revising Your Draft

When the copies of your own essay are returned, carefully look over the responses because they will help you make revisions and write the final version. Check to see if your readers accurately identified your topic and point. If they did not, what is the reason?

1. Did you make a specific point about your topic, or did you instead identify the topic and list facts about it?
2. Did you make many points, without focusing on one of them or without providing evidence to support them?

Look at your evidence.

1. If any of it is in parentheses, could it be that it is not evidence but another point that needs support? If so, provide that support.
2. If any of it is in brackets, could it be that you left out explanations because you thought they were obvious? If so, explain or illustrate your statements in greater detail because readers unfamiliar with the topic will not understand what you think is "obvious."

Look at the comments about your conclusion.

1. If your readers found the conclusion unconvincing, is it because you were unclear about who your audience was?
2. Or is it because you made claims that you really did not illustrate in the body of the essay?

All of these questions should help you determine what you need to add, delete, or change to revise your draft before you turn in the final version of the essay. Remember, however, that *you* control what to revise, and you are under no obligation to act on your classmates' responses, which are advice, not orders. On the other hand, if you received very little response from your classmates, point out areas in your paper about which you would like some advice, and ask them to respond.

Evaluation Criteria

In addition to your group work, here are some criteria for evaluating the essay.

1. The essay should have an introduction containing two features:
   a. an identifiable topic
   b. a point directed toward a particular audience
2. The essay should have a body containing evidence that supports the point.
3. The essay should have a conclusion stressing the importance of the topic and point to the audience.

THE WRITING PROCESS: EDITING

Final-Draft Activities

So far we have emphasized how to get (brainstorm), develop (freewrite), and order (draft) ideas for an essay. Now, the last step you must follow before turning in the final essay is to edit for grammatical, spelling, and punctuation errors. In the following chapters, you may have specific editing assignments for each essay, but for this first essay you should have a friend, parent, or classmate proofread your essay and point out the errors. If you have questions about the errors found, ask your instructor about them or attach a note to the final version of the essay explaining what and where you think your grammar, spelling, and punctuation errors are. That way your instructor will be able to answer your questions and know what kind of editing assignments to give you to help you correct your errors.

Also, so that your instructor can help your work group function smoothly, write a note to him or her evaluating your group's response to this essay. Explain why you found it helpful or unhelpful.

SUMMARY

This chapter provided you with an overview of the purpose and process of essay writing by having you write. In the future, you should return to this information as a guide for any paper you may have to write. In the following chapters, we will review, expand upon, and help you to apply everything you have attempted in this chapter.

Descriptive Essay

WRITING ASSIGNMENT

The writing assignment due at the end of this chapter is a descriptive essay in which you will describe an object or a place that is important to you. You will use vivid details to recreate the object or place in your reader's mind and to show why it is important to you. The reading below, "The Red Car" by Louis Kirchoff, is an example of the kind of paper you will write.

Why Write a Descriptive Essay?

Much of what is written in college begins with a clearly written description of carefully observed detail. Although what is observed can vary from a dissected pig in a zoology class to the reactions of human or animal subjects in a psychology experiment to the composition of an advertisement in a communication class, college writing is often based on description. However, the writing usually does not stop there. When you read Louis Kirchoff's description below, you will see that he does not stop with a mere physical description of his subject, the car. He also develops the car's meaning, or significance, for him and his father. Similarly, college writers in nearly all fields of study develop broader generalizations or insights from the specific details they observe. Writing a descriptive paper to support an insight about a place or object gives you practice in this important kind of college writing.

INVENTION: READING, WRITING, AND TALKING FOR IDEAS

Reading

 The Red Car

Louis Kirchoff, student (age 29)

1   Giving the "For Sale" sign a final tap, I straightened up to look at the home in which I had grown up. I was the youngest by several years

of a family of six kids, but the only one still living in Orfordville, so it had fallen to me to take care of all the arrangements when Mom moved into the Good Samaritan home. Most of the furnishings had been sold at the house auction on Saturday, and the few unsold items had been loaded into the pickup and taken to Good Will. The flower beds, now simply dirt beds at the edge of the lawn, looked barren, and the naked windows without Mom's starched white curtains looked forlorn, but, to my surprise, as I rounded the corner of the house and viewed the weedy acre that had always been the backyard, what looked emptiest of all was the far corner where the old car had rested.

2   Hidden from the rest of the world, that old red sports car had died a slow death. The weeds that grew sparsely over the rest of the yard had surrounded and engulfed the car as though it had been a decaying animal. Once the toy of my dad's youth, it was given a new name in its decrepit state. We simply referred to it as "the red car."

3   My father always promised to resurrect the creature but somehow never found the time. I know that he really meant to, and not just because he talked about it. He sold the tires before I even remember, but left the engine intact. "It was a great engine," he said. "Could do 120 in its day . . . Could do it again, with a little work," he said. As I gazed at the spot where the car has rested, I realized that there were a lot of things that he had really meant to do, but had never seemed to find the time for. I think he just gave up on the car, like he did on so many other ideas. So the car had sat in its open grave, waiting.

4   In my earliest memories the red car was sitting on its rusted orange wheel rims in that back corner of the yard. Its once shiny red coat had already faded, and the small dents and scratches portended the greater ravages to come. As the rains and dusty winds worked at the chips in the paint, they spred rusty cancers that eventually ate through the metal, leaving open holes that allowed easy access for mice, cats, or just about anything that needed shelter. It even served as a nursery for a raccoon family one spring. The adult raccoons had crawled into the trunk from underneath the car, scrabbled up the trunk lining, added their own choice grasses and muds, and made a cozy home for their brood. Dad said to leave them alone—raccoons were too mean to fool with, and besides, they were just doing what came naturally.

5   But, whatever else the car sheltered, it was most important to us kids for housing our games and dreams. My friend Eddie and I played in it often. On the warm spring day when we would try to open the doors for the first time since late summer the previous year, the resistance of the weight of the wide doors together with the hinges seized by the winter's rust would almost overpower our small bodies. But finally, after pulling on the handle enough to open the door a crack, we could hook our fingers around the edge and, the two of us straining together, could

pull the door full open, its hinges squawking their resistance the whole way. Our reward was to be overwhelmed by the rank odors of mildew and animal leavings. That first day we would examine the winter's damage, noting the new holes in the dash that exposed the car's internal organs and the new tears in the sun-bleached upholstery from which stuffing protruded. We would clean out the interior a little, but playing inside was always more than we could stand that first day. So we'd open both doors and play escaping bank robbers, firing on the cops from behind the protection of the open doors. As the car aired out, our games changed. We would slide into the low bucket seats, pull the heavy doors closed, and pretend to gun the engine to readiness for the starting shot of the Indy 500. Or we raced over land and sea in the year 2005, escaping from aliens that wanted to eat our brains. Or we were spies, hiding powerful secret weapons in the holes in the dash.

6   As we got a little older, we would sometimes talk more seriously about fixing up the car. After all, that's what Dad was planning to do with it. We could learn how to repair those internal organs, could easily replace the ragged bucket seats, and could fill the rusted holes in the exterior and restore the shiny red finish. We would talk about all the girls who would fight over taking turns riding to and from school. We planned a trip to the ocean on a surfing safari after graduation. We had elaborate plans for the great times we were going to have and how we would make them come true.

7   The years passed, and Eddie moved to another town and another high school. My father finally sold what was left of the car to a junk dealer who came with a flatbed truck and hauled it away. So I was surprised when that spot where the car had rested seemed emptiest of all to me. It had really been empty for years now. I don't miss the car or wish it back. What I miss are all those things we talked about, all those things I was going to do but didn't. I turned and left the yard, my father's son.

⟡ Journal Assignments

1. Write a journal page about your reactions to "The Red Car." Did you like the reading? Why do you think Louis Kirchoff remembered the car so well? Do you have any similar memories? Were there any special or forbidden places in your home or neighborhood that had special meaning for you? You may write about these questions or other ideas that the reading brings to mind.

2. Write a paragraph explaining, in your own words, what the car meant to Louis Kirchoff. Then select one significant place or object in your life and write about what it means to you.

Reading Questions

Content

1. What do you know about the car itself?
2. What opinions have you formed about Kirchoff's father? Which details made you form these impressions?
3. What is your impression of the family as a whole?
4. What was the significance of selling the tires? Selling the car? What words and phrases help you to understand the significance?
5. Kirchoff never mentions the make of the sports car. Why do you think he does not?
6. What does the car represent to Kirchoff?

Structure

1. This essay moves between past and present time.
   a. In which paragraphs or sentences does Kirchoff speak as an adult looking back on his childhood?
   b. When does it seem more like the child is speaking?
   c. What does Kirchoff gain by speaking as both the child and the adult? In other words, what is Kirchoff able to show or say by using both perspectives that he couldn't have said if he used just one?
2. Why do you think Kirchoff began his description at the front of the house instead of in the spot where the car had been?
3. Underline and discuss words in the reading that appeal to each of the five senses—sight, hearing, touch, taste and smell. Which of the senses does he appeal to the most? Mention some of the words you think most effectively create an impression for the reader.
4. In any essay, all of the details should contribute to the support of the main point. You have already discussed the car's significance for Kirchoff. What does the information in each paragraph contribute to your understanding of its significance? Are there any details that do not seem to belong? Why or why not?

DRAFTING: WRITING, TALKING, REWRITING, AND EVALUATING

 Writing Assignment: More Information

You have used your journal writing to think about the car's significance to Louis Kirchoff and about some objects or places of significance to you. Now it is time to pick one of those places or objects and think about developing an essay describing it. Here are some things to keep in mind.

In this essay, your statement of point will be a sentence telling why the object or place is significant to you. Although explaining this significance may actually take several sentences, you should be able to sum up the ideas in one sentence that concisely states your point.

As you think about what your point should be, consider something that Louis Kirchoff said about his essay. "We all have a red car of some kind in our past"; in other words, we all have something like the car that represents broken dreams or unrealized intentions. Can you discover insights about your topic that might hold true for other people as well as yourself? If you can, you will have found the way to make your own topic significant to your audience (in this case your teacher and classmates) as well as to yourself.

Remember to describe your object or place with specific details so that your reader can know it as you know it. Select details that show why the object or place is significant.

Using Descriptive Details

Break up into writing groups of from three to five students. You will be using writing groups frequently throughout this course. Sometimes your group will practice specific writing techniques; sometimes you will help each other on your papers; sometimes you will work together to discuss or evaluate other writing samples. In every case, the group work is designed to contribute to your ability to write well.

When you work in writing groups, pick one student to be the scribe. Remember, the scribe's job is to record what the rest of the group tells him or her to write, not to come up with the ideas.

The exercises below give you practice in expressing an attitude, feeling, or opinion by using **descriptive details.** As you begin to write, you will find that you need to describe *sounds, smells, tastes,* and *textures* as well as *appearances.* These will result in vivid language.

Exercises

1. Pick one (or more) of the following topics. As a group, write a paragraph using specific details to show (rather than tell) the suggested attitude toward the topic. The purpose of this exercise is to give you practice discovering and selecting details to support a particular point or attitude.

   a. **A man in a deserted alley.**

   He makes you afraid. Describe him to demonstrate why you are afraid, but do not *say* you are afraid in the paragraph. *Show* us what makes you afraid.

He makes you feel sorry for him. Describe him to show why you feel sorry for him. Again, do not tell us in the paragraph that you feel sorry for him. *Show* us why.

b. **A German shepherd standing between you and the door of a house where you must make a delivery.**

She makes you afraid. Describe her to show why you are afraid. (Remember sounds as well as appearances.)

She makes you feel welcome. Describe her to show why you feel welcome.

c. **A used Camaro you are considering buying.**

You are convinced it is a great buy. Describe the car to show why.

You would not take it on a bet. Describe the car to show why. (You would not base your decision merely on exterior appearance. You would get in and start the engine, too. What smells or sounds would you notice?)

d. **Your boyfriend or girlfriend has just cooked his or her first meal for you.**

On the basis of this meal you decided this would be a lifetime relationship. Describe the meal to show why.

On the basis of this meal you broke up later that night. Describe the meal to show why.

2. One characteristic of good descriptive writing is the use of specific, concrete nouns, adjectives, and verbs. To learn how to incorporate such vivid language into your writing, work together as a group to rewrite the following paragraphs to make the language more vivid. Some of the dull words in the paragraph are italicized to give you a few ideas about which words to change, but do not limit yourselves to those words. Feel free to change words or add new words or phrases to help your reader visualize the situation and feel the emotions of the writer.

(a) *Example* The second sentence in the paragraph below might be rewritten as follows:

Hundreds of people in front of me are jamming the subway stairs like a cork in the neck of a bottle.

It is rush hour and I am late for class. The *people* in front of me *moving* toward the subway stairs seem like a *wall*. I wonder if they would *move faster* if I *said* "Fire!" I decide against trying it. As they *move slowly* toward the exit stairs, I try to *get* between some people to *get* a little ahead. Finally, I *am* on the stairs and can see daylight. When I *am* on the street, I *move as fast as I can* toward my class building across the street. I do not have time *to get to* the corner, so I *cross in the middle of the block.* A couple of cars *stop suddenly;* another one *almost hits me. One cabbie is really mad.* Finally, I *make it across the street* and into my *safe class building.*

(b) *Example*   The fourth sentence in the paragraph below might be rewritten as follows:

When I started, the sky was a deep azure, and the sun shimmered overhead.

Usually I love storms, but this one was different. It *came out* of the Southwest *faster than anyone expected.* I was home alone, mowing the yard. When I *started the sun was shining.* I was *working so intently* that I never noticed the sky *become gray.* Suddenly I felt a chill. I looked up. The *clouds got thick and dense.* High winds *made the grain in the fields beyond the fence wave.* I ran to the shelter of the house. The clouds seemed to be *blowing in circles* instead of blowing straight across the sky. *The color of the sky was strange.* For the first time in my life, I *was really scared* of a storm.

3. Another way to practice using vivid language is to revise some of your own writing. You may do this either as a group or individually. Look through your journal pages for sentences that you now think can be improved. Rewrite one or two sentences by changing words or adding details to help the reader visualize your scene or feel your emotions. If you are working as a group, read the sentences you have selected to the group and get their help to rewrite them more vividly.

First-Draft Activities

Writing is usually considered a solitary activity. Students try to isolate themselves in quiet spots to concentrate. No one else sees the written work until it is turned in to the instructor. This isolation creates a lot of anxiety. Am I doing what the instructor wants? Did I understand the assignment? Is every student except me writing something brilliant? Have I said enough? Too much? Is this the best way to organize my ideas? In this class, your writing group will help you answer these questions before you hand in your work to your instructor. When you read each other's first draft, and later each other's second draft, you will find out whether you understood the assignment as they did, and you will see that your writing is no less brilliant than theirs. Your peers will also help you to make judgments about organization and content. And all this happens *before* you have to turn the paper in for a grade.

By now your first draft of your own description should be complete. Meet in your writing group to discuss the draft. Your teacher may assign your group one or more of the following activities. The purpose of each is to give you ways to evaluate your own writing and to figure out how to improve it.

1. Read your draft to the group. They will attempt to draw the place or object you are describing. If they get stuck, explain what they need to do. This means that your description was not detailed enough. Write down the same information you gave them to complete the drawing. Get the group members' help if you cannot figure out how to transform the information into sentences in your paper.

2. Read your draft to the group. Ask the group to pick out a sentence in which they cannot quite picture what you described. Explain it in more detail, and then get them to help you revise the sentence to include the new details.

3. Pass out photocopies of your draft to members of your group. Have them underline details that appeal to each of the five senses (sight, hearing, touch, taste, smell), using a different color pen or pencil for each sense. If your group finds lots of words that appeal to several of the senses, you have probably done a good job of using specific details. If your group finds only a few, it means that part of your revising job is to add vivid details to help the reader visualize your object or place.

Use the help your group has given you to write your second draft.

 Second-Draft Activities

Evaluation Criteria

Here are some criteria for evaluating a descriptive essay.

1. The essay should begin with a paragraph that contains
   a. some background information, that is, a **context,** introducing your topic to a particular audience
   b. a point, or dominant impression about the topic that you will develop in the essay. For this assignment the point is simply a statement telling why the object or place is significant to you.
2. The introductory paragraph should be followed by one or more body paragraphs that
   a. describe a place or object, not an experience or event

b. are developed with vivid descriptive details that reinforce the main point or dominant impression.

3. The essay should close by stressing the importance of your insight or dominant impression to your audience.

Sample Student Essays

Following are two essays written in response to this assignment by other students. Read each essay and decide, on the basis of the above criteria, which one is the better. Rank them 1 and 2.

The Trophy

1   When you walk into my apartment, you walk into the living room and you see an old wobbly desk that sits on long skinny legs. It holds a lot of things that are important to me because I am studying to become an electronic engineer, so I spend a lot of time there.

2   On the desk sits a small computer to which an old cassette recorder is connected to load programs into the computer. There are also two designer cinder blocks that hold a thick board that is used as a shelf. On the shelf sits a 13 inch black and white T.V. that is used as a computer monitor. On each side of the T.V. set are speakers that are connected to the T.V. Next to the right side of the T.V. are some programming books for the computer.

3   But something more important, is a trophy that stands about twelve inches tall. This is a baseball trophy. It has a baseball player standing on a platform poised to hit the ball. This is at the top of the trophy. In the middle of the trophy appears the year and on the bottom of the platform is engraved, "Champs." The baseball player stands about four inches tall. He is standing on a winner's platform that is about one inch tall. All of this is sitting on a marble stone. This stone is 3x3x2 inches. The stone is resting on an alulminum stand that is gold tinted with a black plate in the middle and a "84" emblem in the center of all this. The bottom of the trophy is another marble stone that is 3x3x2 inches and on the front is engraved, "Champs."

4   This trophy meant a lot to me when I was fifteen. It brings back memories of that year. All season long we were a real good team. The whole season riding down to the last play of the championship game. The score was tied, there were two outs the bases were loaded and I was up to bat. I can remember thinking as I walked to bat, "Why did Kirkman strike out?" Then it came to the last play. I didn't want to play another inning and I had three balls and two strikes and I was praying like everything to at least hit the ball. The pitcher threw the ball and it hit me in the nose and that walked in the winning run. I felt like I really deserved that trophy.

Summit County

1   The place which is most significant to me is the place where I grew up. This place happened to be Summit County, Colorado. I refer to Summit County as my home town although I am talking about the whole county rather then just the town where I was raised. My home town is a place where I have memories which are very special to me.

2   I remember the Christmas card scenes of snow covered rooftops and evergreen trees. I also remember the people and myself suffering as the winter came to an end. The torture came not from the disappointment of seeing the winter leave but from the time it took for the snow to go away. We'd see pictures on the evening news of Denver enjoying its spring and we would be jealous. Trips to Denver were planned when ever possible. There would be comments like, "It seems this winter will last forever." After six months of nothing but white landscapes and cold temperatures you would suffer to as the winter held back the spring as long as it possibly could. The suffering was just one of the many experiences which the people of summit county shared. Those types of experiences brings the people closer together.

3   To live in Summit County is to be a member of a special group. A group which, to me, is like no other group in the world.

4   When ever I return to Summit County I feel sad. I am an outsider there. I know my way around the county. I know every square inch of the county. I know what goes on at all the places but I am not among the people. I am not a member of the group anymore. I walk down the streets and watch the people go by. I see them driving home after going to the store. I watch people doing their things and I remember doing them to. They are actions which take place in the county which I don't do anymore because I don't live there. I know what it is like to do them. I wish I could do them again but I am not a Summit County person and I would have no practical purpose in doing them. I'm now just a visiter there and I have no need to perform these actions. I watch people riding skate boards and heading to the mall to hang out. I remember when I would go to the mall to hang out and be with my friends. If I went in the mall right now, no one would know me and I would not fit in with the crowd. I would just be another tourist.

5   Right now, I imagine myself sitting on one of the benches in front of the small, (in relation to a city) tan Frisco Mall. I become hungry and my mouth waters as the smell of sea food drifts up from the basement. Many people are walking by in front of me on the sidewalk and cars are zooming past on the street. A neighborhood kid speeds by on his dirt bike. He sharply makes a right turn and barely stops before hitting the glass front doors of the mall. He is probably going to the arcade or going

to "Teddy Bears" for ice cream. Thats what I used to do. I could go on forever describing the events which happens next. I just sit there looking sad and watching the people and remembering what it is like to live in Summit County. Its like watching my past. If someone sat down next to me and asked, "Why do you look so depressed?" I would say, "I used to live here. Its a great place." It feels so good to be depressed.

Evaluating the Sample Essays

Meet in writing groups. Compare your ratings with those of the other group members.

1. Did you agree on which was better? If so, discuss the characteristics that led you to assign each paper the rating you did.

2. Did you disagree? Take turns explaining why you assigned each paper the rating you did. Be sure to discuss your ratings in relation to the criteria. Try to agree as a group on the right rating for each essay. Be ready to defend your decisions in class discussions.

After each group reports to the class as a whole on its rating decisions, discuss how the papers succeeded or failed to meet the criteria.

Revising Your Second Draft

Reread and check your own second draft according to the criteria you just used to evaluate the sample essays. Use the criteria to help you see what to change as you write your final draft.

Type your final draft. (If you use a word processor, revising and typing can be done in the same step.)

EDITING

Final-Draft Editing

Work with a partner. Read your partner's paper, looking for spelling, typing, and punctuation errors. Do not make corrections on the paper. Just draw a little arrow in the margin pointing to the line with the error and tell your partner what you think is wrong.

If, as the writer, you agree that you have an error, neatly cross it out and make the correction with a black pen or a sharp pencil.

Postfinal-Draft Editing

Your teacher may assign specific corrections or revisions to make after grading the final draft.

C H A P T E R 3

Character Sketch

WRITING ASSIGNMENT

The paper due at the end of this chapter is an essay in which you describe the character of a person you know. Writers use two methods to describe a person's character. They often describe the person's appearance because character is sometimes reflected in physical appearance. They also tell very short true stories, or **anecdotes,** about incidents in the person's life that illustrate character. You will use both of these methods to write your character sketch.

Why Write a Character Sketch?

A character sketch is a more complicated kind of descriptive writing than a descriptive essay. You will again closely observe and vividly describe physical details, but this time the details will describe a person's appearance as part of developing your point about his or her character. And you will do more. You will also describe an incident (tell an anecdote) in which your subject does something that reveals the sort of person he or she is. So you will be using both descriptive details and **narrative,** that is, a story, incident, or anecdote, to make your point. Again, descriptive and narrative writing are two kinds of writing that college and professional writers frequently use to support the more general points they wish to make.

INVENTION: READING, WRITING, AND TALKING FOR IDEAS

Reading

The following reading is very much like the character description you will be writing. Your subject (the person you write about) may or may not be similar to the brother in the reading, but the methods you use to describe your person will be very similar.

My Big Brother

Jennifer Murphy

From the editors of Good Housekeeping: *Jennifer Murphy originally wrote this article for a writing class at the University of Georgia, where she's an Education major. Her family and an author friend suggested she submit it to Good Housekeeping.* We're glad she did.

1   My brother, Mark, was one of those kids other kids called a "Brain." Some just thought he was a little eccentric. Others considered him just plain weird. I thought he was terrific.

2   As a 12 year old, Mark was pudgy and awkward; coordination and agility described his intellect, not his athletic prowess. He wore glasses with thick lenses that were set in brown plastic rims. He also had a tendency to fasten every button of his shirt right up to his Adam's apple.

3   Mark was a solitary child by choice; his playmates were fantasies and "secret missions." A budding scientist, he had no time for a 10-year-old tag-along sister who could not seem to understand the significance of his lofty experiments. Yet, I desperately wanted to be admitted into his private universe.

4   Every Saturday when Mark peddled his 10-speed bike to the local science museum, I would follow, pumping my three-speed furiously behind him. He never bothered to check my progress, and I never removed my eyes from his hunched back as we sped along. At the museum I would sit silently by my brother's side in the planetarium show, and (when he was in an especially benevolent mood) Mark would point out a certain star or constellation. As he did, his deep brown eyes would sparkle just as brightly as the stars that were swirling above our heads.

5   "That's the Big Dipper," he would tell me, and I would nod my head slowly as if he had imparted some great and golden truth. For a brief few moments I was part of Mark's mysterious world, and I snatched the opportunity greedily.

6   Mark's bedroom at home was a museum in itself. Sometimes I would sneak inside when he was on one of his "secret missions" or sitting in front of the TV engrossed in *Star Trek*. He had a big bookcase containing what seemed like millions of books: *Dinosaurs, Lord of the Rings, Jonathan Livingston Seagull,* a series of encyclopedias. Next to the shelves were glass jars filled with glittering quartzite rocks. I remember staring at them, wishing I knew which planets they came from. In the corner was a chemistry set with test tubes, experimental dyes, and colored powders. On the windowsill sat a dried and browning cactus, the unfortunate product of too many experiments. However, a Venus's-flytrap and sprouting baking potato both thrived in their sunlit spot.

7   I knew Mark would be angry if he caught me in his room. But I never bothered anything—except an old shoebox he had labeled, "SECRET: KEEP OUT! CONFIDENTIAL!" The warning was too much for my 10-year-old curiosity to resist, and I lifted the cover to peek. Inside was a mess of papers: Mark's personal poems and stories. I quickly replaced the shoebox lid as if I had performed some kind of sacrilege and left.

8   One day, not long after, I was digging in the garden in our backyard when my shovel hit a hard surface. What was it? I dug deeper. Ah! It was Mark's white-and-black rocketship with USA decals on the sides! He must have lost it, I thought. And he must be searching everywhere for it.

9   I remembered the afternoon I had watched Mark carefully assemble the toy model. I looked at the rocketship now—dirty and moisture-warped—but so *beautiful*. I had an offering to present to Mark—and a chance to win his favor! Clutching the rocketship to my chest, I ran to find my brother.

10   I found him in a magnolia tree swinging from the upper branches and holding a long piece of string with a weight tied at its end. Another one of his unexplainable experiments. When Mark looked down at me, his eyes caught the object in my hand. Suddenly, he raced down the tree. As he touched the ground, I flashed a triumphant smile and held out my gift to him.

11   To my shock, Mark snatched the toy model and snarled. "You stupid! I buried this for a time-warp experiment, and you've ruined the *whole thing!*" He opened the rocketship and pulled out a piece of paper. I stared at its message in disbelief: "Mark E. Murphy, 44th St., Savannah, Ga. 3:01 P.M., August 21, 1974." My stomach turned flip-flops as I realized my mistake. Wanting only to help, I had spoiled my brother's experiment.

12   Mark marched away and turned back only when he heard my howl of anguish. It was the cry of a creature who had seen the demise of something dear. The "death" I'd seen was that of all hope of ever getting close to my brother, and I believe Mark sensed this as he stared at me in surprise.

13   Mark's brow creased, but my pain and disappointment wouldn't allow me to stop the tears. And then Mark silently walked away.

14   That night as I prepared for bed, I found a note, with my name scrawled on the outside, laid on my pillow. As I opened it, I braced myself for the venomous attack I felt I deserved. But what I found was a cherished treasure from Mark's "Top Secret" shoebox: a gentle poem expressing love and apology. For the second time that day, I cried.

15   Later . . . much later . . . I lost the poem—but I never lost the love I felt when I read it. I doubt I ever will.

16   That was all 12 years ago. Mark is no longer the pudgy 12 year old, and I am not the overly sensitive, idol-worshipping little sister. Mark and I have begun our own lives—separate but still very much tied by bonds of affection. At 21, I am about to graduate from college. Mark is married, and he and his wife live in Augusta, Ga., while he works toward a degree in medicine. They're expecting their first baby.

17   Now, I find myself experimenting with different "aunt" names and imagining what sort of person this child will become. It's then that I whisper a silent hope that he or she will someday have a brother like mine . . . and will know the glorious feeling of discovering their special relationship.

Journal Assignments

1. Write a journal page about your responses to this reading. Did you like the reading? Why do you think Jennifer Murphy remembered this incident so well? Do you have any similar memories about brothers or sisters? If so, write a little about the memories. Would a reader who is an only child be interested in this essay? Why or why not? You may write about these questions or other ideas that this essay brings to mind.

2. Write a journal page about two or more interesting people in your life. These people may be a family member, a friend, a boss, a co-worker, a former teacher or coach—anyone whom you know or knew fairly well. Tell your reader why each of them is interesting or memorable. It does not have to be someone you *like*—just someone who is *memorable*, for whatever reason.

3. Focus on just one of the people that you wrote about in the second journal assignment. Write a full page about that person. Try to write both about the person's physical appearance and about at least one incident that illustrates the person's character. The following suggestions should help you think of things to write about:

   a. What does the person's hair look like? How does the facial skin look? What are the eyes like? Are there any other interesting facial features that a reader should know about? What body build does this person have? How does the person dress? Does he or she have any noticeable mannerisms or habits?

   b. Think about the character trait that you want to demonstrate. Is the person generous? stingy? courageous? cowardly? honest? duplicitous (double-dealing or two-faced)? loving? mean? even-tempered? easily angered? calm? highly emotional? selfless? selfish? dependable? unreliable? When you think of a word like one of these to describe the person's character, it will be because you have seen the person do something that made you apply this adjective. Write about what the person has done that makes you describe him or her as generous, mean, or whatever adjective you used.

Reading Questions

Content

1. Describe Mark's physical appearance.

2. What adjectives would you have used to describe Mark's character (what he is like on the inside, what sort of person he is) *if* Jennifer had never received the note?

3. What new adjectives would you add to describe Mark's character after you find out that he sent the note?

4. Putting together all that you know about Mark as a child, how would you summarize the sort of person he was? The adjectives you use to describe a person's character are termed **character traits.**

5. How would you describe Jennifer as a child?

6. How would you describe the relationship between the two children?

7. The headnote to the reading tells you two of Murphy's audiences: her writing teacher (and maybe classmates) and the readers of *Good Housekeeping*. Why would the editors of *Good Housekeeping* think their readers would be interested in this character sketch? (Hint: You need to think about who the readers of *Good Housekeeping* are.) Who else would be interested in this character sketch besides *Good Housekeeping*'s audience? Why?

Structure

Both the descriptive language and the anecdotes help readers to know Mark. We will examine how these techniques work in the reading.

Writers frequently use details about a person's physical appearance to reflect what the person is like on the inside. In the second paragraph, Murphy describes Mark's appearance.

1. What would you conclude about Mark's character based on his appearance? (Hint: Some of the character traits you named in response to content question 2 might have been based on his appearance.)

2. Notice Murphy's choice of words to describe Mark's appearance. Why did she use "pudgy and awkward" rather than "fat and clumsy"?

3. Murphy not only describes Mark's personal appearance, but also describes his room. What do the details about Mark's room add to our knowledge about him?

Further evidence of Mark's character is given by means of the anecdotes that Murphy tells. Let us look carefully at how each one illustrates Mark's character.

1. The first anecdote in the reading is the story of the Saturday rides to the planetarium. From which details in the story can you infer Mark's interest (or lack of it) in Jennifer?

2. Let us examine a specific example of Murphy's **diction,** or word choice, as she tells this anecdote. Which child has a harder time biking to the planetarium? Which specific words give you the answer? What impressions about Mark or Mark's relationship to Jennifer are created by these details? Note that Murphy *shows* us the sibling relationship through her use of descriptive language.

3. What did Murphy want the reader to learn from the first anecdote? Why did she include the second anecdote about the rocket ship and the poem?

The following questions direct your attention to how anecdotes are constructed. There are two anecdotes in this reading, the story of the Saturdays at the planetarium and the story of digging up the rocket ship. Answer the following questions for each anecdote.

1. What is (are) the setting(s) of each of these anecdotes?

2. Who are the characters in each anecdote?

3. When does each anecdote occur? Which words indicate time?

4. What is the action of each anecdote?

DRAFTING: WRITING, TALKING, REWRITING, AND EVALUATING

Preparing to Write a Character Sketch

Describing People

The following exercises for your writing groups give you practice in the kinds of writing you will use for your own character sketch.

Physical Description   Pick a scribe. As a group, write a detailed physical description of the characters described below (as assigned by your instructor). Visualize what you think the person would look like. Then add the details you visualize to those of the rest of your group members in order to develop as detailed a portrait as possible. This will probably require four steps.

First, each member contributes all the descriptive details he or she can think of to describe the type of person named. Use journal assignment 3a (p. 25) to help you think of details. (This is really brain-storming.)

Second, select the details you want to include in your group's description. You may decide to use all of them, or you may decide that some do not really fit.

Third, decide on a logical order for the details in order to help your readers visualize the person you are describing.

Fourth, write your details into a descriptive paragraph.

Here, to serve as an example, is a paragraph describing a colicky baby. Note the logic of the order. Describe it.

A Colicky Baby

My baby boy lay on his back in the crib, blanket twisted around his body and between his jerking legs. He inhaled in short panting breaths and exhaled in frantic wails. His face had lost its soft baby contours; instead, its features were tense behind his wide open, toothless mouth. Tears coursing from his tightly closed eyes made his bulging, tomato red cheeks glisten. New tears made little pools on his clenched eyelids and stuck his lashes together. His sparse hair was matted to his head by sweat. His whole little body tightened in a spasm of pain.

Now write a paragraph describing each of the following characters (or the ones your teacher assigns).

1. A 50-year-old woman who has smoked two packs of cigarettes a day for thirty years
2. A 55-year-old rancher or farmer who has worked in the outdoors all of his life
3. A 32-year-old, short-tempered manager of a fast-food chain store
4. An old musician
5. A high-pressure high-school football (soccer, basketball, volleyball) coach
6. the beer-drinking sports fan behind you at a football game
7. the student who sits next to you in chemistry (psychology, history) lecture and is *always* prepared.

Anecdotes Pick a scribe. As a group, make up a single incident to illustrate one characteristic below. You will be writing a very short story, or anecdote, to exemplify the characteristic. In all stories, even very short ones, you need to tell your reader the setting, the characters, and the action. Here is a paragraph to serve as an example.

The Selfish Basketball Player

East High trailed by one point with nine seconds left in the basketball game—long enough to inbound the ball at midcourt and pass it up court for a shot. During the time-out, Coach told Brooke to inbound the ball to either Natalie or Jackie, who was to relay it to Erin, positioned for her best shot just outside the free-throw lane. Brooke tossed the ball to Jackie, who whirled to face the home basket—but didn't pass. Instead she put the ball to the floor, cutting sharply past the defending guard with a move that got her almost to the three-point line. She heard the fans chanting down the seconds, "Five, four, three . . ." Erin waved her arms in the air. She was on her spot, open. "Here! Here!" she screamed. Jackie glanced at her, hesitated a split second, then put the ball in the air from 20 feet out as the last second ticked off the clock. It was wide, off the rim. East lost, 48–47.

Which player is the selfish one? How do you know? As a group, now write an incident to illustrate each of the following character traits (or the ones your teacher assigns):

1. A compulsively neat person
2. A rude driver
3. A rude sales clerk
4. A rude customer
5. An honest customer
6. A mean fifth grader
7. An overly cautious driver
8. A selfish brother or sister
9. A slick salesperson
10. A generous friend
11. A sexist employer
12. A character of your own choosing

Now choose one of the characters you described earlier in the Physical Description section. Think of a character trait that might be typical of that person. (The fast-food manager already has one—a short temper.) As a group, make up an anecdote to illustrate this character trait.

Character Description in Your Journals Read your third journal assignment for this chapter to your group. After everyone has read an entry, select the one that made you feel you know the individual described best. Your instructor will ask you to read this entry to the entire class.

Using Direct Quotations

Writers use a **direct quotation** to record someone else's exact words. (An **indirect quotation** is the record of what someone has said without using the speaker's exact words.) Note that Jennifer Murphy used several direct quotations in her article. Direct quotations make readers feel as though they are present at the scene of the story, overhearing exactly what was said at the time. You may want to use direct quotations when you write your own character sketch.

Here are some rules for recording in writing exactly what someone else has said.

1. Use quotation marks around only the exact words spoken.

    As his face turned a delicate seafoam green, Jerry said, "I don't feel well."

2. Do *not* put quotation marks around an indirect quotation.

    As his face turned a delicate seafoam green, Jerry said that he didn't feel well.*

3. The first quotation mark comes just before the first quoted word. The second comes after the end punctuation of the quoted sentence.

    As the ice cream dripped from the bottom of her cone, Karen sighed, "I hate it when that happens."

4. The first word within the quotation is capitalized.

    Andy yelled, "Watch out for that car!"

5. A comma follows words introducing a quotation.

    The cop said, "May I see your driver's license?"

6. When the quotation is a statement at the beginning of a sentence, a comma follows the quoted words.

    "This license seems to have expired," the cop said.

7. When the quotation is a question, it is followed by a question mark. When it is an exclamation, it ends with an exclamation point.

    "Can you give me a ride?" she asked.

    "Don't get near me!" Matt screamed in terror.

8. If the quotation is more than one sentence long, use just one pair of quotation marks at the beginning and end of the entire speech.

    The teacher directed, "Get out a sheet of clean paper. Put your name in the upper right-hand corner. Number the left-hand margin from one to ten. I will pronounce each word, give it in a sentence, and then pronounce it again. Listen carefully and then write down the word."

9. When you interrupt the quoted words with the speaker's name, set the name off with commas and put quotation marks around the spoken words.

---

*"I don't feel well" are exactly the words Jerry said. *That he didn't feel well* are not the words Jerry actually said. They constitute an indirect, rather than a direct, quotation. So we do not put quotation marks around them.

"I'll never understand," Alicia said, "how you manage to get so dirty so fast."

Exercises

1. Punctuate each of the following sentences correctly.
   a. Turn down that boombox Walter demanded.
   b. Tony said that he'd be here by ten.
   c. Don't ever do that again Joe said quietly.
   d. Can you tell me how to get to the stadium the driver asked, looking bewildered.
   e. Go straight ahead to the second stoplight. You'll be at Sunset Avenue. Turn left onto Sunset and go straight ahead until you hit the freeway entrance. Get onto the freeway heading north. In about two miles, you'll start seeing exit signs for the stadium Eddie answered.
   f. The counselor advised me to drop calculus and take it again next quarter.
   g. As the pounding at the door got louder, Andrew yelled keep your shirt on! I'm coming.
   h. If Richie calls, tell him I'll be there in ten minutes Theresa called as she slammed the door on her way out.
   i. That darned washing machine always eats my socks Alice cried in exasperation.
   j. Don't leave this house said Mom before you clean up your room.
2. Either alone or with your writing group, reread the anecdotes that you wrote with the group. Did you include any direct quotations in them? If so, check to see if they were punctuated correctly. If they were not, correct the punctuation now.

   If you did not include quotations, think about which anecdotes could be made more immediate, more like real life, by adding quoted conversation. Write the conversation into your anecdote, punctuating it correctly.

☙ Writing Assignment: More Information

You have by now written three journal assignments for this chapter, the third one focusing on the person about whom you will write your formal paper, and you have helped to write several physical descriptions and anecdotes with your writing group. You are now ready to write the first draft of your own character sketch. The main thing to keep in mind as you write your drafts is the single character trait that your description will illustrate. Pick physical details about the person's appearance and think of a short anecdote or two to illustrate this important character trait.

When you worked in writing groups, you *made up* anecdotes to illustrate a character trait. The purpose for doing this was to practice putting together a good very short story. However, when you write your character sketch, you must use real incidents. You must search your memory for past actions that led you to conclude that your subject possesses the character trait you describe. When you think of a particularly illustrative action, write it up as an anecdote to show what your person is like.

Organizing the Introduction

Begin your character sketch with an introductory paragraph that names the person (you may use a pseudonym if you would rather not use the person's real name), tells the person's relationship to you, and indicates the important character trait that you will be describing.

Organizing the Body and Conclusion

You will probably find that it is most logical to organize the body of your paper in one of two ways:

1. In the first body paragraph, describe the person's physical appearance. In the second paragraph, tell an anecdote that illustrates the person's character. A slightly longer anecdote may take more than one paragraph. If you use two or more anecdotes, you will probably give each anecdote at least one paragraph of its own. Your concluding paragraph should again state the person's main character trait and explain why this person is important to you.

2. The body of your paper may consist of just one longer anecdote that illustrates your person's character. If this is the case, you will include physical description wherever it fits into the story. You will divide the body into paragraphs according to slight shifts in the action of the story. Your concluding paragraph will restate the character trait you have illustrated and explain why this person, with this trait, is important to you. This pattern is probably more difficult to write successfully than the first organizational pattern.

First-Draft Activities

Your teacher will assign one or more of the following activities:

1. Read your draft to your group members. Have group members answer the following questions. If they cannot find the answers to any of these questions, it means you need to revise your draft to include the missing information.

   a. Personal details.
      (1) What is the name of the person being described?
      (2) What is his or her relationship to the writer?

    (3) What is the main character trait being described?

    (4) What does the person look like?

  b. Anecdote. If you have included more than one anecdote, have group members answer the following questions about each one. [You may need to read the anecdote(s) again to the group.]

    (1) What is the setting?

    (2) When does the anecdote take place?

    (3) Who are the characters?

    (4) What is the action, or **plot?**

    (5) What is the point of the anecdote? (*Hint:* In a character sketch, the point is to illustrate an important character trait. What trait does the anecdote illustrate?)

  c. Organization.

    (1) Does the paper have an introductory paragraph, several body paragraphs, and a conclusion?

    (2) Do you have any trouble following the topic of each paragraph, the time of events, or the action within the events? If so, is the problem the transitions between ideas or events?

    (3) Does the conclusion tell you why this person is significant to the writer?

2. Make copies of your draft for each member in your writing group. The job of group members is to help each writer make his or her language as specific and vivid as possible.

  a. Read the parts of the draft that include physical description. Can you visualize the important features of this person? What words or phrases could be made more specific?

  b. Can you visualize the setting and action of the anecdote? If not, point out to the writer where more specific or vivid language is needed.

  c. Are there any spots where you would like to know exactly what the participants said? If so, suggest that the writer include direct quotations.

After you have talked about your first draft with your writing group, you are ready to revise it, taking into account the advice your group members gave you.

Second-Draft Activities

Evaluation Criteria

Below are some criteria for writing a good character sketch.

1. The introductory paragraph names the person being described (you may use a pseudonym), tells the person's relationship to the writer, and gives some indication of the important character trait that the paper will describe.

2. The body of the paper includes pertinent physical characteristics and an anecdote that illustrates the inner character of the person.

    a. The physical details contribute to the reader's understanding of the subject's character.

    b. The anecdotes include setting, time, characters, and action.

    c. The point of the anecdote is clear to readers.

3. The concluding paragraph restates the character trait and tells why the person is significant to the writer.

Sample Student Essays

Here are two character sketches written by students. Both successfully meet some of the criteria but do not meet others.

My Brother-in-Law Danny

1   My brother-in-law Danny is one of those people you just can't help but like. When I was younger it seemed like he knew everybody, and if he didn't he soon would. There is something about Danny that once you meet him you just have to know more about him. He always goes out of his way to make you feel comfortable and welcome no matter where you are.

2   Danny is a heavy man, but seems as swift and agile as a slender teenager in his prime. He has a bushy moustache, and beard, but is losing most of his blondish red hair. He likes to joke a lot, just to see people smile and laugh. Whenever we meet the first thing we do is shake hands. Then Danny will sometimes ask me what that spot is on my shirt? After all these years some times I still fall for it and he will run his finger from the middle of my chest to my forehead. He always has this special twinkle in his eyes and is always smiling.

3   I remember one day in May when Danny had invited me to go trapshooting at the gunclub. I had never been trapshooting before and I was a little nervous. So I asked my best friend, Mike to go along. As soon as we got there, Danny ran over to us, and I introduced Mike to Danny. Danny could not wait to introduce us to everyone he knew which seemed like everyone at the club.

4   Although Danny had just met my freind they got along like they had know each other for years. Neither Mike nor I had ever shot trap before. So Danny went over all the safety rules for the range, put a shotgun in each of our hands, and gave us a couple boxes of shells that he had loaded the night before. He took us right out on the practice range

to teach us the basics. He said "Mike you go first." Then Mike and I walked to the first station (designated places to shoot the targets from). Danny laughed because both our names are Mike, and said "No my brother-in-law Mike." I stood on the first station, pulled my gun up, and called for the bird (clay target). When I pulled the trigger nothing happened. I turned around feeling sort of stupid, but when I saw Danny and my freind chuckling together I knew what had happened. Danny had expected the first one that shot not to remember to take the safety off the gun. We all laughed together and continued to practice.

5   Afterwards we offered him some money for the shells and range tickets, but he wouldn't take it. By the look on his face, and the tone of his voice, we knew if we insisted it would only insult him. He said, "What's mine is yours," and you could sense how sincere he was.

6   Danny and his family love animals which anyone could tell if they have ever been to their home. They have seven cats, three dogs, and they had three horses. At first there were two mares, a mother and offspring. Then a few years later the mom was going to have another foal. During this last pregnancy the expecting mare became very lame. Danny was always out back trying to make the mother as comfortable as possible. He was always brushing her hair and puting straw in a pile so she could lay down and be more comfortable. He would make sure she had plenty of good hay to eat. My family and I just happened to be there when the mother went into labor. Danny was glad we were there. He said, watching the foal be born would be an exciting experience for my family and I. Danny said, "Mike run in the house and grab the camera? We'll need pictures of the kid's watching the foal be born."

7   The other mare was very jealous of the new foal, and seemed to know she would no longer get all of her mother's attention. So she began running and kicking like she was mad at the world. Danny said, "She'll have to be seperated from her mom and new sister." Danny and I worked most of the night building a barrier between the horses. Danny told me "You know Mike I think of you as one of my brothers." That was the best thank-you he could have given me.

8   After the foal was weened the mother had to be put to sleep. Eventually the two sisters got where they could be in the same corral. The friendship that then grew became very strong. My brother-in-law had a lot to do with this because he not only took care of their physical needs, but gave them a sense of love and emotional stability that their mother was no longer able to give. I think the loss of a loved one is sad. But to have someone to share this greif with is essential to be able to go on.

9   Danny has always been a caring person not only towards people but with any living thing. As the years passed I knew why I wanted to be as much like him as I could. I wish there were more people as generous and friendly as he is. You just know how happy it makes him to do thing's for someone or something else.

The Warmth of a Friend

1   When I was 16, Sue Perry was my best friend. We did most everything together. There wasn't a day that would go by that she wouldn't call or stop by. It is easily said that Sue was the most caring person I have ever known.

2   Sue wasn't what most people would call stunning, but she wasn't bad. She was short and heavy set. Her short brown hair framed her round face. Sue's eyes were her most attractive feature. They were a soft steel blue that showed her warm and caring nature.

3   Sue was a quiet, soft spoken person. She had very few friends, but the friends she did keep ment more to her than life itself. I felt lucky to be included in that circle.

4   One particular incident that stays with me was the night of my seventeenth birthday. She had planned to take me to dinner then to see Swan Lake. I wasn't feeling well so when she called, I told her that I was sorry I would not be able to go. She said that it was all right and that she would come over to my place to keep me company.

5   When she arrived, she had a bag full of food. She set the bag on the kitchen table then came into the living room where I was lying on the couch. She turned on the television saying "If we can't go to see it, we'll just have to bring it here." The ballet was being broadcast from a local station. She then walked back into the kitchen to make dinner. We watched the ballet while we ate. After it was over we talked about how beautiful the dancers were. I don't remember falling asleep, but when I woke up she was sitting by me with her head on the couch. She looked up at me and asked how I felt. I just smiled.

6   Sue was always doing things like this, even for people she hardly knew. I can say that Sue Perry was the most caring person I have ever known.

Evaluating the Sample Essays

In your writing group, discuss each example in relation to each of the evaluation criteria above (see pp. 33–34). Which of the criteria does each sample meet? Which criteria does each fail to meet? Pick a scribe to write down your answers.

Revising Your Second Draft

Make enough photocopies of your second draft for each member of your writing group. In class, meet with your writing group to discuss each member's second draft. Your purpose is to help each other meet the requirements for writing an effective character sketch, one that makes readers understand the characteristic the writer is describing and why this person is significant to the writer.

Use the evaluation criteria for writing a character sketch on pages 33–34 as a checklist. Read through each member's draft to make sure that all of the required features are included. Tell the writer about any features that are omitted or unclear.

As homework, revise your final draft. As you revise, keep in mind the criteria for a good character sketch and the advice your writing group has given you. You do not need to use every piece of advice you received, but you must carefully consider all of it and decide for yourself whether the paper would be improved by using it.

EDITING

Final-Draft Editing

In class, before turning in your final draft, exchange it with a partner. Proofread your partner's draft for spelling, punctuation, and grammatical errors. Pay particular attention to the punctuation of quotations. Do not correct errors on the paper, but pencil in a little arrow in the margin next to the line where the error occurs. Then tell the writer what the error is.

As the writer, your job is to decide whether you agree with your partner that you have an error and, if you do, to make neat corrections on the paper with pencil or black pen. If you are unsure about an error, ask your teacher.

Postfinal-Draft Editing

Your instructor may draw your attention to particular errors in your paper that need correction. He or she may ask you to correct sentences in your paper or to write exercises from the handbook that will help you with your problem.

Using Personal Experience to Make a Point About Stereotyping

WRITING ASSIGNMENT

In the writing assignment due at the end of this chapter you will make a point about the effects of **stereotyping** by writing an essay about a time when you have stereotyped someone or have been stereotyped yourself. The reading in this chapter raises the social issue of stereotyping as well as illustrates some descriptive and narrative techniques you can use in writing your own essay. You will use the following familiar kinds of evidence to support your point: descriptive details, personal experience, and anecdotes. You will also learn a new kind of evidence, typical examples.

Why Write a Personal Experience Essay About Stereotyping?

In the previous chapters' assignments, you worked hard to write vivid images that communicated to your audience; you used descriptive details and anecdotal evidence to make a point to your readers about important places and people from your own life. Beginning with this assignment, you will need to use your descriptive skills to write about social issues that affect all of us. Because most of us have been affected by stereotyping, this assignment provides a way to add your judgment about the effects of stereotyping to the pool of knowledge about this issue. This assignment, like most college writing assignments, requires you to formulate and support your point about an issue raised by our culture, and to do so within the framework of a particular academic discipline.

INVENTION: READING, WRITING, AND TALKING FOR IDEAS

Reading

The author of the reading below, Brent Staples, is assistant metropolitan editor of the *New York Times*.

 ## Just Walk on By: A Black Man Ponders His Power to Alter Public Space

Brent Staples

1   My first victim was a woman—white, well dressed, probably in her early twenties. I came upon her late one evening on a deserted street in Hyde Park, a relatively affluent neighborhood in an otherwise mean, impoverished section of Chicago. As I swung onto the avenue behind her, there seemed to be a discreet, uninflammatory distance between us. Not so. She cast back a worried glance. To her, the youngish black man—a broad six feet two inches with a beard and billowing hair, both hands shoved into the pockets of a bulky military jacket—seemed menacingly close. After a few more quick glimpses, she picked up her pace and was soon running in earnest. Within seconds she disappeared into a cross street.

2   That was more than a decade ago. I was 22 years old, a graduate student newly arrived at the University of Chicago. It was in the echo of that terrified woman's footfalls that I first began to know the unwieldy inheritance I'd come into—the ability to alter public space in ugly ways. It was clear that she thought herself the quarry of a mugger, a rapist, or worse. Suffering a bout of insomnia, however, I was stalking sleep, not defenseless wayfarers. As a softy who is scarcely able to take a knife to a raw chicken—let alone hold it to a person's throat—I was surprised, embarrassed, and dismayed all at once. Her flight made me feel like an accomplice in tyranny. It also made it clear that I was indistinguishable from the muggers who occasionally seeped into the area from the surrounding ghetto. That first encounter, and those that followed, signified that a vast, unnerving gulf lay between nighttime pedestrians—particularly women—and me. And I soon gathered that being perceived as dangerous is a hazard in itself. I only needed to turn a corner into a dicey situation, or crowd some frightened, armed person in a foyer somewhere, or make an errant move after being pulled over by a policeman. Where fear and weapons meet—and they often do in urban America—there is always the possibility of death.

3   In that first year, my first away from my hometown, I was to become thoroughly familiar with the language of fear. At dark, shadowy

intersections in Chicago, I could cross in front of a car stopped at a traffic light and elicit the *thunk, thunk, thunk, thunk* of the driver—black, white, male, or female—hammering down the door locks. On less traveled streets after dark, I grew accustomed to but never comfortable with people who crossed to the other side of the street rather than pass me. Then there were the standard unpleasantries with police, doormen, bouncers, cab drivers, and others whose business it is to screen out troublesome individuals *before* there is any nastiness.

4   I moved to New York nearly two years ago and I have remained an avid night walker. In central Manhattan, the near-constant crowd cover minimizes tense one-on-one street encounters. Elsewhere—visiting friends in SoHo, where sidewalks are narrow and tightly spaced buildings shut out the sky—things can get very taut indeed.

5   Black men have a firm place in New York mugging literature. Norman Podhoretz in his famed (or infamous) 1963 essay, "My Negro Problem—And Ours," recalls growing up in terror of black males; they "were tougher than we were, more ruthless," he writes—and as an adult on the Upper West Side of Manhattan, he continues, he cannot constrain his nervousness when he meets black men on certain streets. Similarly, a decade later, the essayist and novelist Edward Hoagland extols a New York where once "Negro bitterness bore down mainly on other Negroes." Where some see mere panhandlers, Hoagland sees "a mugger who is clearly screwing up his nerve to do more than just *ask* for money." But Hoagland has "the New Yorker's quick-hunch posture for broken-field maneuvering," and the bad guy swerves away.

6   I often witness that "hunch posture," from women after dark on the warrenlike streets of Brooklyn where I live. They seem to set their faces on neutral and, with their purse straps strung across their chests bandolier style, they forge ahead as though bracing themselves against being tackled. I understand, of course, that the danger they perceive is not a hallucination. Women are particularly vulnerable to street violence, and young black males are drastically overrepresented among the perpetrators of that violence. Yet these truths are no solace against the kind of alienation that comes of being ever the suspect, against being set apart, a fearsome entity with whom pedestrians avoid making eye contact.

7   It is not altogether clear to me how I reached the ripe old age of 22 without being conscious of the lethality nighttime pedestrians attributed to me. Perhaps it was because in Chester, Pennsylvania, the small, angry industrial town where I came of age in the 1960s, I was scarcely noticeable against a backdrop of gang warfare, street knifings, and murders. I grew up one of the good boys, had perhaps a half-dozen fist fights. In retrospect, my shyness of combat has clear sources.

8   Many things go into the making of a young thug. One of those things is the consummation of the male romance with the power to

intimidate. An infant discovers that random flailings send the baby bottle flying out of the crib and crashing to the floor. Delighted, the joyful babe repeats those motions again and again, seeking to duplicate the feat. Just so, I recall the points at which some of my boyhood friends were finally seduced by the perception of themselves as tough guys. When a mark cowered and surrendered his money without resistance, myth and reality merged—and paid off. It is, after all, only manly to embrace the power to frighten and intimidate. We, as men, are not supposed to give an inch of our lane on the highway; we are to seize the fighter's edge in work and in play and even in love; we are to be valiant in the face of hostile forces.

9   Unfortunately, poor and powerless young men seem to take all this nonsense literally. As a boy, I saw countless tough guys locked away; I have since buried several, too. They were babies, really—a teenage cousin, a brother of 22, a childhood friend in his mid-twenties—all gone down in episodes of bravado played out in the streets. I came to doubt the virtues of intimidation early on. I chose, perhaps even unconsciously, to remain a shadow—timid, but a survivor.

10   The fearsomeness mistakenly attributed to me in public places often has a perilous flavor. The most frightening of these confusions occurred in the late 1970s and early 1980s when I worked as a journalist in Chicago. One day, rushing into the office of a magazine I was writing for with a deadline story in hand, I was mistaken for a burglar. The office manager called security and, with an ad hoc posse, pursued me through the labyrinthine halls, nearly to my editor's door. I had no way of proving who I was. I could only move briskly toward the company of someone who knew me.

11   Another time I was on assignment for a local paper and killing time before an interview. I entered a jewelry store on the city's affluent Near North Side. The proprietor excused herself and returned with an enormous red Doberman pinscher straining at the end of a leash. She stood, the dog extended toward me, silent to my questions, her eyes bulging nearly out of her head. I took a cursory look around, nodded, and bade her good night. Relatively speaking, however, I never fared as badly as another black male journalist. He went to nearby Waukegan, Illinois, a couple of summers ago to work on a story about a murderer who was born there. Mistaking the reporter for the killer, police hauled him from his car at gunpoint and but for his press credentials would probably have tried to book him. Such episodes are not uncommon. Black men trade tales like this all the time.

12   In "My Negro Problem—And Ours," Podhoretz writes that the hatred he feels for blacks makes itself known to him through a variety of avenues—one being his discomfort with that "special brand of paranoid touchiness" to which he says blacks are prone. No doubt he is speaking here of black men. In time, I learned to smother the rage I felt at so often

being taken for a criminal. Not to do so would surely have led to
madness—via that special "paranoid touchiness" that so annoyed
Podhoretz at the time he wrote the essay.

13   I began to take precautions to make myself less threatening. I move
about with care, particularly late in the evening. I give a wide berth to
nervous people on subway platforms during the wee hours, particularly
when I have exchanged business clothes for jeans. If I happen to be
entering a building behind some people who appear skittish, I may walk
by, letting them clear the lobby before I return, so as not to seem to be
following them. I have been calm and extremely congenial on those rare
occasions when I've been pulled over by the police.

14   And on late-evening constitutionals along streets less traveled by, I
employ what has proved to be an excellent tension-reducing measure: I
whistle melodies from Beethoven and Vivaldi and the more popular
classical composers. Even steely New Yorkers hunching toward
nighttime destinations seem to relax, and occasionally they even join in
the tune. Virtually everybody seems to sense that a mugger wouldn't be
warbling bright, sunny selections from Vivaldi's *Four Seasons*. It is my
equivalent of the cowbell that hikers wear when they know they are in
bear country.

Journal Assignments

1. Write a journal page responding to "Just Walk on By." Do you
think that there is any solution to Staples' problem? How is writing
about his problem an attempt to provide a solution? How has writing been used to create a problem? (*Hint:* See paragraphs 5 and 12.)
Do you think that this article provides a response to Podhoretz's
(and Hoagland's) commentary?

2. Write about a time when you have been stereotyped. Why were you
stereotyped? What effect did it have on you? How did you resolve
the effects of the stereotyping? Or if you prefer, write about a time
when you have stereotyped someone else. Why did you stereotype
that person? What, if anything, caused you to change your mind
about the person you stereotyped or the group of people the person
belonged to?

Thinking About Stereotyping

Defining Stereotypes

Before discussing the reading, define *stereotype* and as a class brainstorm a list of stereotypes commonly used to categorize people. Pick one
from the list and describe the stereotype. Here is an example.

A Typical Nerd

A nerd is easy to identify. Even before you see one, you can hear the stomp and squeak, especially the squeak, of his clumsy shoes. As you scan the floor looking for the source of the offending noise, black leather lace-up shoes, orthopedic looking, slightly turned up at the toe, and scuffed, will appear—nerd shoes and socks. His socks, usually white Orlon, barely cover his ankles, which must always be cold since no nerd has ever worn a pair of pants long enough to reach his ankles. The length missing in the pant legs is made up for at the other end because a nerd belts his pants, always a loud-colored plaid, somewhere between his naval and chest. His shirts, usually striped, have the same problem as his pants. His bony wrists stick out of his shirtsleeves a long way, and his collar, always buttoned right up to his chin, squeezes his Adam's apple cruelly. You see a lot of wrist and hand action from a nerd, whether he is pulling a calculator out of his shirt pocket, flipping open his heavy briefcase and flicking open a notebook, or pushing up his thick-lensed glasses with the taped arm and then flipping an unevenly cut lock of stringy hair out of his eyes. His eyes, though magnified by his thick lenses, look vague and unfocused, like the rest of his face, an effect that is probably due to the long hours he spends staring at computer screens or chessboards. Most social graces are beyond nerds, who are at their best with inanimate objects. His only contribution to most conversations will be a braying laugh delivered at an inappropriate moment while he digs for ear wax with his pinkie finger. Finally you need to know that if you want to avoid nerds, never go to conventions, especially "Star Trek" conventions, or lectures on any subject. These places are nerd havens!

What you have just read is a **typical example.** A typical example describes a type or category of person or event as opposed to a particular person or single event.

> **Exercise** Pick a stereotype from your class list, and as a class or in small groups, write a detailed description of that stereotype. You will be developing a typical example.

Sources of Stereotyping

Now that you have a sense of what a stereotype is, consider how and why stereotyping occurs. Here are some questions to guide your group or class discussion.

1. Why do we stereotype others?
2. Under what circumstances do we tend to stereotype?
3. Whom do we tend to stereotype?
4. How do stereotypes affect our perception of particular people?
5. Can stereotyping have both positive and negative effects?

Reading Questions

As a writer, you need to analyze not only the content of what you read but, for the purposes of imitation, the structure of what you read as well. Now you will apply your analytical skills to the content and structure of "Just Walk on By." As you read the questions below notice how the words *effect* and *affect* are used and see if you can explain the difference between them.

Content

1. How do strangers, especially women, stereotype the author?
2. What effect does this stereotype have on strangers?
3. Why do they stereotype him as they do?
4. When did the author first become aware of his effect upon strangers?
5. How does the author see himself with respect to the stereotype?
6. Does the author understand why he is stereotyped? Why is he?
7. How does this stereotype develop?
   a. What stereotypical characteristics are men supposed to have?
   b. How do these characteristics affect "poor and powerless young men"?
8. How was the author affected by the stereotype as he was growing up?
9. How is he affected by the stereotype now?
10. In what ways is the stereotype dangerous?
11. How has the author changed his behavior as a result of the way strangers stereotype him?

Structure

1. The author begins his article with an anecdote. What purpose does it serve? That is, why is the anecdote important? (*Hint:* Look at paragraphs 2 and 3.)
2. In which paragraph is the topic of this essay identified? What is the topic?
3. In which paragraph does the author make his point about how stereotyping has affected him? What is the point?
4. What kind of evidence does the author use to support his point? Find a paragraph developed with a typical example. (*Hint:* What typically happens to the author at lightly trafficked intersections?)
5. How does the author organize his evidence? (Hint: Look for paragraphs that explain the effects and causes of stereotyping. Look also for paragraphs beginning with an indication of time.)

6. Where does the conclusion begin? How does it emphasize the importance of the author's topic and point?

7. Who is the audience for this essay? Where did you find the information indicating who the audience might be?

Writing Assignment: More Information

As a result of your class discussion on stereotyping and on "Just Walk on By," you should have formed some clear opinions about the effects of stereotyping. Those opinions together with your second journal assignment will give you the material necessary to interpret your experience in order to make a point about, and explain the effects of, stereotyping.

> **Exercise** Add to the information your discussions and journal writings have yielded by freewriting, keeping in mind these questions.
>
> 1. What is the stereotype you want to write about? Describe it.
>
> 2. How did it affect the way you were judged or the way you judged someone else? Explain the effects of this judgment.
>
> 3. Explain how and why you were reevaluated or how you reevaluated the person you stereotyped. If you were not reevaluated, or if you did not reevaluate the person you stereotyped, explain why. Give specific examples.
>
> 4. What did you learn about the effects of stereotyping as a result of your experience? Why is what you learned important?

As you write, keep in mind that these questions are not always easy to answer. They are designed to help you analyze and evaluate your past experience.

DRAFTING: WRITING, TALKING, REWRITING, AND EVALUATING

First-Draft Activities

Make photocopies of your first draft for group work so that your classmates can carefully read your essay and answer the following questions about it:

1. Does the introductory paragraph(s) provide enough background information (context) leading up to the statement of point? Underline the essay's point, or write "no point" in the margin.

2. What is the stereotype? Is it easily recognizable and clearly and adequately described? If not, write "develop stereotype" at the end of the paper.

3. Can you follow the narration (detailed explanation) of the writer's experiences? Put a question mark in front of the sentences you find difficult to follow, or write "more information!" in the right-hand margin beside the paragraphs that need further development or explanation.

4. Does the experience(s) show the effects of stereotyping and support the point the author makes about those effects? If not, what point do you think the experience supports? Write it down at the end of the paper.

5. Who is the audience for this essay? Write it down at the end of the paper.

6. Does the concluding paragraph adequately convince the audience that the author's point and topic is important? If not, explain why not.

Second-Draft Activities

Organizing the Introduction

Revise your first draft according to the responses of the group on your first draft. If you had trouble with your *introduction,* you might consider doing the following as you revise:

1. You might write an introductory paragraph providing a background for your experience by telling a brief story (anecdote) that sets the scene for the essay. This will give the reader insight into your situation at a particular time in your life. It is the technique that the author of "Just Walk on By" uses.

2. Alternately, you might introduce the topic immediately and address your reader directly by writing something such as "Like so many others, I never used to think about the effects of stereotyping until _____ (you fill in the blank), and then because of my experience with _____ (name), I discovered that stereotyping causes _____" (the blank you fill in here will probably be the statement of your point). Of course, you should not use those exact words, but you get the idea. This kind of introduction will leave no doubt in your reader's mind as to what your point is.

Organizing the Body and Conclusions

Next, in order to develop the *body* of your essay more fully, consider the following:

1. Make sure you have chosen a recognizable stereotype; *dumb jock* is more recognizable than *swimmer,* for example. One way to make sure your readers understand the attributes of the stereotype is to

describe completely not only the typical physical characteristics, but also the typical actions and attitudes expected from that stereotype. If you set up a typical example describing the stereotype, the contrasts between it and the specific characteristics of the person you are describing will help you to order the body of your essay.

2. To clarify the organization of your essay further, you might order it *chronologically* using words and phrases such as "First," "Next," "Later that day," or "When I first met . . ." They help the reader follow the action. The author of "Just Walk on By" uses this strategy very effectively in paragraphs 2–4.

3. If the *evidence* in the body of your essay does not support your *point,* you probably began writing thinking that your experience supported a particular point, but your perception of that experience gradually changed as you wrote. This frequently happens to writers—what we think we are going to write and what we end up writing are not always the same, and that is good. It means we are actively thinking as we write instead of trying to make our evidence support preconceived ideas. Be sure, then, to reevaluate your point in the light of the evidence you have developed, so that you let your experience lead you to a point instead of forcing your experience to support a point.

4. If your point is accurate, but somewhere you wandered off track as you wrote the body of your essay, it probably means you did not keep in mind the directed first-draft activities on pages 45–46. Go back through those questions to pinpoint where you strayed.

Taking this last step should also ensure that your *conclusion* convinces your readers that your topic and point are significant.

Evaluation Criteria

Finally, here are some criteria for evaluating an essay on the effects of stereotyping.

1. The essay should have an introduction containing
   a. some background information (context) introducing your topic to a particular audience
   b. a point about the topic you wish to develop in the essay

2. The essay should have a body containing the following evidence, all of which should reinforce your point:
   a. a typical example describing the stereotype you are examining
   b. specific examples showing how an individual conforms to or differs from that stereotype
   c. personal experiences that led you to come to your conclusions about the effects of stereotyping

3. The essay should have a conclusion stating the importance of your point to your audience.

Sample Student Essays

Following are two essays written in response to this assignment by other students. Read each essay and decide, on the basis of the above criteria, which is the better essay.

The Class Nerd

1   Let's face it, a stereotype is more or less a judgment call you make or is made about you. Those judgment calls can be very wrong because they take into consideration only external appearances.

2   You see in Jr. High I got stereotyped as one of the class nerds. A nerd was one of those people that were a bit backward when it came to school. We were not the best at anything, we were just there, back in the woodwork. We were the ones that would go to study hall during the dances, not because we liked studying, but it was easier than going to the dance and not being asked. We were the ones that the gym teacher would give the "best tryer award" to so we wouldn't feel left out. Because of our coke bottle glasses and stuttering every other word we spoke, we became easy targets for ridicule. We seemed always one step behind everyone else. We were the last one to start dating, if we dated at all.

3   There was a part of me that knew that this stereotype did not apply to me. But sometimes the evidence would seem to tell me different. I remember in the school there were benches by the library where all the jocks hung out, with their merciless tauntings and catcalls. I began to dread that part of the school building and even started to avoid it by taking the long way around. Those things said about me were not true, but I heard those comments so many times that a part of me began to believe them.

4   To prevent anything happening in class, I spent many hours perfecting a talk or speech I would have to give, knowing that if I didn't prepare well, I would be the laughing stock of the class. Art projects that I tried my best in, would seem to be never good enough but would be jeered at. As a result even to this day, there is a part of me that still doubts my ability to accomplish anything.

5   Society, I think, uses stereotypes to put a quick handy label on people, and uses this label to dismiss people from their minds or to rationalize their actions. Those people who were stereotyped also could rationalize. Sometimes I rationalized some of the things I did, because I saw myself as being the "class nerd". I sometimes would give up too easily

on myself because I started to think of myself as incapable of completing the project. Stereotypes can have damaging effects on one's ego, as a person continually hears that he or she is one thing or the other, they start to believe in the stereotype. It became a self fulfilling prophecy, as it were.

6   When we use stereotypes to group people into simple packages, we don't see them as individuals, with individual strengths and weaknesses. Yes, I may have had problems in communicating in the spoken word, but when given a chance, to see beyond the stereotype, one would have seen my abilities.

7   In summary, people who use negative stereotypes judge others to make them feel that they are better than others and need to justify their Superiority. In fact they are just showing their weakness.

Being Oldest

1   Unlike other stereotypes, being stereotyped as "the oldest" is a sterotype that exist both within a family and outside of the family. The oldest in the family or the oldest in a group of friends is going to be looked upon as the responsible one. He will be the one who is elected to something because he is suppose to be the responilbe one.

2   Stereotyping someone as a "Mormon" or a "black" will only happen outside the family. Take a group of Jr. High School students. Now a Mormon in a group of Mormon and non-Mormon kids may be elected to do something because he is Mormon. But, when he goes home he won't be elected because he is Mormon, but because he's the oldest. Being of a differnet race is the same thing. A person may be picked to do something because he's black. But when he gets home his parents can't very well say "do this because your black". But they will say "because your the oldest".

3   I am the oldest of three kids in our family. I was also the oldest in a few of the groups I ran around with in my school years. Being the oldest is not only a big pain as a child but something you tend to have to live up to not only in your own eyes but in the eyes of others. As a child in a family situation, the oldest is always expeced to do the work in the house, set the examples for the younger brothers and sisters, be in charge of the younger brothers and sisters and be a guinea pig for the mom & dad.

4   All three of us could be sitting in the living room watching T.V. and mom would need something, it was me she called. When asked "why me"? she answered "because your the oldest". I always had to wash the dishes, clean the bathrooms, vacuum the house, etc., because I was "the oldest". Well I didn't realize the oldest was the only one who could do

these chores. Since when did a rule come out that eight and nine year olds couldn't do these things? When I was eight and nine I was washing dishes, and vacuuming.

5   I always hated to be left in charge when mom & dad had to go somewhere. My sisters didn't like it either. They always wanted to be left in charge and dad would always say no. They would get mad and tell dad they didn't think it was fair and dad would reply "well, she's the oldest". Being in charge was always hard. Especially because dad would say "now remember, your in charge, don't let these other two get out of hand". In charge, a twelve year old in charge of two resentful sisters who were only one and two years younger then myself. My parents didn't realize that I didn't know anymore than my sisters. After all we were all raised in the same house, and by the same rules. As far as I'm concerned there's no reason why they couldn't be in charge.

6   Being an example was another hard one to live up to. Mom & dad were constantly reminding me that I was an example for my sisters. I always tried to be aware of the thintgs I did around my sisters. If I goofed I could always count on my parents saying "now that's not a good example for your sisters". What a guilt trip that can leave. The examples I'd set for my sisters are basically the same examples my parents set for me. Unless my parents didn't like the examples they set for me, I don't understand why the burden of setting the examples were put on me.

7   Being the oldest also meant being the one who the parents could use as a test. If mom and dad found that something they tried on me didn't work, they wouldn't use it on the other two. The biggest thing I can remember is when I ended up marrying my first husband. I was eighteen and still living at home. I was seeing a man who was ten years older than me and my parents didn't know. They soon found out and forbid me to see him as long as I lived in their home. Well I moved out and married him. My sisters of course saw anyone they pleased with no arguments from mom & dad.

8   I think that we, as a society, stereotoype people because it gives us a set image to picture someone by. When describing a person and the first thing described is that this person is Mormon, well then the image that can be first pictured may be squeaky clean and self-righteous because of the way we have sterotyped Mormons. Being introduced as the oldest, the image that comes to mind is responsible. This is because of stereotyping. Stereotyping has become a way to describe a person in a quick and easy way.

9   Well, not every Mormon is squeaky clean or self-righteous nor is every child born the oldest responsible. We need to learn that when someone is described as being Mormon or the oldest, to look beyond that stereotype that we have of these people and find who that person is as an individual.

10   Being the oldest will be with me forever. I am more responsible

than my two sisters. When I visit may parents I'm the one who still does most of the work. When I eat over at someone elses house I'm the one who gets the dishes started. Being sterotyped the oldest may have been a good thing for me as an adult. It did make me responsible, but to have to live up to all those expectations as a child in my opinion is not so good.

Evaluating the Sample Essays

Meet in writing groups. Compare your ratings with those of the other group members.

1. Did you agree? If so, discuss the characteristics that led you to assign each paper the rating you did.
2. Did you disagree? Take turns explaining why you assigned each paper the rating you did. Be sure to discuss your ratings in relation to the criteria. Try to agree as a group on the rating for each essay. Be ready to defend your decisions in class discussion.

After the groups report to the class as a whole on their rating decisions, discuss how the papers succeeded or failed to meet the criteria.

Revising Your Second Draft

Reread your own second draft and evaluate it according to the criteria you just used to evaluate the student essays. Use the criteria to help you see what to change as you write your last draft.

Type your final essay. (If you use a word processor, revising and typing can be done in the same step.)

Editing

Final-Draft Editing

Work with a partner. Read your partner's paper, looking for spelling, typing, and punctuation errors. Do not make corrections on the paper. Just draw an arrow in the margin pointing to the line with the error and explain what you think is wrong.

If you agree that you have an error, cross it out and make the correction neatly.

Postfinal-Draft Editing

After grading the final draft, your instructor may assign you to make specific corrections or revisions on your essay.

C H A P T E R   5

Personal Narrative

WRITING ASSIGNMENT

The writing assignment due at the end of this chapter is a narrative essay about a personal experience that made a difference in your life. Generally, for an experience to make a difference, it must have caused some significant change in your life, or you must have learned something important from it.

At first it may seem difficult to come up with something significant to write about, but as you work through this chapter, you will discover that an experience does not have to be exciting or unusual to be significant. Significance can be found in the most ordinary events, especially if they involve a problem or a conflict.

Why Write a Personal Narrative Essay?

People write about personal experience, first of all, because it helps them make sense out of the events of their lives. If you review the readings in this text based on personal experience, such as those by Louis Kirchoff, Jennifer Murphy, and Brian Staples, you will recognize this common thread among them. Each of these pieces was written several years after the experience occurred, so that the writers have had time to reflect on the experience. But this does not necessarily mean that they had figured out its meaning before they began to write. It is very likely that some of the writers came to understand the experience *only as they were writing about it.* As people think about an experience during the act of writing, they often discover new meaning in it. So do not be too concerned if you are not sure what an experience means to you when you begin to write. You will figure it out as you write.

Personal narratives are written for readers as well as writers. The writers you have already read and those whom you will read in this chapter wrote in part to understand themselves better, but what they said was also valuable to readers. This is possible because their own experience was not merely the experience of one person, but also a part of shared human experience. Although Jennifer Murphy's specific experience with her brother was unique, many people are troubled by their relationship with their siblings. In this chapter's readings, too, you will see that the authors' individual experiences reflect larger social problems. Langston Hughes's "conversion" happened to him alone, but it resulted from social pressures common to all. In the second reading, Maya Angelou and the secretary were the only two people involved in the confrontation in the railway office, but many people suffer the kind of injustice she describes. As you write your journal entries, think about the larger problems or issues of which your particular experience might be an example. You make connections with your readers through these larger contexts.

INVENTION: READING, WRITING, AND TALKING FOR IDEAS

Reading

Langston Hughes wrote the following narrative essay about an experience that had happened years before. Like Louis Kirchoff ("The Red Car," Chapter 2), Hughes attempts to recapture emotions of his youth and reflect on them from a more mature adult perspective. You will probably need to use such a dual perspective—both the child's and adult's—in your own narrative essay.

The episode below is excerpted from Hughes's autobiographical book, *The Big Sea*.

 ### Salvation

Langston Hughes

1   I was saved from sin when I was going on thirteen. But not really saved. It happened like this. There was a big revival at my Auntie Reed's church. Every night for weeks there had been much preaching, singing, praying, and shouting, and some very hardened sinners had been brought to Christ, and the membership of the church had grown by leaps and bounds. Then just before the revival ended, they held a special meeting for children, "to bring the young lambs to the fold." My aunt spoke of it for days ahead. That night I was escorted to the front row and placed on the mourners' bench with all the other young sinners, who had not yet been brought to Jesus.

2   My aunt told me that when you were saved you saw a light, and something happened to you inside! And Jesus came into your life! And God was with you from then on! She said you could see and hear and feel Jesus in your soul. I believed her. I had heard a great many old people say the same thing and it seemed to me they ought to know. So

I sat there calmly in the hot, crowded church, waiting for Jesus to come to me.

3   The preacher preached a wonderful rhythmical sermon, all moans and shouts and lonely cries and dire pictures of hell, and then he sang a song about the ninety and nine safe in the fold, but one little lamb was left out in the cold. Then he said: "Won't you come? Won't you come to Jesus? Young lambs, won't you come?" And he held out his arms to all us young sinners there on the mourners' bench. And the little girls cried. And some of them jumped up and went to Jesus right away. But most of us just sat there.

4   A great many old people came and knelt around us and prayed, old women with jet-black faces and braided hair, old men with work-gnarled hands. And the church sang a song about the lower lights are burning, some poor sinners to be saved. And the whole building rocked with prayer and song.

5   Still I kept waiting to *see* Jesus.

6   Finally all the young people had gone to the altar and were saved, but one boy and me. He was a rounder's son named Westley. Westley and I were surrounded by sisters and deacons praying. It was very hot in the church, and getting late now. Finally Westley said to me in a whisper: "God damn! I'm tired o' sitting here. Let's get up and be saved." So he got up and was saved.

7   Then I was left all alone on the mourners' bench. My aunt came and knelt at my knees and cried, while prayers and songs swirled all around me in the little church. The whole congregation prayed for me alone, in a mighty wail of moans and voices. And I kept waiting serenely for Jesus, waiting, waiting—but he didn't come. I wanted to see him, but nothing happened to me. Nothing! I wanted something to happen to me, but nothing happened.

8   I heard the songs and the ministers saying: "Why don't you come? My dear child, why don't you come to Jesus? Jesus is waiting for you. He wants you. Why don't you come? Sister Reed, what is the child's name?"

9   "Langston," my aunt sobbed.

10   "Langston, why don't you come? Why don't you come and be saved? Oh, Lamb of God! Why don't you come?"

11   Now it was really getting late. I began to be ashamed of myself, holding everything up so long. I began to wonder what God thought about Westley, who certainly hadn't seen Jesus either, but who was now sitting proudly on the platform, swinging his knickerbockered legs and grinning down at me, surrounded by deacons and old women on their knees praying. God had not struck Westley dead for taking his name in vain or for lying in the temple. So I decided that maybe to save further trouble, I'd better lie, too, and say the Jesus had come, and get up and be saved.

12   So I got up.

13   Suddenly the whole room broke into a sea of shouting, as they saw me rise. Waves of rejoicing swept the place. Women leaped in the air. My aunt threw her arms around me. The minister took me by the hand and led me to the platform.

14   When things quieted down, in a hushed silence, punctuated by a few ecstatic "Amens," all the new young lambs were blessed in the name of God. Then joyous singing filled the room.

15   That night, for the last time in my life but one—for I was a big boy twelve years old—I cried, in bed alone, and couldn't stop. I buried my head under the quilts, but my aunt heard me. She woke up and told my uncle I was crying because the Holy Ghost had come into my life, and because I had seen Jesus. But I was really crying because I couldn't bear to tell her that I had lied, that I had deceived everybody in the church, and I hadn't seen Jesus, and that now I didn't believe there was a Jesus any more, since he didn't come to help me.

Journal Assignments

1. Write a journal page about your responses to the narrative. What do you think Hughes's main point is? Do you find more than one point? What did you like about the story? Dislike? This story was first published fifty years ago. In what ways does it relate to life today?

2. Your teacher may have you pick one or more of the following topics about which to write journal entries. These entries will help you to think of topics for your own personal narrative.

   a. Hughes was disillusioned by this experience. Write a journal entry in which you first define "disillusionment" in your own terms. Then write about an experience that caused you to be disillusioned about something.

   b. Hughes's beliefs changed (at least temporarily) as a result of this experience. Write a journal entry about an experience of yours that made you change your beliefs about something.

   c. Sometimes experiences lead us to appreciate something we had not appreciated before or to understand something that had been confusing. Write about an experience that led you to greater appreciation or understanding of something or someone.

   d. We tend to learn more by working through difficulties, problems, or conflicts than we do from good times. Write about a difficulty or conflict that you have experienced. What did you learn from it?

Reading Questions

The following questions are designed to help you analyze how a good narrative essay is written. You will use many of the same techniques that you discover in Hughes's writing when you write your own essay.

Content

1. How would you describe the character of the boy Langston at the beginning of the story?

2. What differences might have existed between what the adults meant by "seeing Jesus" and what Langston the boy thought they meant? Hughes does not tell us what his own interpretation of "seeing Jesus" is as an adult, but we can speculate about it. Do you think he still feels as he did right after the revival meeting? Do you think he agrees with the adults of his youth? Or do you think his adult interpretation is different from both?

3. What does Langston the boy learn by the end of the story? (*Hint:* This question has several answers. You might think about what he learned about himself, about religion, or about the adult world.)

4. What does the story say about the effects of social pressure on a child? Why does Langston resist social pressure? Why does he give in? What conflicts are involved here?

5. Why is this story titled "Salvation"?

Structure

1. This narrative starts with some background information essential to the reader's understanding of the situation and then moves to the main incident. With which sentence does Hughes begin the main incident? Summarize the essential background information that he supplies before this sentence. Why must readers know the information in paragraph 2?

2. How much time does Hughes cover in the first two paragraphs? In the rest of the story? Note that he takes many more words to cover the short time span of the main incident than to describe the weeks leading up to it. Why? Imagine the reverse, that he had spent 13 paragraphs on the previous weeks, and only 2 on the children's meeting. How would that have changed the emphasis and point of the story?

3. Scan the story to pick out the quoted speech. What similarities do you find among the quotations? For what purpose does Hughes use quotation?

4. Paragraphs 3, 4, and 7 are especially descriptive. To which senses do the descriptive words appeal?

5. What are the **conflicts** in this story? There must be *two* opposing sides to any conflict. The three typical kinds of conflicts are **person against nature, person against person,** and **person against self.** Into which categories do the conflicts in this story fall?

6. You might have noticed that paragraphs 5 and 12 are each only one

sentence long. Why? What is the **turning point,** or climax, of this story?

Reading

Maya Angelou wrote the following narrative about an experience that had happened years before. Like Louis Kirchoff (''The Red Car,'' Chapter 2), Angelou attempts to recapture emotions of her youth and reflect on them from a more mature adult perspective. You will probably need to do the same—adopting both the child's and the adult's perspective in your own narrative essay.

The narrative reprinted below is an episode from Angelou's autobiography, *I Know Why the Caged Bird Sings*.

 ### Step Forward in the Car, Please

Maya Angelou

1   My room had all the cheeriness of a dungeon and the appeal of a tomb. It was going to be impossible to stay there, but leaving held no attraction for me, either. Running away from home would be anticlimactic after Mexico, and a dull story after my month in the car lot. But the need for change bulldozed a road down the center of my mind.

2   I had it. The answer came to me with the suddenness of a collision. I would go to work. Mother wouldn't be difficult to convince; after all, in school I was a year ahead of my grade and Mother was a firm believer in self-sufficiency. In fact, she'd be pleased to think that I had that much gumption, that much of her in my character. (She liked to speak of herself as the original ''do-it-yourself girl.'')

3   Once I had settled on getting a job, all that remained was to decide which kind of job I was most fitted for. My intellectual pride had kept me from selecting typing, shorthand or filing as subjects in school, so office work was ruled out. War plants and shipyards demanded birth certificates, and mine would reveal me to be fifteen, and ineligible for work. So the well-paying defense jobs were also out. Women had replaced men on the streetcars as conductors and motormen, and the thought of sailing up and down the hills of San Franciso in a dark-blue uniform, with a money changer at my belt, caught my fancy.

4   Mother was as easy as I had anticipated. The world was moving so fast, so much money was being made, so many people were dying in Guam, and Germany, that hordes of strangers became good friends overnight. Life was cheap and death entirely free. How could she have the time to think about my academic career?

5   To her question of what I planned to do, I replied that I would get a job on the streetcars. She rejected the proposal with: ''They don't accept colored people on the streetcars.''

6   I would like to claim an immediate fury which was followed by the noble determination to break the restricting tradition. But the truth is, my first reaction was one of disappointment. I'd pictured myself, dressed in a neat blue serge suit, my money changer swinging jauntily at my waist, and a cheery smile for the passengers which would make their own work day brighter.

7   From disappointment, I gradually ascended the emotional ladder to haughty indignation, and finally to that state of stubbornness where the mind is locked like the jaws of an enraged bulldog.

8   I would go to work on the streetcars and wear a blue serge suit. Mother gave me her support with one of her usual terse asides, "That's what you want to do? Then nothing beats a trial but a failure. Give it everything you've got. I've told you many times, 'Can't do is like Don't Care.' Neither of them have a home."

9   Translated, that meant there was nothing a person can't do, and there should be nothing a human being didn't care about. It was the most positive encouragement I could have hoped for.

10   In the offices of the Market Street Railway Company, the receptionist seemed as surprised to see me there as I was surprised to find the interior dingy and the décor drab. Somehow I had expected waxed surfaces and carpeted floors. If I had met no resistance, I might have decided against working for such a poor-mouth-looking concern. As it was, I explained that I had come to see about a job. She asked, was I sent by an agency, and when I replied that I was not, she told me they were only accepting applicants from agencies.

11   The classified pages of the morning papers had listed advertisements for motorettes and conductorettes and I reminded her of that. She gave me a face full of astonishment that my suspicious nature would not accept.

12   "I am applying for the job listed in this morning's *Chronicle* and I'd like to be presented to your personnel manager." While I spoke in supercilious accents, and looked at the room as if I had an oil well in my own backyard, my armpits were being pricked by millions of hot pointed needles. She saw her escape and dived into it.

13   "He's out. He's out for the day. You might call tomorrow and if he's in, I'm sure you can see him." Then she swiveled her chair around on its rusty screws and with that I was supposed to be dismissed.

14   "May I ask his name?"

15   She half turned, acting surprised to find me still there.

16   "His name? Whose name?"

17   "Your personnel manager."

18   We were firmly joined in the hypocrisy to play out the scene.

19   "The personnel manager? Oh, he's Mr. Cooper, but I'm not sure you'll find him here tomorrow. He's . . . Oh, but you can try."

20   "Thank you."

21   "You're welcome."

22   And I was out of the musty room and into the even mustier lobby. In the street I saw the receptionist and myself going faithfully through paces that were stale with familiarity, although I had never encountered that kind of situation before and, probably, neither had she. We were like actors who, knowing the play by heart, were still able to cry afresh over the old tragedies and laugh spontaneously at the comic situations.

23   The miserable little encounter had nothing to do with me, the me of me, any more than it had to do with that silly clerk. The incident was a recurring dream, concocted years before by stupid whites and it eternally came back to haunt us all. The secretary and I were like Hamlet and Laertes in the final scene, where, because of harm done by one ancestor to another, we were bound to duel to the death. Also because the play must end somewhere.

24   I went further than forgiving the clerk, I accepted her as a fellow victim of the same puppeteer.

25   On the streetcar, I put my fare into the box and the conductorette looked at me with the usual hard eyes of white contempt. "Move into the car, please move on in the car." She patted her money changer.

26   Her Southern nasal accent sliced my meditation and I looked deep into my thoughts. All lies, all comfortable lies. The receptionist was not innocent and neither was I. The whole charade we had played out in that crummy waiting room had directly to do with me, Black, and her, white.

27   I wouldn't move into the streetcar but stood on the ledge over the conductor, glaring. My mind shouted so energetically that the announcement made my veins stand out, and my mouth tighten into a prune.

28   I WOULD HAVE THE JOB. I WOULD BE A CONDUCTORETTE AND SLING A FULL MONEY CHANGER FROM MY BELT. I WOULD.

29   The next three weeks were a honeycomb of determination with apertures for the days to go in and out. The Negro organizations to whom I appealed for support bounced me back and forth like a shuttlecock on a badminton court. Why did I insist on that particular job? Openings were going begging that paid nearly twice the money. The minor officials with whom I was able to win an audience thought me mad. Possibly I was.

30   Downtown San Francisco became alien and cold, and the streets I had loved in a personal familiarity were unknown lanes that twisted with malicious intent. Old buildings, whose gray rococo façades housed my memories of the Forty-Niners, and Diamond Lil, Robert Service, Sutter and Jack London, were then imposing structures viciously joined to keep me out. My trips to the steetcar office were of the frequency of a person on salary. The struggle expanded. I was no longer in conflict only with

the Market Street Railway but with the marble lobby of the building which housed its offices, and elevators and their operators.

31   During this period of strain Mother and I began our first steps on the long path toward mutual adult admiration. She never asked for reports and I didn't offer any details. But every morning she made breakfast, gave me carfare and lunch money, as if I were going to work. She comprehended the perversity of life, that in the struggle lies the joy. That I was no glory seeker was obvious to her, and that I had to exhaust every possibility before giving in was also clear.

32   On my way out of the house one morning she said, "Life is going to give you just what you put in it. Put your whole heart in everything you do, and pray, then you can wait." Another time she reminded me that "God helps those who help themselves." She had a store of aphorisms which she dished out as the occasion demanded. Strangely, as bored as I was with clichés, her inflection gave them something new, and set me thinking for a little while at least. Later when asked how I got my job, I was never able to say exactly. I only knew that one day, which was tiresomely like all the others before it, I sat in the Railway office, ostensibly waiting to be interviewed. The receptionist called me to her desk and shuffled a bundle of papers to me. They were job application forms. She said they had to be filled in triplicate. I had little time to wonder if I had won or not, for the standard questions reminded me of the necessity for dexterous lying. How old was I? List my previous jobs, starting from the last held and go backward to the first. How much money did I earn, and why did I leave the position? Give two references (not relatives).

33   Sitting at a side table my mind and I wove a cat's ladder of near truths and total lies. I kept my face blank (an old art) and wrote quickly the fable of Marguerite Johnson, aged nineteen, former companion and driver for Mrs. Annie Henderson (a White Lady) in Stamps, Arkansas.

34   I was given blood tests, aptitude tests, physical coordination tests, and Rorschachs, then on a blissful day I was hired as the first Negro on the San Francisco streetcars.

35   Mother gave me the money to have my blue serge suit tailored, and I learned to fill out work cards, operate the money changer and punch transfers. The time crowded together and at an End of Days I was swinging on the back of the rackety trolley, smiling sweetly and persuading my charges to "step forward in the car, please."

36   For one whole semester the streetcars and I shimmied up and scooted down the sheer hills of San Francisco. I lost some of my need for the Black ghetto's shielding-sponge quality, as I clanged and cleared my way down Market Street, with its honky-tonk homes for homeless sailors, past the quiet retreat of Golden Gate Park and along closed undwelled-in-looking dwellings of the Sunset District.

37   My work shifts were split so haphazardly that it was easy to believe

that my superiors had chosen them maliciously. Upon mentioning my suspicions to Mother, she said, "Don't worry about it. You ask for what you want, and you pay for what you get. And I'm going to show you that it ain't no trouble when you pack double."

38   She stayed awake to drive me out to the car barn at four thirty in the mornings, or to pick me up when I was relieved just before dawn. Her awareness of life's perils convinced her that while I would be safe on the public conveyances, she "wasn't about to trust a taxi driver with her baby."

39   When the spring classes began, I resumed my commitment with formal education. I was so much wiser and older, so much more independent, with a bank account and clothes that I bought for myself, that I was sure that I had learned and earned the magic formula which would make me a part of the gay life my contemporaries led.

40   Not a bit of it. Within weeks, I realized that my schoolmates and I were on paths moving diametrically away from each other. They were concerned and excited over the approaching football games, but I had in my immediate past raced a car down a dark and foreign Mexican mountain. They concentrated great interest on who was worthy of being student body president, and when the metal bands would be removed from their teeth, while I remembered sleeping for a month in a wrecked automobile and conducting a streetcar in the uneven hours of the morning.

Vocabulary

Look up each of the following words in your dictionary. Copy each word on your own paper, copy the sentence from the reading in which it appears, and copy the dictionary meaning that fits the sentence. You are studying how words are used *in context* because this is an excellent way to increase your vocabulary.

hordes (paragraph 4)	concoct (paragraph 23)
ascend (paragraph 7)	apertures (paragraph 29)
terse (paragraph 8)	alien (paragraph 30)
aside (paragraph 8)	aphorism (paragraph 32)
supercilious (paragraph 12)	shimmy (paragraph 36)
swivel (paragraph 13)	retreat (paragraph 36)
paces (paragraph 22)	haphazard (paragraph 37)
encounter (paragraph 22)	maliciously (paragraph 37)
recur (paragraph 23)	conveyance (paragraph 38)

Journal Assignments

1. Write a journal entry about your responses to the reading. You might discuss any or all of the following questions: What do you

think Angelou's main point is? Did you find more than one significant point in the story? What did you like about the story? Dislike?
This story was written during World War II, close to 50 years ago,
and many of the historical conditions Angelou describes have
changed. What aspects of her story are still relevant to readers
today?

2. Your teacher may ask you to pick one or more of the following
   topics for your journal entries. These entries will help you think of
   topics for your own personal narrative essay.

   a. One of the subthemes of this essay is Angelou's relationship with
      her mother. Write about a time in your own life when you re-
      ceived unexpected support from an adult. It does not have to
      be a parent; it might be another relative, a teacher, or an adult
      friend.
   b. Racial discrimination is an important theme in the essay. Write
      about a time when you were a victim of discrimination. How did
      you react to the discrimination? What did you learn from it? As
      you think about this subject, remember that there are grounds
      for discrimination other than race. Age and sex are two exam-
      ples.
   c. Discrimination usually involves a group of "insiders" and a
      group of "outsiders": the "insiders" discriminate in some way
      against those they consider "outsiders." Nearly everyone has
      experienced this in high school where there is always a "popu-
      lar" in-group that excludes others, who become the outsiders.
      Have you ever been the member of an in-group? Or have you
      ever been an outsider? Describe an incident that let you know
      that you were either inside or outside of a group. What did you
      learn about yourself or others from the experience?
   d. Write about a time when you have had a conflict with a person
      in a position of authority. How did you react? What did you learn
      from the experience?
   e. We often learn a lot about the adult world from our first work
      experience. Describe your own experience job hunting and what
      you learned from it. Or describe an on-the-job experience that
      taught you something about the work world.

3. We tend to learn more by working through difficulties, problems,
   or conflicts than we do from good times. Write about a difficulty or
   problem that you have experienced. (You might elaborate on one
   of the experiences you have described in previous entries.) What
   did you learn from it?

Reading Questions

Content

Although this essay covers a timespan of at least seven or eight months, only one incident is described in detail: the encounter with the receptionist at the railway office. This single incident, lasting maybe five minutes, takes up several paragraphs of the essay. The following questions will help you understand why Angelou thought this incident important enough to merit so much space.

1. What is Angelou's initial reaction to the railway office itself?

2. When does Angelou first suspect that the receptionist is lying? What makes her suspicious?

3. How does Angelou force the issue?

4. In paragraph 17, Angelou calls the office scene "hypocritical." In what ways is each actor (Angelou and the receptionist) being hypocritical?

5. In paragraphs 21 through 23, Angelou makes an attempt to explain to herself the office scene. How does she explain it? According to this explanation, where does the responsibility for the hypocrisy lie?

6. In just a few words in paragraph 25, Angelou entirely reverses her first interpretation. What is the new interpretation? What happened to make her rethink the situation? What were the results of her new interpretation?

7. Why does the writer make the confrontation at the railway office the central incident of her narrative?

8. What did Angelou learn from her mother during her job hunt and employment? What did she learn *about* her mother?

9. This narrative focuses on Angelou's relationship to the adult world of work, but she does not ignore the fact that she was supposed to be a high-school student at the time.

    a. What does she tell you about her school life at the beginning of the story?
    b. What is her status among her peers at the end of the story?
    c. What are Angelou's feelings about this status? Are they the same for the 15-year-old girl as for the adult writer?
    d. Why does Angelou close this narrative with her return to school? What did she learn about herself when she returned to school?

10. What is the significance of the title "Step Forward in the Car, Please?" In what ways does the sentence extend beyond what the conductor says to streetcar passengers?

Structure

1. You have noted that the 20 or so minutes spanning the time from Angelou's walking into the railway office through her rethinking of the confrontation with the receptionist takes up a quarter of the story, though the entire story covers 7 or 8 months. These 20 minutes are the turning point of her story, so Angelou emphasizes this incident by taking extra space to tell it. The following questions help you see how she achieved this emphasis.

   a. Find all of the examples of quoted speech in the narrative. In what part of the story do you find most quotations? What else does Angelou emphasize through the use of quotations?

   b. Reread paragraphs 9 through 27. Angelou uses descriptive details to describe people, places, and actions. Point out a few details in each of these categories.

2. One of the characteristics that make a story different from other kinds of writing, like descriptive writing, is that a story always has conflict. Remember, there must be *two opposing sides* to any conflict and the three typical conflicts are person against person, person against nature, and person against him or herself. Identify the conflicts in Angelou's story.

3. Stories also must have a plot; something must happen. The conflict is acted out in some way. How is conflict acted out in this narrative?

4. The action in a story usually proceeds to a turning point, a point at which an important decision is made. In which paragraph does the turning point of Angelou's story occur?

5. A story must also have at least one **setting,** a place where the events occur. What are the settings of Angelou's story? Which setting(s) can you visualize best?

6. Stories must also have **characters,** the people who do the action.

   a. Who are the characters in Angelou's story? Describe some of the main character traits of each character.

   b. How does Angelou make you aware of these traits? By describing actions? By describing appearance? By quoting characters? Find examples of the techniques she uses.

DRAFTING: WRITING, TALKING, REWRITING, AND EVALUATING

As you know from previous assignments, the first step in the process of writing a paper is discovering ideas to write about. Several strategies are available to you for doing this. You have already begun to use them for your narrative essay by reading and discussing Hughes's or Angelou's ideas or both and by writing one or more journal entries. The class brainstorming exercise below will add to your supply of ideas. Then, as you continue to explore ideas in your journals, you will also read and discuss the discovery and drafting processes of one student, Sharon Nelson, as she wrote this assignment.

Brainstorming

Significant stories usually come out of conflict, difficulty, or struggle. Recall the three traditional kinds of conflicts: person against person, person against self, and person against nature. These categories may remind you of more specific conflicts. For instance, two examples of relationships in the person-against-person category are between mother and daughter and between mother and son. As a class, think of as many specific examples of possible conflicts in each of the three categories as you can.

After your class has collected as many such conflicts as it can, pick a few and think of specific incidents that could arise from the situation. For instance, conflict between mother and daughter may be over the amount of responsibility the daughter is expected to take for the care of younger siblings. The narrative would then be about a single incident in which this conflict came to a head.

One Student's Writing Process

You will need to write about an experience that was *significant* to you in order to write a good narrative essay. Important experiences are often also very personal, and though you might be willing to have a teacher or a stranger read them, you might not want other students to read them just now. So you will not work in writing groups on your drafts for this essay.

Sharon Nelson's Essay

Instead of sharing your writing with each other, you will follow the writing process of a former student of ours, Sharon Nelson, as you write your own drafts. Reprinted below is Sharon's final draft exactly as she turned it in (though names have been changed). After you read it, we will trace the development of this final paper from her first journal entries.

Fifteen Dollars

1   It was a hot, sizzling, July afternoon when my now ex-husband Earl and I arrived with out baby daughter Becky at Paul's Foodcity.

2   After Earl had precisely parked our old gray bomber in the shade of the only tree in the parking lot, he lunged out of the car with the grace of a pregnant hippo. Slamming the door he catapulted straight for the store. As he reached the IN door he was ushered into the store by the mad rush of Saturday shoppers. However, pretty soon he meandered timidly back to the car. He took my hand and helped me out. He smiled a sheepish sort of smile. He knew he was in trouble. I knew the smile was only for insurance.

3   With Becky in tow I took a deep breath and tried to quickly collect my thoughts. But, because of an argument over money before leaving for the store, the churning in my stomach felt more than ever like a pool of acid. The gases expanded up through my whole diaphragm. The sour taste of rotten eggs reached up and grabbed ahold of my esophagus, then my mouth and finally clenched its sickly cold fingers around my tongue. How could Earl have wasted almost his whole paycheck on himself, doing heaven knows what? How was I going to make the last fifteen dollars stretch for one month's groceries?

4   Emptiness entrapped my heart. I felt the vomit rolling in a slow, bubbling, volcanic action up my throat. I was going to be sick! Earl's emotionless face strained to hide the look of impatience. This whole money thing wasn't even phasing him. With his hand gripped tightly about my arm, my body moved in a robotic motion toward what now appeared to be an emotionless piece of concrete. A towering, single level of doom, whose gaping jaws would swallow what bit of dignity I had left.

5   As I made my way inside the store and placed Becky in a shoppng basket, I glanced at the shoppers rushing about. They were not paying much attention to anyone. Suddenly the room began to spin, slowly at first, then with ever increasing speed until the ringing in my ears whined with such a tinniness it felt like the onset of madness. I looked about once more only to see distorted, concave looking faces everywhere.

6   My legs plopped one in front of the other. My hands, now clammy and slippery with cold sweat, grasped cautiously each item, removing and replacing, deciding if it was an absolute necessity. After an hour and one-half I found myself at the check-out counter. I looked hungrily at the basket ahead of us, the over-weight family, laughing and fighting joyously as though they had not a care in the world. Then I looked at the

contents of my basket, baby food (a necessity), milk, eggs, fruit and vegetables. An uncontrollable rage welled up in my breast as I looked at my sweet baby and then thought of my selfish husband.

7   Suddenly my wandering shopper threw two steaks into our basket. I could almost smell the smoke from the barbecue as my eyes, welling up with tears, envisioned the succulent, rare morsels. Earl kept saying, "The Lord will help us, wait and see." The dry, hot lump in my throat scratched and tore its way down. As the cool tears trickled down my hot, flushed face, my mind burned with an unceasing heat as it whirled and spun like a cyclone. Sparks pelleted my brain as though to laser it into sections. It felt as though I was short circuiting. The blood rushed to my brain only to again plumet back down to my feet. Dizziness swooped over me as I tried desperately to gain control. As I laid my head in my hands, on the basket handle, sweat escaped every pore of my body. Tears were coming like a leak from a dike as they were held desperately back, and wiped away quickly with a shaking hand.

8   It was my turn. As the checker asked, "hi, how are you?" a small timid "pretty good, thanks" escaped through a trembling lip held tight in place by several teeth and a clenched jaw.

9   "15.87," said the checker. I turned to find Earl, but he was nowhere to be found. I didn't have enough.

10   "Can you take off the steaks?" The words trembled out like an old-fashioned car trying to start up.

11   Although the checker was very polite, it felt as though she could see right through me. Right through the embarrassment of my poverty.

12   As my eyes hesitantly looked up there stood Earl, like a pompous version of Buddah, with his beer belly sagging below his belt and a scowl that reminded me of a stern, primpy old maid with her mouth screwed up like a lemon. A strange, almost savage, feeling penetrated the very core of my heart. I deserved better than this, better than him! No one should ever have to endure the helpless feeling of being a doormat to anyone. Life with all its wonderous facets has far too much to offer. Each person is a unique, individual personality and no one has the right to take that away. With this feeling deeply embedded in my mind, though I also allow myself the right to make mistakes, I took the change from the fifteen dollars, clutched my baby, my grocery bag and vowed never, never to be that poor again.

Discussion Questions

1. What is the setting of Sharon's essay? What do you know about it?

2. Sharon began her narrative with the arrival at the grocery store parking lot, but she could have begun it at other points in time. She might have begun it earlier, with the argument over money at

home, or later, with standing in line at the checkout counter. Why is the arrival at the parking lot a good point at which to begin?

3. Who are the characters? What do you know about them?

4. The most obvious conflict in this story is the one between Sharon and her husband over money. What other conflicts can you discover?

5. What are the emotions Sharon Nelson is feeling? What are their causes? How does Sharon make them clear to the reader?

6. Discuss the writing itself. What words or phrases are especially vivid? If you were the author, would you leave any of the descriptive words and phrases out? Which ones? Why?

7. It is often difficult to decide when to begin a new paragraph in a narrative essay because the whole story seems to be a single action. Study Sharon's paragraphs. Why did she begin new paragraphs where she did?

8. What is the turning point of Sharon's essay? Which parts of the trip are described in most detail? If you were the author, would you change the emphasis of the story in any way? What can an author do to change the emphasis of a piece of writing?

9. What is the significance of this experience for Sharon? Were you surprised by her final sentence? If so, what had you expected her to say?

10. Everybody goes to the grocery store. This is hardly an interesting event in itself. Why is it significant to readers? In other words, what important problems does Sharon discuss that her readers might share?

Sharon's Journals

We will be able to follow Sharon's writing process from her first journal entries through her rough draft. Sharon was asked to write journal assignments somewhat different from yours. Her assignment was simply to write several daily entries in which she was to think about possible paper topics.

You will find as you read Sharon's entries that some of her writing problems are the same as yours and some are different. Note what she thinks of doing to solve her problems.

First Entry

I could do it on a number of things except I don't know what maybe my experience as a divorced single mom. No, maybe on my life as a college student at 40. Oh the heck with it. I don't know, I don't even know who would be interested in any of my life. One day I'd like to write a book but I guess that will be when I can look at things without feeling it any more.

Maybe I'll do it on something that maybe the world knows alot about but needs to know more about. If I can stand it I'll write on an experience with my ex. It seems like there's so much to write when I think about it, but, of course, if I write to much it would probably compile to such a point that it could make a book.

Second Entry

Now comes the task of narrowing it down. I hate him still for what he did to us but I'm not sure if I'll ever get over that hate. I guess it will be easier if I take a event that is not as bad as some. Yet, even that was horrible. But how can I write this without showing my discust and hatred for him. Maybe if I just free write first I'll be able to work it out.

Discussion Questions

1. What are Sharon's concerns as she begins to write?
2. Sharon is *not* worried about having nothing at all to write about. Why not?
3. What strategies does Sharon consider using to overcome her problems with getting started?

Sharon's Freewrite

Sharon agreed to share her freewrite with you even though she wrote it not as a journal entry but for herself only. It was an important part of her discovery process.

Well here goes. I only wish I knew a way to really tell on paper what I feel in my heart. Earl did so many rotten things I could probably write a whole novel except then theres the problem of wondering how people might react if things were on paper. Oh who cares, they're big boys and girls. Sometimes the truth is absolutely shocking. I could write about the time he tryed to kill me by drowning or about the time I found out he was hurting Becky, God I hate him for that. What gave him the right to think he could abuse such a tiny sweet child. I know it may take time to forgive him but it is only because of the rotten, awful things he did. For example he thinks that no one matters but himself. All he thinks of is his sex and his gut— That's it! Like the time he thought manna would fall from Heaven—even if he wasted his whole paycheck just on his selfish self. Sometimes I don't know what I ever saw in him to love. As long as he didn't starve he didn't care if Becky or I did. It didn't matter to him if a check would bounce or if anything he would just run to mommy and daddy if he had to for a hand out. Why didn't they ever teach him to grow up. Why didn't they ever leave him alone long enough to become responsible for some one other than himself. I know I'll never forget that day. I didn't want his folks handout and yet I hated him for being so selfish and not even caring if we would starve. Thank God I had the sense—though it took 10 years to get away from him. Now we aren't constantly beaten, abused or starved. Times are still hard while I'm in school but I will never ever let Becky and I go hungry again.

Discussion Questions

1. How many different incidents does Sharon mention in her freewrite? At what point does she decide on the subject for her paper?
2. In what ways does the grocery store incident fit the requirements she had mentioned in her journal entries?
3. Though she has a topic, what Sharon has written so far is not even close to looking like her final paper. Put yourself in Sharon's shoes (or behind Sharon's pen) at this point. What do you need to think about in order to turn this topic idea into a narrative essay?
4. Sharon was very much wrapped up in her own experience and feelings as she freewrote. Do you think she succeeded in making the grocery store incident significant to her readers, as well as to herself, when she wrote it into her narrative essay? If so, what accounts for her success? If not, what could she have done to make the final draft more meaningful to readers?

Sharon's First Draft

As you think about your topic, you might find that your ideas do not develop in exactly the same order, or pattern, as Sharon's. You might focus on a single topic more quickly than Sharon, or you might need to keep writing journal entries (or freewrites for yourself as audience) longer than Sharon did. You might not be happy with your topic or approach after writing your first draft and make major revisions at that point. All of these variations are normal. We are following Sharon's process as only one example of how writing develops. Every writer works in a slightly different pattern, and the same writer's pattern might vary from one assignment to the next.

The first two paragraphs of Sharon's first draft are reprinted below. You will see that by the time she finished her journals and her freewrite and actually began the draft, she had the general form and content of the narrative pretty well in mind.

Note the changes Sharon made in these paragraphs from the first to the final draft. Attention to these changes will help you to revise your own first draft.

Most people consider a trip to the grocery store quite mundane and rather dull. Many do it only out of necessity.

It was a hot, sizzling July afternoon when my now ex-husband Earl and I arrived with our baby daughter Becky at Paul's Foodcity. Earl, after precisely parking our gray bomber in the shade of the only tree in the parking lot lunged out of the car door with the grace of a hippo in waiting. Slamming the door he catapulted straight for the store. He reached the IN door, he was ushered in the store by the mad rush of Saturday shoppers. Pretty soon, however, he meandered to the car. He had forgotten me, the baby and the check book. He smiled one of those sheepish smiles as he took my hand and helped me out of the car. He knew he was in trouble (but that I wouldn't say too much.) So with Becky in tow I took a deep breath and stood up in the open car doorway. As my eyes scanned the parking lot I noticed the usual Saturday bustling of people, with their baskets upon baskets of groceries coming out of the store and loading their cars. My stomach that had been churning on the ride to the store began to feel like a pool of acid with the gases expanding up through my whole diaphram (it felt like the creeping gas of death) as the sour taste of rotten eggs reached up and grabbed hold of my esophagus, then my mouth and tongue. I felt sicker than I ever remember feeling against any one person—Earl. What kind of thoughtless waste could have possessed him. How could he have wasted that much money on himself, forgetting his responsibilities to his wife and most importantly to his tiny child. How could he have wasted almost his entire check on himself? With thoughts like this flooding my brain, surely I was entering the twilight zone. How could I do what Earl was expecting me to do? How could I make 15 dollars stretch for one month's groceries?

Discussion Questions

1. Sharon started her final draft with an entirely different paragraph from her first draft. What are the effects of the change? Do you think she made the right decision?

2. A major problem confronting writers is *how much* to say. Writers seem to fall into two categories: those who tend to say too much and those who tend to say too little. Which is Sharon's problem?

3. To know when you have said enough, but not too much, you need to think about your *readers*. When they read your narrative, your readers need to understand (a) the event itself (what happened), (b) your emotions during the event, and (c) why the event is important (what issues are involved).

   Look closely at the material that Sharon decided to leave out. (a) Why did she decide that it was not necessary? (b) What did she add to the final draft that did not appear in the first draft? (c) Why did she make the additions?

4. Sharon also made some changes in wording. What are they? Why did she make them?

Evaluating a Narrative Essay

Evaluation Criteria

A good personal narrative essay does the following:

1. Includes a point that is
   a. clearly focused and stated in the introduction of the essay, the conclusion, or both
   b. significant to readers
2. Includes an introductory section that in some way sets the scene and introduces the characters
3. Tells a story that has
   a. a conflict
   b. a turning point
4. Focuses on the turning point by telling this part of the story in more detail than any other part
5. Excludes information that does not contribute to the main point of the story
6. Uses active, vivid words that show actions and emotions
7. Uses paragraphs appropriately
8. Includes a conclusion that summarizes the significance of the event
9. Has a title that
   a. gives the reader some sense of the subject and point
   b. makes the reader curious about the essay
10. Has no major grammatical, spelling, or punctuation errors

Sample Student Essay

Here is another student essay written for this assignment.

Influenced by Fear

1   During winter quarter of 1989 I reluctantly enrolled in a required history class. Two weeks into the quarter I found myself behind in my reading, lost in the class discussions and faced with an essay test in a week. Needless to say, I felt very overwhelmed and discouraged.

2   It was obvious I needed help; however, the fear inside kept me silent. My head began to pound as a constant debate ran through my mind. "Everyone else seemed to be grasping the material. I can't raise my hand and reveal how lost I am. I'll just study extra hard this weekend and get all caught up."

3   By the time the test day had come my fear had escalated. Feeling defeated I chose to avoid the test and the class the rest of the quarter. After I rationalized inside that failing out of choice was easier to accept than trial and error. However, the conflict seemed only to intensify through out the quarter. I tried to face my fear by making several attempts during the quarter to the professors office but I always ended up walking past his office. I couldn't force myself to tell him his discussions were confusing and that I feared asking for help. I believed his sympathy would be limited because my actions had proven far from responsible. Therefore, I chose to remain silent and deal with the consequences later.

4   A few weeks after the quarter I walked into my apartment after work and noticed the mail on the table. My heart started pounding when I saw the familiar red and white envelope. Quickly passing the table I went to my room with out picking up the envelope. The time had come to face the consequences but I was still trying to avoid them. After a few minutes I went and picked up the letter and slowly ripped it open. There it was in black and white. The conflict I felt during the previous quarter was symbolized in one letter, F.

5   My stomach dropped to the floor and my body turned weak as I felt the shock of reality. My illusion of being erased from the class role as well as my responsibilities, because of my absence had lost its power. The consequences for my actions had been chosen. However, along with the shock of disillusionment came a sense of relief. I was no longer in the dark about the out come of my decision. The conflict had ceased when I saw the end result.

6   In time I was able to see the grade as a representation of my performance and not my potential. The result of my avoidance was hard to accept but it helped me look inside myself and realize how important education is to me. I had resisted asking for help at the risk of looking stupid. However, the feeling of defeat through silence was a lot more costly.

7   This experience taught me how important it is in school and every day life to confront fears instead of avoiding them. Trying to go around the fear and pretending its not there only intensifies the conflict going on inside. However, by taking steps to overcome a fear can leave a person with a sense of accomplishment.

Evaluating the Sample Essay

Meet in writing groups to evaluate the sample essay according to the criteria. Which criteria does the essay meet? Point out sections, sentences, or words or all three that meet the criteria. Which criteria does it fail to meet?

You might also evaluate Sharon Nelson's essay according to these criteria.

Revising Your Own Essay

Once you have finished your first draft, evaluate it according to the same criteria you used for the student example. Which criteria have you met? Which have you not met? Revise your draft to meet each of the criteria.

EDITING

Editing the Narrative Essay

Time Words: Verbs

One way that time is indicated in English is through the form of a verb. In writing a narrative, verbs are always a problem. You know that the spelling, the endings, and the number of words used in a verb change to show whether the action happens in the past, the present, or the future:

Past tense
Karl *drove* to Baltimore.
Edwin *looked* for his glasses.

Present tense
Karl *is driving* to Baltimore.
Edwin *is looking* for his glasses.

Future tense
Karl *will drive* to Baltimore.
Edwin *will look* for his glasses until he finds them.

Note the changes in spelling, endings, and number of words used for each of the different tenses. Note especially that a change in spelling (usually in one or more vowels in the middle of the word) or the addition of an *-ed* ending means the past tense. The addition of an *-ing* ending means the present tense.

When you write a narrative, you are writing about an event that happened at some time in the past, so it is natural to put your verbs in the past tense.

Exercise The sentences below are from Sharon's essay, rewritten to illustrate the problem of inconsistent tense. Decide whether the verb (italicized) in each sentence is in the past or present tense. Since all of the action actually happened in the past, every underlined verb should be in the past tense. If the verb is in past tense, write *correct* in the blank at the end of the sentence. If it is in the present tense, change it to the past tense in the appropriate blank at the end of the sentence.

1. My legs *plopped* one in front of the other. _PAST_

2. My hands, now clammy and slippery with cold sweat, *grasp* cautiously each time, removing and replacing, deciding if it *was* an absolute necessity. _PRESENT PAST_

3. After an hour and one-half I *find* myself at the check-out counter. _PAST_

4. I *look* hungrily at the basket ahead of us, the over-weight family, laughing and fighting joyously as though they *had* not a care in the world. _PRESENT PAST_

5. Then I *looked* at the contents of my basket, baby food (a necessity), milk, eggs, fruit and vegetables. _PAST_

6. An uncontrollable rage *wells* up in my breast as I *look* at my sweet baby and then *think* of my selfish husband. _PAST PRESENT PRESENT_

Time Words: Adverbs and Prepositions

The verb is not the only way that time is indicated in English. The English language also contains words whose only job is to indicate time sequence: actions happening before, at the same time as, or after other actions. These words are usually classified as **adverbs** or **prepositions.** Below is a partial list of these words.

before	during	after
until	as	then
	now	next
	while	

Here is Sharon's paragraph again, just as she wrote it. Read it and circle any of the time words listed above. What verb comes before the time word? After? What does the time word tell you about the sequence of the actions named by each verb?

> My legs plopped one in front of the other. My hands, now clammy and slippery with cold sweat, grasped cautiously each item, removing and replacing, deciding if it was an absolute necessity. After an hour and one-half I found myself at the check-out counter. I looked hungrily at the basket ahead of us, the over-weight family, laughing and fighting joyously as though they had not a care in the world. Then I looked at the contents of my basket, baby food (a necessity), milk, eggs, fruit and vegetables. An uncontrollable rage welled up in my breast as I looked at my sweet baby and then thought of my selfish husband.

Editing Your Own Draft

Check the verbs in your own essay. Are main verbs consistently in the past tense? If not, make corrections where necessary.

Analyzing and Classifying Product Names

WRITING ASSIGNMENT

In this essay you will use your own knowledge, some research, and your analytical skills to support a point. Specifically, you will analyze product naming as an advertising strategy. To do this assignment, you will gather and classify evidence to support the point that advertisers compose descriptive product names to evoke images that appeal to particular consumers.

Why Write About Product Names

An important skill valued in academic and professional thinking and writing is to uncover connections among diverse topics or situations. One important aspect of this assignment is to help you develop the facility for making such connections. In previous chapters you have developed and refined an important writing skill: writing vividly and concretely. Now you will analyze how this skill is used in contexts other than descriptive and character sketch writing.

To apply what you have learned from Chapters 2–4 about the power of writing descriptively, you will analyze one way advertisers use descriptive language to sell a product. In addition, this chapter will help you learn how to make sense of a large topic, such as product names, by using an effective organizing strategy—**classification.** Classification helps you to organize the data you have assembled into related groups. This strategy allows you to begin analyzing various parts of your topic in order to discover and support a point about the whole.

INVENTION: READING, WRITING, AND TALKING FOR IDEAS

Reading

The following reading will be useful for this essay assignment as well as the one in Chapter 7. In Chapter 7 you will use the information in this reading to help you analyze how language works to sell a product. But for now, the essay is useful primarily because of its organizational strategy—classification. You will be able to use this reading as a structural model to order the information you gather for your own essay.

 Weasel Words: God's Little Helpers

Paul Stevens

1   First of all, you know what a weasel is, right? It's a small, slimy animal that eats small birds and other animals, and is especially fond of devouring vermin. Now, consider for a moment the kind of winning personality he must have. I mean, what kind of a guy would get his jollies eating rats and mice? Would you invite him to a party? Take him home to meet your mother? This is one of the slyest and most cunning of all creatures; sneaky, slippery, and thoroughly obnoxious. And so it is with great and warm personal regard for these attributes that we humbly award this King of All Devious the honor of bestowing his name upon our golden sword: the weasel word.

2   A weasel word is "a word used in order to evade or retreat from a direct or forthright statement or position" (Webster). In other words, if we can't say it, we'll weasel it. And, in fact, a weasel word has become more than just an evasion or retreat. We've trained our weasels. They can do anything. They can make you hear things that aren't being said, accept as truths things that have only been implied, and believe things that have only been suggested. Come to think of it, not only do we have our weasels trained, but they, in turn, have got you trained. When *you* hear a weasel word, you automatically hear the implication. Not the real meaning, but the meaning *it* wants *you* to hear. So if you're ready for a little re-education, let's take a good look under a strong light at the two kinds of weasel words.

WORDS THAT MEAN THINGS THEY REALLY DON'T MEAN

Help

3   That's it. "Help." It means "aid" or "assist." Nothing more. Yet, "help" is the one single word which, in all the annals of advertising, has

done the most to say something that couldn't be said. Because "help" is the great qualifier; once you say it, you can say almost anything after it. In short, "help" has helped help us the most.

Helps keep you young
Helps prevent cavities
Help keep your house germ-free

4   "Help" qualifies everything. You've never heard anyone say, "This product will keep you young," or "This toothpaste will positively prevent cavities for all time." Obviously, we can't say anything like that, because there aren't any products like that made. But by adding that one little word, "help," in front, we can use the strongest language possible afterward. And the most fascinating part of it is, you are immune to the word. You literally don't hear the word "help." You only hear what comes after it. And why not? That's strong language, and likely to be much more important to you than the silly little word at the front end.

5   I would guess that 75 percent of all advertising uses the word "help." Think, for a minute, about how many times each day you hear these phrases:

Helps stop . . .
Helps prevent . . .
Helps fight . . .
Helps overcome . . .
Helps you feel . . .
Helps you look . . .

I could go on and on, but so could you. Just as a simple exercise, call it homework if you wish, tonight when you plop down in front of the boob tube for your customary three and a half hours of violence and/or situation comedies, take a pad and pencil, and keep score. See if you can count how many times the word "help" comes up during the commercials. Instead of going to the bathroom during the pause before Marcus Welby operates, or raiding the refrigerator prior to witnessing the Mod Squad wipe out a nest of dope pushers, stick with it. Count the "helps," and discover just how dirty a four-letter word can be.

Like

6   Coming in second, but only losing by a nose, is the word "like," used in comparison. Watch:

It's like getting one bar free
Cleans like a white tornado
It's like taking a trip to Portugal

7   Okay. "Like" is a qualifier, and is used in much the same way as "help." But "like" is also a comparative element, with a very specific purpose; we use "like" to get you to stop thinking about the product per se, and to get you thinking about something that is bigger or better or different from the product we're selling. In other words, we can make you believe that the product is more than it is by likening it to something else.

8   Take a look at that first phrase, straight out of recent Ivory Soap advertising. On the surface of it, they tell you that four bars of Ivory cost about the same as three bars of most other soaps. So, if you're going to spend a certain amount of money on soap, you can buy four bars instead of three. Therefore, it's like getting one bar free. Now, the question you have to ask yourself is, "Why the weasel? Why do they say "like"? Why don't they just come out and say, 'You get one bar free'?" The answer is, of course, that for one reason or another, you really don't. Here are two possible reasons. One: sure, you get four bars, but in terms of the actual amount of soap that you get, it may very well be the same as in three bars of another brand. Remember, Ivory has a lot of air in it—that's what makes it float. And air takes up room. Room that could otherwise be occupied by more soap. So, in terms of pure product, the amount of actual soap in four bars of Ivory may be only as much as the actual amount of soap in three bars of most others. That's why we can't—or won't—come out with a straightforward declaration such as, "You get 25 percent more soap," or "Buy three bars, and get the fourth one free."

9   Reason number two: the actual cost and value of the product. Did it ever occur to you that Ivory may simply be a cheaper soap to make and, therefore, a cheaper soap to sell? After all, it doesn't have any perfume or hexachlorophene, or other additives that can raise the cost of manufacturing. It's plain, simple, cheap soap, and so it can be sold for less money while still maintaining a profit margin as great as more expensive soaps. By way of illustrating this, suppose you are trying to decide whether to buy a Mercedes-Benz or a Ford. Let's say the Mercedes cost $7,000, and the Ford $3,500. Now the Ford salesman comes up to you with this deal: as long as you're considering spending $7,000 on a car, buy my Ford for $7,000 and I'll give you a second Ford, free! Well, the same principle can apply to Ivory: as long as you're considering spending 35 cents on soap, buy my cheaper soap, and I'll give you more of it.

10   I'm sure there are other reasons why Ivory uses the weasel "like." Perhaps you've thought of one or two yourself. That's good. You're starting to think.

11   Now, what about that wonderful white tornado? Ajax pulled that one out of the hat some eight years ago, and you're still buying it. It's

a classic example of the use of the word "like" in which we can force you to think, not about the product itself, but about something bigger, more exciting, certainly more powerful than a bottle of fancy ammonia. The word "like" is used here as a transfer word, which gets you away from the obvious—the odious job of getting down on your hands and knees and scrubbing your kitchen floor—and into the world of fantasy, where we can imply that this little bottle of miracles will supply all the elbow grease you need. Isn't that the name of the game? The whirlwind activity of the tornado replacing the whirlwind motion of your arm? Think about the swirling of the tornado, and all the work it will save you. Think about the power of that devastating windstorm; able to lift houses, overturn cars, and now, pick the dirt up off your floor. And we get the license to do it simply by using the word "like."

12   It's copywriter's dream, because we don't have to substantiate anything. When we compare our product to "another leading brand," we'd better be able to prove what we say. But how can you compare ammonia to a windstorm? It's ludicrous. It can't be done. The whole statement is so ridiculous it couldn't be challenged by the government or the networks. So it went on the air, and it worked. Because the little word "like" let us take you out of the world of reality, and into your own fantasies.

13   Speaking of fantasies, how about that trip to Portugal? Mateus Rosé is actually trying to tell you that you will be transported clear across the Atlantic Ocean merely by sipping their wine. "Oh, come on," you say. "You don't expect me to believe that." Actually, we don't expect you to believe it. But we do expect you to get our meaning. This is called "romancing the product," and it is made possible by the dear little "like." In this case, we deliberately bring attention to the word, and we ask you to join us in setting reality aside for a moment. We take your hand and gently lead you down the path of moonlit nights, graceful dancers, and mysterious women. Are we saying that these things are all contained inside our wine? Of course not. But what we mean is, our wine is part of all this, and with a little help from "like," we'll get you to feel that way, too. So don't think of us as a bunch of peasants squashing a bunch of grapes. As a matter of fact, don't think of us at all. Feel with us.

14   "Like" is a virus that kills. You'd better get immune to it.

Other Weasels

15   "Help" and "like" are the two weasels so powerful that they can stand on their own. There are countless other words, not quite so potent, but equally effective when used in conjunction with our two basic weasels, or with each other. Let me show you a few.

16   **Virtual** *or* **Virtually**   How many times have you responded to an ad
that said:

Virtually trouble-free . . .
Virtually foolproof . . .
Virtually never needs service . . .

Ever remember what "virtual" means? It means "in essence or effect,
but not in fact." Important—"but not in fact." Yet today the word "virtually" is interpreted by you as meaning "almost or just about the
same as. . . ." Well, gang, it just isn't true. "Not," in fact, means not,
in fact. I was scanning, rather longingly I must confess, through the
brochure Chevrolet publishes for its Corvette, and I came to this
phrase: "The seats in the 1972 Corvette are virtually handmade." They
had me, for a minute. I almost took the bait of that lovely little weasel.
I almost decided that those seats were just about completely handmade. And then I remembered. Those seats were not, *in fact,* handmade. Remember, "virtually" means "not, in fact," or you will, in
fact, get sold down the river.

17   **Acts** *or* **Works**   These two action words are rarely used alone,
and are generally accompanied by "like." They need help to work,
mostly because they are verbs, but their implied meaning is deadly,
nonetheless. Here are the key phrases:

Acts like . . .
Acts against . . .
Works like . . .
Works against . . .
Works to prevent (or help prevent) . . .

You see what happens? "Acts" or "works" brings an action to the
product that might not otherwise be there. When we say that a certain
cough syrup "acts on the cough control center," the implication is that
the syrup goes to this mysterious organ and immediately makes it better. But the implication here far exceeds what the truthful promise
should be. An act is simply a deed. So the claim "acts on" simply
means it performs a deed on. What that deed is, we may never know.

18   The rule of thumb is this: if we can't say "cures" or fixes" or use
any other positive word, we'll nail you with "acts like" or "works
against," and get you thinking about something else. Don't.

Miscellaneous Weasels

19   **Can Be**   This is for comparison, and what we do is to find an
announcer who can really make it sound positive. But keep your ears
open. "Crest can be of significant value when used in . . .," etc., is

indicative of an ideal situation, and most of us don't live in ideal situations.

20   **Up To**   Here's another way of expressing an ideal situation. Remember the cigarette that said it was aged, or "cured for up to eight long lazy weeks"? Well, that could, and should, be interpreted as meaning that the tobaccos used were cured anywhere from one hour to eight weeks. We like to glamorize the ideal situation; it's up to you to bring it back to reality.

21   **As Much As**   More of the same. "As much as 20 percent greater mileage" with our gasoline again promises the ideal, but qualifies it.

22   **Refreshes, Comforts, Tackles, Fights, Comes On**   Just a handful of the same action weasels, in the same category as "acts" and "works," though not as frequently used. The way to complete the thought here is to ask the simple question, "How?" Usually, you won't get an answer. That's because, usually, the weasel will run and hide.

23   **Feel** *or* **The Feel of**   This is the first of our subjective weasels. When we deal with a subjective word, it is simply a matter of opinion. In our opinion, Naugahyde has the feel of real leather. So we can say it. And, indeed, if you were to touch leather, and then touch Naugahyde, you may very well agree with us. But that doesn't mean it is real leather, only that it feels the same. The best way to handle subjective weasels is to complete the thought yourself, by simply saying, "But it isn't." At least that way you can remain grounded in reality.

24   **The Look of** *or* **Looks Like**   "Look" is the same as "feel," our subjective opinion. Did you ever walk into a Woolworth's and see those $29.95 masterpieces hanging in their "Art Gallery"? "The look of a real oil painting," it will say. "But it isn't," you will now reply. And probably be $29.95 richer for it.

WORDS THAT HAVE NO SPECIFIC MEANING

25   If you have kids, then you have all kinds of breakfast cereals in the house. When I was a kid, it was Rice Krispies, the breakfast cereal that went snap, crackle, and pop. (One hell of a claim for a product that is supposed to offer nutritional benefits.) Or Wheaties, the breakfast of champions, whatever that means. Nowadays, we're forced to a confrontation with Quisp, Quake, Lucky-Stars, Cocoa-Puffs, Clunkers, Blooies, Snarkles and Razzmatazz. And they all have long one thing in common: they're all "fortified." Some are simply "fortified with vitamins," while others are specifically "fortified with vitamin D," or some other letter. But what does it all mean?

26   "Fortified" means "added on to." But "fortified," like so many other weasel words of indefinite meaning, simply doesn't tell us

enough. If, for instance, a cereal were to contain one unit of vitamin D, and the manufacturers added some chemical which would produce two units of vitamin D, they could then claim that the cereal was "fortified with twice as much vitamin D." So what? It would still be about as nutritional as sawdust.

27   The point is, weasel words with no specific meaning don't tell us enough, but we have come to accept them as factual statements closely associated with something good that has been done to the product. Here's another example.

Enriched

28   We use this one when we have a product that starts out with nothing. You mostly find it in bread, where the bleaching process combined with the chemicals used as preservatives renders the loaves totally void of anything but filler. So the manufacturer puts a couple of drops of vitamins into the batter, and presto! It's enriched. Sounds great when you say it. Looks great when you read it. But what you have to determine is, is it really great? Figure out what information is missing, and then try to supply that information. The odds are, you won't. Even the breakfast cereals that are playing it straight, like Kellogg's Special K, leave something to be desired. They tell you what vitamins you get, and how much of each in one serving. The catch is, what constitutes a serving? They say, one ounce. So now you have to whip out your baby scale and weigh one serving. Do you have any idea how much that is? Maybe you do. Maybe you don't care. Okay, so you polish off this mound of dried stuff, and now what? You have ostensibly received the minimum, repeat, minimum dosage of certain vitamins for the day. One day. And you still have to go find the vitamins you didn't get. Try looking it up on a box of frozen peas. Bet you won't find it. But do be alert to "fortified" and "enriched." Asking the right questions will prove beneficial.

29   Did you buy that last sentence? Too bad, because I weaseled you, with the word "beneficial." Think about it.

Flavor and Taste

30   These are two totally subjective words that allow us to claim marvelous things about products that are edible. Every cigarette in the world has claimed the best taste. Every supermarket has advertised the most flavorful meat. And let's not forget "aroma," a subdivision of this category. Wouldn't you like to have a nickel for every time a room freshener (a weasel in itself) told you it would make your home "smell fresh as all outdoors"? Well, they can say it, because smell, like taste and flavor, is a subjective thing. And, incidentally, there are no less than three weasels in that phrase. "Smell" is the first. Then, there's "as" (a substitute for the ever-popular "like"), and, finally, "fresh,"

which, in context, is a subjective comparison, rather than the primary definition of "new."

31   Now we can use an unlimited number of combinations of these weasels for added impact. "Fresher-smelling clothes." "Fresher-tasting tobacco." "Tastes like grandma used to make." Unfortunately, there's no sure way of bringing these weasels down to size, simply because you can't define them accurately. Trying to ascertain the meaning of "taste" in any context is like trying to push a rope up a hill. All you can do is be aware that these words are subjective, and represent only one opinion—usually that of the manufacturer.

Style and Good Looks

32   Anyone for buying a new car? Okay, which is the one with the good looks? The smart new styling? What's that you say? All of them? Well, you're right. Because this is another group of subjective opinions. And it is the subjective and collective opinion of both Detroit and Madison Avenue that the following cars have "bold new styling": Buick Riviera, Plymouth Satellite, Dodge Monaco, Mercury Brougham, and you can fill in the spaces for the rest. Subjectively, you have to decide on which bold new styling is, indeed, bold new styling. Then, you might spend a minute or two trying to determine what's going on under that styling. The rest I leave to Ralph Nader.

Different, Special, and Exclusive

33   To be different, you have to be not the same as. Here, you must rely on your own good judgment and common sense. Exclusive formulas and special combinations of ingredients are coming at you every day, in every way. You must constantly assure yourself that, basically, all products in any given category are the same. So when you hear "special," "exclusive," or "different," you have to establish two things: on what basis are they different, and is that difference an important one? Let me give you a hypothetical example.

34   All so-called "permanent" antifreeze is basically the same. It is made from a liquid known as ethylene glycol, which has two amazing properties: It has a lower freezing point than water, and a higher boiling point than water. It does not break down (lose its properties), nor will it boil away. And every permanent antifreeze starts with it as a base. Also, just about every antifreeze has now got antileak ingredients, as well as antirust and anticorrosion ingredients. Now, let's suppose that, in formulating the product, one of the companies comes up with a solution that is pink in color, as opposed to all the others, which are blue. Presto—an exclusivity claim. "Nothing else looks like it, nothing else performs like it." Or how about, "Look at ours, and look at anyone else's. You can see the difference our exclusive formula makes." Granted, I'm exaggerating. But did I prove a point?

A Few More Goodies

35 *At Phillips 66, it's performance that counts*
Wisk puts its strength where the dirt is
At Bird's Eye, we've got quality in our corner
Delicious and long-lasting, too

Very quickly now, let's deflate those four lines. First, what the hell does "performance" mean? It means that this product will do what any other product in its category will do. Kind of a back-handed reassurance that this gasoline will function properly in your car. That's it, and nothing more. To perform means to function at a standard consistent with the rest of the industry. All products in a category are basically the same.

36   Second line: What does "strength" or "strong" mean? Does it mean "not weak"? Or "superior in power"? No, it means consistent with the norms of the business. You can bet your first-born that if Wisk were superior in power to other detergents, they'd be saying it, loud and clear. So strength is merely a description of a property inherent in all similar products in its class. If you really want to poke a pin in a bubble, substitute the word "ingredients" for the word "strength." That'll do it every time.

37   Third line: The old "quality" claim, and you fell for it. "Quality" is not a comparison. In order to do that, we'd have to say, "We've got better quality in our corner than any other frozen food." Quality relates only to the subjective opinion that Bird's Eye has of its own products, and to which it is entitled. The word "quality" is what we call a "parity" statement; that is, it tells you that it is as good as any other. Want a substitute? Try "equals," meaning "the same as."

38   Fourth line: How delicious is delicious? About the same as good-tasting, or fresher-smelling is fresher-smelling. A subjective opinion regarding taste, which you can either accept or reject. More fun, though, is "long-lasting." You might want to consider writing a note to Mr. Wrigley, inquiring as to the standard length of time which a piece of gum is supposed to last. Surely there must be a guideline covering it. The longest lasting piece of gum I ever encountered lasted just over four hours, which is the amount of time it took me to get it off the sole of my shoe. Try expressing the line this way: "It has a definite taste, and you may chew it as long as you wish." Does that place it in perspective?

39   There are two other aspects of weasel words that I should mention here. The first one represents the pinnacle of the copywriter's craft, and I call it the "Weasel of Omission." Let me demonstrate:

Of America's best-tasting gums, Trident is sugar-free

40   Disregard, for a moment, the obvious subjective weasel "best-tasting." Look again at the line. Something has been left out. Omitted very deliberately. Do you known what that word is? The word that's missing is the word "only," which should come right before the name of the product. But it doesn't. It's gone. Left out. And the question is, why? The answer is, the government wouldn't let them. You see, they start out by making a subjective judgment, that their gum is among the best-tasting. That's fine, as far as it goes. That's their opinion, but it is also the opinion of every other maker of sugar-free gum that his product is also among the best-tasting. And, since both of their opinions must be regarded as having equal value, neither one is allowed the superiority claim, which is what the word "only" would do. So Trident left it out. But the sentence is so brilliantly constructed, the word "only" is so heavily implied, that most people hear it, even though it hasn't been said. That's the Weasel of Omission. Constructing a set of words that forces you to a conclusion that otherwise could not have been drawn. Be on the lookout for what isn't said, and try to fill the gaps realistically.

41   The other aspect of weasels is the use of all those great, groovy, swinging, wonderful, fantastic, exciting and fun-filled words known as adjectives. Your eyes, ears, mind, and soul have been bombarded by adjectives for so long that you are probably numb to most of them by now. If I were to give you a list of adjectives to look out for, it would require the next five hundred pages, and it wouldn't do you any good, anyway. More important is to bear in mind what adjectives do, and then to be able to sweep them aside and distinguish only the facts.

42   An adjective modifies a noun, and is generally used to denote the quality or a quality of the thing named. And that's our grammar lesson for today. Realistically, an adjective enhances or makes more of the product being discussed. Its the difference between "Come visit Copenhagen," and "Come visit beautiful Copenhagen." Adjectives are used so freely these days that we feel almost naked, robbed, if we don't get at least a couple. Try speaking without adjectives. Try describing something; you can't do it. The words are too stark, too bare-boned, too factual. And that's the key to judging advertising. There is a direct, inverse proportion between the number of adjectives and the number of facts. To put it succinctly, the more adjectives we use, the less we have to say.

43   You can almost make a scale, based on that simple mathematical premise. At one end you have cosmetics, soft drinks, cigarettes, products that have little or nothing of any value to say. So we get them all dressed up with lavish word and thought images, and present you with thirty or sixty seconds of adjectival puffery. The other end of the scale is much harder to find. Usually, it will be occupied by a new product that is truly new or different. . . . Our craving for adjectives has become so overriding that we simply cannot listen to what is known as "nuts and bolts'' advertising. The rest falls somewhere in the middle; a combination of adjectives, weasels, and semitruths. All I can tell you is, try to brush the description aside, and see what's really at the bottom.

Journal Assignments

1. In your own words, define ''weasel word'' and then outline the contents of the reading as follows. (You will be able to use your outline as a quick reference when you analyze the text of an advertisement, part of the next chapter's writing assignment.)

   I. Major Headings
      A. Subheadings (when they occur)
         1. Word(s) and brief definition(s)

2. Brainstorm a list of products (toothpaste, deodorant, cars . . .); then pick one product and list all the names for it that come to your mind. Finally, explain the following:

   a. What each name means (go to the dictionary if necessary)
   b. What image or qualities that name causes you to associate with the product
   c. To which consumer the name appeals
   d. Under what categories of similar qualities you can group the names

3. Based on the information from journal assignment 2d, pick one name from each category and describe how a commercial for that product further develops the image the product name evokes.

Reading Questions

Content

1. What is the author's attitude toward his subject? How does his anecdote about the Corvette illustrate his attitude?

2. This reading is almost two decades old. Point out some evidence that dates the reading. Does this dated material invalidate the author's claims about advertising language? Point out evidence that makes the reading valid or invalid.

3. Even if we did not know the author had been in advertising, we could probably tell by the informal tone and style he uses in his writing. Examine the introductory paragraphs to determine what kind of relationship the author sets up with his audience. How does he set up this relationship? Give specific examples. Who is his audience?

4. Point out diction that illustrates the author's informality.

5. Are the author's sentences long and complicated, or short and conversational? Give specific examples.

Structure

1. How does the structure of this essay differ from the others we have read? How is it the same? For instance, how does the author set up the context (background) for this reading? Can you still find a statement of point, and of significance? Where?

2. Why is classification an appropriate form of organization for this essay?

3. Can we figure out the logic behind the essay's development by looking at the headings and subheadings? Explain.

4. How does the author organize his material within each heading or subheading? Take the information under ''help,'' for example, to explain his strategy for developing evidence.

Thinking About Advertising

Like stereotyping, advertising is a common cultural phenomenon. You are all experts on advertising. After all, we are bombarded with commercials day after day and have been all our lives unless we have never watched TV, listened to the radio, read a magazine, or seen a billboard. Like many people, you may shrug your shoulders at advertising ''hype,'' thinking you are too sophisticated to be taken in by commercials, but we all do choose to buy one product over another—perhaps for rational reasons, perhaps for reasons of which we are not fully aware.

In the course of this chapter and the next you will analyze and write about some selling strategies advertisers use. In this chapter you will analyze and classify product names to see what effect they are intended to have on consumers. Your own knowledge of products and commercials along with the readings, journal assignments, and group activities will all work together to give you the information you need to write this essay assignment.

An Example of Analysis and Classification

One way to begin analyzing advertising strategies is to examine the names advertisers give their products. You will need to answer the following questions for each product.

1. What does the name mean?
2. What image does the name evoke?
3. What qualities, based on that image, are consumers supposed to associate with the product?
4. To which audience is the product name supposed to appeal? and
5. What categories of images emerge?

Not all four of these will apply to all products

Now, you need a product. Take a bath or hand soap,* for example.

Dove	Zest
Coast	Ivory
Lava	Irish Spring
Dial	Caress
Fiesta	Tone
Lifebuoy	Safeguard

This list is not complete, and you can add to it; however, you have enough to make a start. First on the list is Dove. Your answers to the first four questions might look like this:

1   The **denotative,** or literal, meaning of the word is a bird, specifically a member of the pigeon family, but the **connotative,** or suggestive meaning, is of

2, 3   peacefulness/gentleness/softness/purity/delicacy, and these images and qualities

4   are commonly, and stereotypically, associated with women.

The second name is Coast.

1   The name literally means the place where the land meets the sea

2, 3   and we associate the word with the cleansing properties of fresh breezes and with invigorating waves of water;

4   these images would probably be appealing to ''outdoors'' people, and not just to one sex or the other.

The next name is Lava.

1   The name literally means the molten rock that pours from an erupting volcano, and

2, 3, 4   we associate it with a scouring force that clears everything in its path, definitely an image with stereotypically masculine thrust.

As you can see, these names evoke powerful images harnessed in the service of a small bar of soap.

As you continue down the list, you will see relationships between the names and the images they evoke and be able to classify the names into categories of images, as asked for in question **5.** For example, one clear category that emerges from the list revolves around the image of pure, gentle softness embodied in such names as Ivory, Dove, and Caress. Can you add to the list of names in this category? What about Cashmere Bouquet? What does it mean? What images and qualities are associated with the name? To

*Note that manufacturers' names, such as Jergens, are not included in the list. Why not?

whom do these images appeal? Does it belong in the same category as the other three names?

> **Exercise**   As a whole class, or in your writing groups, continue adding to the list of hand or bath soap names. Then follow the five steps illustrated above until the class's or writing group's information or inspiration runs dry.

DRAFTING: WRITING, TALKING, REWRITING, AND EVALUATING

Structuring the Essay

Developing the Evidence

As a result of the class discussion of product names and of your journal assignments, you should be ready to write your first draft. As you begin, concentrate first on the evidence you will use in the body of your paper; that is, make sure you

1. have chosen a product for which you can think of a number of descriptive names as opposed to manufacturers' names
2. can explain what each name means and describe what images or qualities we are supposed to associate with that product as a result of its name
3. can describe the commercials for some of the names and explain how they develop the image the name evokes
4. can categorize the names according to like images or qualities
5. can identify which group of consumers is likely to be the target of a particular category of product names

Ordering the Evidence

After you have gone through the above five steps to develop the evidence in the body of your essay, you will be able to see how to group your information into paragraphs. For example, each category of names should have its own paragraph.

Furthermore, you will probably have a good sense of how the information should be ordered within each paragraph. For example, you should probably begin with a statement that identifies and generally describes the category and the audience it appeals to. The rest of the information in the paragraph should support this first statement. You should follow it with specific examples of names, what they mean, what images they evoke, and how commercials build on that image.

Setting Up the Introduction

Next, you will write an introduction, which will need careful planning. First you need to provide a context, or background, for your particular topic. Perhaps the context should include comments about the broader topic of advertising and readers' familiarity with it. Then you can go on to state, and make a point about, the topic of your essay: an advertising strategy that you believe may not seem so obvious to your readers. This kind of introduction, one that begins with information about a topic familiar to most readers then moves on to an unfamiliar aspect of that topic, is quite a traditional way to organize an introduction.

Setting Up the Conclusion

Finally you must have a conclusion that explains the significance of your essay. Why is it important to know that product names often evoke images "targeted" toward certain people?

First-Draft Activities

Make copies of your draft for your group members. Exchange papers and answer the following questions for each draft:

1. How does the introduction set up a context for the topic and point of the essay?
2. Circle the topic, or if you do not find it, write "topic?" in the left margin of the introductory paragraph(s).
3. Underline the point, or write "point?" in the left margin of the introductory paragraph(s).
4. Where is the product the author uses as illustration introduced? Put brackets around this information, and write "move?" by it if you think it is in the wrong place.
5. Is each body paragraph adequately developed? Check to see whether the author has done the following, and put the number and letter of any missing or unclear information (e.g., 5c) in the left margin of each paragraph:
   a. The categories are accurately defined and the audience for each is identified, probably in the **topic sentence,** or beginning sentence, of each paragraph
   b. The product names within each category are well defined, and the images they evoke are well described, thus convincingly showing why they belong in that particular category
   c. There are too many or too few examples of product names, their definitions, and the images each evokes

    d. There is a description of a commercial that builds upon the image evoked by at least one product name in every category

    e. There are transitions between ideas within each paragraph and from one paragraph to the next

6. How does the conclusion explain the importance of the topic?

7. After you have read each draft and answered the questions for each, choose the draft that has the best introduction, the most successfully developed body paragraphs, and the most convincing conclusion. These may not all be in the same draft. Then, compare your choices with the other group members and explain why you chose the draft(s) you did.

Second-Draft Activities

The comments on your first draft will help you see how you need to revise. Chances are you will be revising in two major areas, evidence and transitions.

Revising the Evidence

You may need more evidence, which simply means a return to the store to search out more product names. On the other hand, you may have too much evidence, which means you should choose the best names within each category and leave out the rest.

Providing the Transitions

You may have all the information you need, but be having trouble moving smoothly and clearly from one idea to the next. This is likely to happen in your introduction when you mention the particular product you are going to write about. Here is one way of ending your introduction and providing a transition into the body paragraphs.

> One particular *strategy* advertisers use is. . . . To illustrate this *strategy,* we will look at brand names of product X. . . .

Repeating key words is one way to provide a transition between ideas. In the example above, the two sentences could conclude the introductory paragraph(s), or the second sentence could be a one-sentence transitional paragraph between the introduction and the first body paragraph, or it could be the first sentence of the first body paragraph, coming before you introduce your first category of names.

After the topic sentence, you may also need transitions between the different kinds of information within each body paragraph.

> [Topic sentence identifying and describing the category and its target audience.] *For example,* the name X, *meaning* (define), *evokes an image of* (explain image). *The commercial builds on this image by. . . . Another* name *in this category* is. . . .

To provide transitions here, we used a phrase, "for example," indicating relationship to the previous sentence; we repeated a key word, "image"; and we used "another," which indicates the addition of a different example.

You may also need to provide transitions between body paragraphs.

The *next* (or *another, the second, third, last*) major category. . . .

These highlighted words simply indicate the ordered movement of information.

The preceding sample sentences illustrate some options you have for supplying transitions among ideas in your essay. Turn to pages 243–244 for a more detailed list of transitional words and phrases.

Evaluation Criteria

Here are some criteria for evaluating a classification essay on product names.

1. The introduction of the essay must
   a. provide a context explaining the essay's focus
   b. state the topic and the writer's point (opinion) about the topic
   c. identify the product whose names are to be examined
2. The body must contain at least two paragraphs that
   a. define the category and audience it targets
   b. provide examples of names (at least two) within each category and explain
      (1) the definition of each name
      (2) the image each name evokes
      (3) how the commercial (for at least one name in a category) develops the image suggested by the name
   c. provide appropriate transitions among ideas
3. The conclusion must state the significance of the essay to its audience, stressing why having knowledge about particular strategies that advertisers use to convince us to buy a product is important.

Sample Student Essays

Following are two examples of this essay assignment written by students.

Psychological Effects of Products

1　　Advertising is a means of placing a specific product or service in front of the public in order to make a gain (monetary or ego). The advertisers use the various media (newspaper, radio, television and publication) in order to promote their clients products. Most products have a name that means something or represents the use or description of the product. Manufacturers use psychological techniques to give their products name and/or brand recognition. One of the favorite methods is to name a product for the job it does or in relationship to the uses the product has.

2   A good example of manufacturers using descriptive names to psychologically promote their products is underarm deodorants. Each of the manufacturers generate a name that they hope will have the effect of creating need for their product. They also consider the job it is to do prior to its naming of the product. An underarm deodorant or anitperspirant is meant to keep underarms dry, odor free, fresh and non-showing. For those people that are insecure, manufacturers have come up with names to suit these peoples needs. The image of assurance is given by the products names Secret, Sure, Ban, Hi & Dri, and Arrid Extra Dry. "Secret" evokes images of hiding odors and perspiration, keeping underarm odors a secret. Sure implies that if you use this product that you can be confident. Ban gives the idea of preventing your odors and banning them. Hi & Dri and Arrid Extra Dry are just about the same giving the idea that you will be kept odorless and dry. Both meaning that you will be able to raise up your arm and you will smell fresh and not show any unwanted "sweat".

3   Other images that manufacturers try to create are from names like; Right Guard, Old Spice, and Brut. These names evoke an image of masculenity. Right Guard says it protects and guards your underarms from odor, like a football player guards his quarterback. Old Spice implys an "aroma", a spice as aged cinnamon with its aromatic scent. Brut showing strength or toughness against odor and perspriation. Making you a "macho" type individual.

4   I've been told by lady friends that "women do not sweat, they glow." Even women have underarm problems, so antiperspirants such as Lady's Choice, Babe, and Lady's Speed Dry were made to evoke an image for those women who do not wish to "glow".

5   The images that these names create in you and I (the consumer) are meant to trigger a need; (whether real or imaginary). For thes products. By buying and using these products we are able to fulfill small fantacies that show us as "macho", suave and debonaire, or as a self-confident successful business person. If we feel this way, then the time and expense used in creating these brand names has been well worth the effort spent by the manufacturers who will surely profit from the endevors.

What's in a Name?

1   Adversting is a business which uses psychological principles to influence our behavior to buy a certain product. One method to enhance

memory studied by psychologists is that of association. If a product is associated with a strong image, that product is more likely to be remembered.

2   The advertising of cat food products often uses association to influence our thoughts. Many cat foods have names which suggest the type of personality or character the cat will possess. A cat who eats "Friskies Buffet" is always in your yarn and jumping around the house. A Cat who eats "9-Lives" will live for a long time. "Atta Cat Cusine" is the good cat which does as it is told: therefore, you may hear the owner say, "Atta good cat". "Alley Cat" food is for those people who feel cats should be independent and tough; while, "Pussn Boot Supreme" will make cats wise and knowledgeable. A cat which eats Happy Cat is good tempered. There is a cat food brand to match every kind of cat.

3   These images for the names of products are expounded in commercials by the media. For example, in one 9-lives commercial a cat will be shown escaping a near miss from a car; next, a ball will swish past his head. Then, a limb of a tree will break from under his feet, while the cat narrowly escapes death by falling onto a hammock below. The cat finally makes it safely home while his loving master feeds him 9-Lives for dinner.

4   The quality of cat food and it's appetite appeal are a concern for cat owners; therefore, the product names often promote images of food quality and taste appeal. The name Chef's Blend implies that it is prepared not by factory workers who don't care about your cat, but by a four star chef creating a special blend of food. Fancy Feast may not state how it was made, but is the best food elegantly fixed. Tender Vittles is a supply of food fixed in country style goodness. Crave will be a type of food the cat can't resist like humans can't resist junk food, while, Meox Mix and Pet's Choice would be what your cat would choose if he went shopping instead of you.

5   Meox Mix commercials are based on the cat's choice; they show a smart cat dialing on the phone to order his choice of food. Commercials for Fancy Feast will show a long white haired, pure-bred, persian cat being served dinner on a silver platter. The food is elegantly placed in a cyrstal goblet and delivered by a butler, thus reinforcing the image that a cat who eats Fancy Feast is very special.

6   Cat foods provide nutrition which give your cat health and longevity. Is one cat food really better than another? If you looked at the ingredients of a cat food it would contain some yellow ground corn, meat by-products, corn gluten meal, soybean meal, animal fat, etc. The difference in ingredients from one brand to another would probably not vary greatly. Why do people buy one brand over another brand? The image produced by the product's name and commercials aid in the decision of which cat food is the best. The technique of memory association is used when a person shops for cat food. The image of the cat's personality and food quality is matched to the product's name, thus, the impulse to buy

a product may not be based on the quality of the merchandise, but the image associated with the product.

Evaluating the Sample Essays

Use the evaluative criteria for a guideline, and within your group, discuss which sample essay is better and why. Also, be ready to discuss with the whole class suggestions as to how the authors of these examples could have improved their essays. You might want to pick a scribe to write down these suggestions and act as spokesperson for your group.

Revising Your Second Draft

Review the information in this chapter, the advice your group members have given you, and insights from evaluating the sample essays in order to decide how you should revise your essay.

EDITING

Final Draft Editing

Before turning in your final essay, exchange it with a partner. Proofread your partner's essay for spelling, punctuation, and grammar errors. Read carefully for appropriate transitions, as well. Do not correct the errors, but mark the lines in which they occur. If your partner does not recognize the errors you have indicated, tell the writer what they are.

When your essay is returned to you, neatly cross out and correct those things you agree are errors. Ask your instructor when you are unsure about an error.

Postfinal-Draft Editing

Your instructor may have you revise a section of your essay or have you correct particular errors.

Structural Analysis of an Advertisement

WRITING ASSIGNMENT

The paper due at the end of the chapter will make a point about the influence advertisements have on consumers. You will analyze an advertisement to explain its underlying *message* and how it conveys that message to its audience. The language the advertisement uses and the image the product name evokes will provide some of the evidence you need to support your point. The rest of your evidence will come from a physical description of the advertisement, explaining how it captures the *attention* of consumers and tries to build consumer *confidence* in and stimulate *desire* for the product.

Why Write a Structural Analysis of an Advertisement?

Because advertisements provide such accessible and abundant research material, and because they are such a large part of our consumer culture and have such an impact on us, the way they make their impact is well worth analyzing. Analyzing how a whole advertisement works to convey its message is more complicated than assembling and classifying data as you did in the previous chapter's assignment. Your purpose in writing this assignment is to identify and explain the structure and strategies, visual and verbal, that advertisers use to make an effective advertisement.

This kind of assignment, in which you analyze a representative sample of a particular topic in order to make a point about the whole subject, is typical of college writing. For example, in an economics class, students might analyze one representative fiscal policy to make a point about the economic health of a country. In an art class, students might analyze one artist's work—even one work of an artist—to show how it is representative of a whole **genre,** or particular kind, of art. Thus, your job in this writing assignment is to analyze one advertisement to draw conclusions and make a point about how advertising as a whole works.

INVENTION: READING, WRITING, AND TALKING FOR IDEAS

Reading

Jay Rosen, a professor of journalism and mass communications at New York University, first published this essay, "The Presence of the Word in TV Advertising," in *Et cetera*, an academic journal published by the International Society of General Semantics. In his essay, Rosen analyzes a few TV commercials to show how they link certain concepts (images or ideas) with the product the advertisers want to sell. As you read, pay close attention to the author's descriptions of the commercials because they serve as excellent models for the kind of description you will be writing when you analyze an advertisement.

The Presence of the Word in TV Advertising

Jay Rosen

1   It is safe to say that most inquiries into the language of television advertising would look at the sort of language actually used in the ads. I could imagine, for example, a rather interesting article on how an advertising slogan like "Where's the Beef?" became almost instantly part of the American language in the summer of 1984. Indeed, in a journal like *Et cetera*[1] there could easily be an entire issue devoted to "Where's the Beef?" For cultural observers, then, there is quite a lot of material in the language employed by television advertising. But that is not the direction I want to take in this article.

2   I would like to begin by observing the following fact. All over America there are people who have discovered a new way of watching television. The advertising industry calls them "flippers," people who drift restlessly around the dial by remote control, changing the channel at the slightest provocation—the appearance on screen of Angie Dickinson,[2] for example. I know one man—not an academic, as it turns out—who says he hits the button as soon as he feels the smallest hint of content coming on. My own habits are not quite so severe, but I am, I confess, a flipper. (By the way, most flippers are male, something no one has thought to study yet.) If the advertising industry is concerned about flippers, it would be doubly concerned about me. For I am not only a

---

[1]*Et cetera:* a periodical dedicated to the role of words and symbols in human behavior.

[2]*Angie Dickinson:* star of the 1970s series *Policewoman.*

flipper, but I often flip with the sound off. I find it easier to recognize patterns that way, and pattern recognition is, so to speak, my profession.

3   Now, flipping with the sound off is a good way of investigating television ads. Frequently I find myself asking, "what is this ad about?" as I watch the images float by. "What is this ad about?" is a different question, of course, from, "what *product* is this an ad for?" To ask what an ad is "about" is to inquire into the underlying message of the ad. . . . Deodorant ads, as almost everyone knows, are about shame and the body, no matter what they may seem to be saying. The art of flipping makes it easier to recognize such things, and I recommend it to everyone as an inexpensive research tool.

4   You don't have to be a flipper to recognize that one trend in television advertising is toward increasing visualization—more images, arriving at a faster clip, and packing more of a punch. Often they are accompanied by music, and frequently this music is borrowed or adapted from hit songs on the radio. MTV is thus an obvious influence on this sort of advertising, but there's an important difference. A certain vagueness or incoherence is possible, even desirable, in a music video. As a result, it is often impossible to say what music videos are really about, despite the presence of a lot of striking images. In advertising there is not as much license. The images must succeed, not only in grabbing attention, but in communicating a single concept or theme which can then be linked to the product. This is what I mean by "deep structure" in TV advertising.

5   A good example is a new series of ads for Michelob beer. You may recall that Michelob's slogan used to be "Weekends Were Made For Michelob." In the new campaign the line is, "The Night Belongs to Michelob," suggesting that by the 1990s, Michelob will have colonized the entire week. In any event, the ads now feature a series of images, very well shot, all of which vivify life in the big city at night. Well-dressed women step out of cabs, skylines twinkle and glow, performers take the stage in smoky nightclubs, couples kiss on the street, backlit by the headlights of cars. These are not only images *of* the night; they are *about* the night as an idea or myth. Their goal is to create a swirl of associations around the world "night," which is actually heard in the ad if you have the sound on. Phil Collins of the rock band Genesis sings a song in which the word "tonight" is repeated over and over.

6   But what's interesting about the ads is that neither the lyrics of Phil Collins nor the slogan "The Night Belongs to Michelob" are necessary to get the message. The word "night" comes through in the very texture of the images. It's there even when the sound is off and no language is being heard. What Walter Ong[3] once called "the presence of the word" does not, in this case, depend on the presence of language. For example,

---

[3]*Walter Ong:* American literary critic and student of literacy (b. 1912).

a singer is shown silhouetted in a spotlight on stage at a nightclub. This is not merely a picture *taken* at night, in a place associated *with* the night. It is almost an abstract diagram of the concept of night. The beam of the spotlight, because it is visible, demonstrates the presence of darkness all around. The singer appears as a silhouette, a black shape who is in, of, and surrounded by the night. The spotlight, then, is the very principle of intelligibility at work: It lights up the night, not in order to obliterate it, but to give it form, to demonstrate what "night" is, almost like a Sesame Street vocabulary lesson. This giving of form to an abstract concept is the logic behind a number of ads on television.

7   Levi's, for example, has created a series of ads about the idea of "blue." Naturally they are shot in blue tones on city streets. They also feature blues songs being strummed in the background. And, of course, the actors are all wearing blue jeans. But blue is communicated on a deeper level, as well. The feeling of blue—the meaning blue has taken on in popular culture—is brought out in the way a girl walks wistfully down the street, blowing soap bubbles into the air. In these ads, blue would come through without the sound of blues songs or the product name—Levi's 501 blues. Indeed, I am tempted to say that blue would come through even on a black and white set. Why? Because the director has found images which "mean" blue at the deepest cultural level. It is not the surfaced presence of the *color* blue that matters, but a kind of inner architecture of blue, on top of which blue scenes, blue jeans and blues songs have been placed.

8   This may seem easy enough with a concept, like blue, that is primarily visual. But what about notions that are essentially verbal? The Hewlett-Packard company[4] has attempted something along these lines. It is now running a series of ads whose slogan is "What if . . .?" In these ads, Hewlett-Packard people are seen pondering difficult problems, hitting upon a possible answer, and rushing to their colleagues to announce, "I've got it: What if . . ." and the sound fades out.

9   Of course, if you turn the sound off, there is no "what if" to be heard and no fade out. And yet the idea of "what if" is not necessarily gone. Picture this: An intelligent-looking woman in glasses is shown alone in her office, tapping a pencil and sort of looking skyward, as if contemplating a majestic possibility. Here the attempt is to produce a visual image of "what-if ness," a notion ordinarily expressed in words or mathematical symbols. It has often been said that pictures have no tense. But Hewlett-Packard is attempting to prove that a tense—in this case, the conditional—can in fact be a visual idea—borrowed from language, but expressed in images. Perhaps we will soon see ads visualizing a host of ideas we ordinarily think of as linguistic. How about a series of pictures about the concept of "nevertheless" or "because"?

[4]*Hewlett-Packard company:* American electronics firm.

10   What I am trying to point out is a certain irony in the trend toward increased visualization. As TV ads become shorter, they become more visual, as a way of saying more in a smaller amount of time. But as they become more visual, the ads seem to be about concepts which are inescapably verbal. Advertising may appear to be relying less on language, but language is simply functioning on a deeper level. It has not, in any sense, gone away. And a final irony is this: In order to discover this deeper level of language it is necessary to ignore the language on the surface. In a strange way, turning the sound off allows you to hear what's really being said.

✎ Journal Assignments

1. After reading Jay Rosen's essay, try his technique for analyzing TV commercials. Turn off the TV's sound during a commercial and see if you can explain and describe how you know what concept the commercial is associating with its product. For example, Rosen says the Michelob beer commercial links the idea of ''nightlife'' to beer and the Levi commercial links the idea of ''the blues'' to jeans. Do all commercials work this way? To answer this question you might think about commercials for department store sales versus commercials about perfume. What is the difference?

2. Look through some magazines to find at least three advertisements that catch your attention. Choose one (or more if your instructor says so) and write an analysis of it using the four steps in the ''Beginning the Analysis Process'' section of this chapter (pp. 102–104).

3. Describe the kinds of advertisements you find in various types of magazines. Choose at least two, such as *Vogue, Time, National Geographic, Sports Illustrated,* and so on. Then describe the kinds of advertisements you find on TV during particular times of day or days of the week. What does this research tell you about the way advertisers target their audiences?

Reading Questions

1. How many paragraphs are in the introduction?

2. Explain how Rosen sets up the background for his point.

   a. What does he do in paragraph 1? In paragraph 2? In paragraph 3?

   b. Why is the introduction so long? To explain this, answer the following:

      (1) Who is his audience?

      (2) What approach does the audience expect him to take to his topic?

      (3) How does he reshape the audience's expectations?

3. According to Rosen, what is the trend in TV advertising?

4. What point does the author make about this trend?

5. To support his point, the author describes, in great detail, three examples of TV advertisements. How does he organize the information in each paragraph? To help you answer this question, do the following:

   a. Put parentheses around the sentences *describing* the advertisement.

   b. Underline the statements *analyzing* the description.

6. Look at Rosen's concluding paragraph. Can you explain the difference between visual and verbal concepts? Think of examples to illustrate the difference. For example, is ''truth'' a visual or a verbal concept? Can you think of any visual images that could represent the abstract idea of ''truth''?

Beginning the Analysis Process

The first step in any analysis is to identify the parts of the subject being analyzed. This identification is necessary in order to discover and explain how the parts work and to what purpose. To begin this process for advertisements, specifically a printed ad, we must

1. describe its visual layout

2. describe its language (the information in ''Weasel Words'' from Chapter 6 will help us here)

3. analyze how the layout and language

   a. capture consumers' attention,

   b. build their confidence or desire,

   c. convey the advertisement's message.

To illustrate how these three steps work, we will examine an advertisement for Crest toothpaste (Figure 7.1).

We begin by articulating the layout (the arrangement of one element in relationship to others on the page) of the advertisement. First our *attention* is captured by a gold tooth, centered in and comprising fully one half of the page. Directly underneath the gold tooth is a caption in large boldfaced lettering. ''Crest. Because enamel is more precious than gold.'' These two elements, the image and the caption, fill two thirds of the page and so are obviously the most important features of the ad. We can analyze how these features make their impact by noting that gold, something most people *desire,* is associated with great value, but not necessarily when it is in a tooth. A false tooth, even a gold one, is still inferior to a natural tooth. So the layout sets up the equation that gold, in this context, is less valuable than

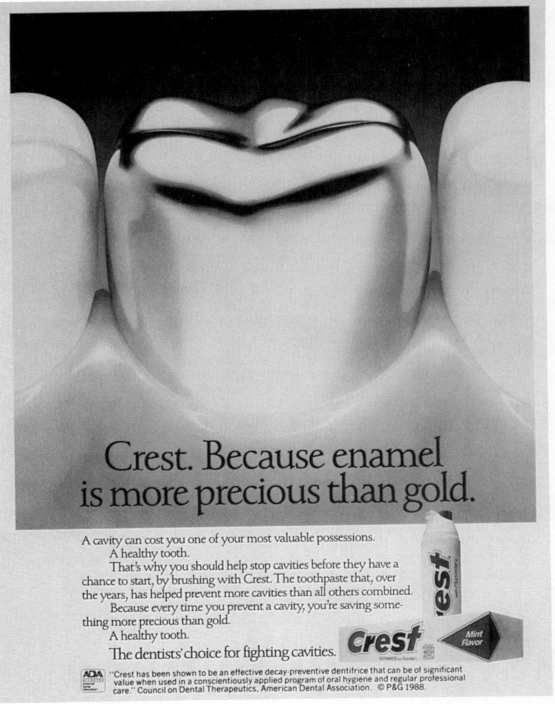

Figure 7.1.
An advertisement for Crest toothpaste. (© The Procter & Gamble Company. Used with permission.)

Crest because Crest equals healthy teeth. Also, the position of the caption, superimposed over the bottom of the image, conveys the *message* that Crest is all that stands between a false tooth and a natural one.

But what about the other elements in the advertisement? Immediately to the right of the caption we see the nozzle of a toothpaste pump, which acts as an arrow drawing our eye downward over the name, Crest, emphasized by thickset boldfaced print, on the toothpaste pump. Our visual progres downward is halted by a triangular arrow, containing the words "mint flavor," pointing left to a boxed tube of toothpaste. On this box we again see the name Crest in thickset boldfaced letters. This part of the layout serves three purposes. First, it repeats the name, and repetition, as we are all too well aware, is a common selling strategy. Next, it provides consumers with product options, telling them that they can buy Crest in the pump or tube, and with mint flavor if they choose. Finally, the juxtaposition, at right angles, of the toothpaste pump and box, serves as an arrow directing our eye from the first caption to the endline caption, not boldfaced and in smaller print. The endline reads "The Dentists' choice for fighting cavities."

This endline serves a couple of purposes. First, it associates the product, Crest, with the testimony of experts, dentists, which gives consumers *confidence* in the product. Also, the endline implies that Crest prevents cavities, which again increases the consumers' *confidence* in and *desire* for, the product. But the wording deserves closer attention. For example, what does the word "fighting" really mean in this context? The outcome of the "fight" is not stated. "Fighting cavities" does not mean stopping them. So even though the implication of the endline is that Crest prevents cavities, that meaning is never actually stated.

To this point, our analysis has identified the most dominant features of this advertisement. From analyzing its layout and language, we discover the advertisers' selling strategies: to provide a dominant visual image, to associate it with a valued object, to identify the valued object with the product being sold, to provide a testimonial about the product, to use language that implies more than it states. Thus the advertisers stimulate the consumers' *confidence* in and *desire* for the product and convey their *message*.

If we were to finish analyzing the remaining parts of this advertisement according to our three steps, would we see the same strategies emphasized?"

Exercise A   As a class, or in small groups, continue to analyze this advertisement.

1. What is the visual layout of the remaining text, or copy? For example, examine the purpose behind the paragraphing in the center copy.

2. What can you discover about the language used in this copy? For example, how does it work to reinforce our previous analysis?

Exercise 2 As a class, or in writing groups, choose another advertisement and using the four steps highlighted above, analyze it as we did for the Crest advertisement.

✎ Writing Assignment: More Information

The advertisements easiest to focus on for this assignment are print advertisements—those from magazines—because you can examine them at your leisure and because you can easily let your classmates and instructor see them. However, if your instructor agrees, you may choose to analyze TV or radio advertisements.

Continuing the Analysis Process

Before you begin to draft a first version of your essay, you need to have plenty of practice developing an analysis. Following are some questions that encompass and expand steps 1–3 on page 102.

1. Are you the target audience for the advertisement? If not, who is? Where did you find this advertisement?

2. What visual elements are working in the advertisement?

    a. What are the dominant visual images?

    b. What colors are used?

    c. What responses do these colors evoke? Why?

    d. How does the color scheme (in this context, a color or group of colors used over and over again) work in the advertisement? For example, if you see a picture of a woman wearing a pink hat and a green dress, and if you next see a flower with a pink blossom and green stem, and then you see a deodorant stick with a pick cap topping a green container, what message is the advertisement trying to convey about the product?

3. What verbal elements are working in the advertisement?

    a. Are there headlines, boldfaced type, small print, a descriptive product name, a combination of these? What is their purpose? For example, do the written parts of the advertisement point out relationships with the visual elements? How? Do they tell a story about the images in the advertisement, or do they interpret or reinforce certain visual elements of the advertisement? Explain.

    b. Does the language used in the advertisement imply more than it actually states? (Refer to your outline of "Weasel Words.")

Having answered these three questions, you should have generated enough evidence to be able to state the advertisement's message and show how the elements in the advertisement's layout work to convey the message. Before you draft this information into essay form, however, bring the advertisement and the answers to the above questions to class for group work.

Exercise In pairs or in groups of three, exchange advertisements and write answers to the assignment questions for each partner's advertisement. When you have finished, pass back your partners' advertisements and your analysis of them.

Then, to see if you can gather insight into the workings of your advertisement, compare and discuss answers about your advertisement with your partners' answers to see on which questions you agree or disagree, and on which questions your partner has answered with more information than you.

DRAFTING: WRITING, TALKING, REWRITING, AND EVALUATING

First-Draft Activities

With the information from your own and your classmate's answers to the questions, you should be ready to write a first draft of your essay. The following guidelines should help.

Guidelines for Writing the First Draft

In your introduction, you need to provide a context, or background, for your essay; that is, you need to do the following:

1. Decide who your audience is—perhaps those people who have never thought much about how advertisements influence them.
2. Tell your audience your topic and purpose for writing the essay; that is, state what you want the audience to learn about advertising.
3. Introduce your advertisement; state its source, its target audience, and its message.

In the body of the paper, you need to provide evidence that shows how the advertisement conveys its message to its audience. One effective way to do this is as follows:

1. Describe the major features emphasized in the advertisement's layout; that is describe what you see first, second, third . . .
2. Explain why the advertisement was composed in this order. Remember, there is not just one "correct" way to analyze, so atten-

tion to detailed, complete description of both the visual and written parts of the advertisement is necessary for your readers to understand your point of view. Even though they can look at the advertisement you are analyzing, your readers will not necessarily be able to follow your analysis easily unless you fully describe what you see and what it means to you.

In the conclusion of the essay, you should explain whether or not the advertisement is effective and summarize why. Then tell why being able to analyze advertisements is important for your reader.

Responding to the First Draft

Bring copies of your first draft and your advertisement to class and exchange them with your group members. Discuss the drafts according to the following guidelines:

1. As you read through each essay, put parentheses ( ) around the sentences you think are unclear.
2. Read through the essay again and underline and label
   a. the sentence(s) implying the essay's audience and stating the essay's purpose
   b. the product advertised and the advertisement's source
   c. its target audience
   d. the sentence(s) stating the advertisement's message. If you cannot find some of this information, write the corresponding number and letter with a question mark (e.g. ''2b?'') in the left margin of the introductory paragraph(s).
3. Does the body of the paper contain the information indicated by the ''Guidelines for Writing the First Draft'' (pp. 106–107)? Write briefly, explaining what is missing or what needs to be further developed. Specifically comment about whether or not there is a balance between description of the advertisement and analysis of what is described. To highlight each kind of information, put brackets [ ] around sentences describing the advertisement, and underline sentences that **analyze,** that is, explain or comment upon, the description.
4. After having looked carefully at the advertisement and the essay analyzing it, do you find the writer's conclusion convincing? That is, do you agree with the writer's assessment of the advertisement and the importance of analyzing advertisements? Write briefly explaining why you agree or disagree.
5. Which parts of the essay are the most successful? Write briefly explaining why.

Second-Draft Activities

Before you begin revising your first draft, read the following two essays, written by students for this assignment.

Evaluation Criteria

Use the following guidelines to evaluate a structural analysis essay about an advertisement.

1. Your essay should have an introduction that
   a. sets up the essay's context and purpose
   b. states the advertisement's subject, its source, its target audience, and its message
2. It should also have a body that explains how the advertisement conveys its message by
   a. describing the major visual features of the advertisement to explain the purpose of its layout
   b. analyzing the written text, if any, to explain how it relates to the other visual elements in the advertisement
3. Finally, it should have a conclusion that evaluates the effectiveness of the advertisement and explains the value of analyzing advertisements.

Sample Student Essays

It's the Image That Counts

1   An advertisement is only effective if it captures the audience's attention, for only then can a message be understood. One way advertisers capture an audience is by matching the advertisement to the magazine. Another method is by presenting the advertisement in such a way that their product or image will stand apart from all others. When the audience is captured by the style or uniqueness of the advertisement; the advertisers will have an opportunity to make a statement about their product. These statements are sometimes constructed by logical reasoning and at other times deal with emotions and desires.

2   Advertisements which build on emotions and desires often characterize men as strong, tough, sophisticated, or successful in business. The character of sexy and seductive has been a trademark for women. A man is handsome while a woman is sensuously sexy. This sterotyping creates a strong image which is associated to the product.

3   *Sports Illustrated* is a magazine targeted for males, and an advertisement found in its pages will address itself to this audience. An advertisement for Just Jockey underwear [Figure 7.2] creates a bold image by dis-

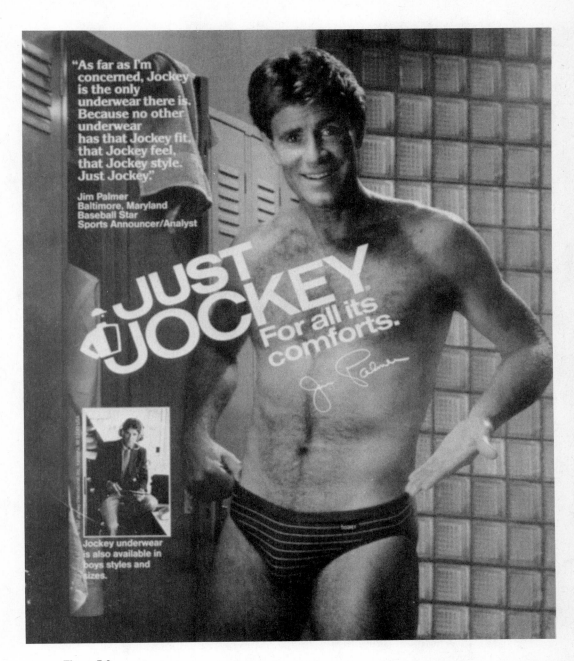

Figure 7.2.
Has the writer of Essay A identified the most important features of this advertisement? (Reprinted by permission of Jockey International Inc.)

playing a man as sexy, which brakes the traditional sterotype for men. In doing so, this advertisement creates a strong eye catching image.

4   While flipping through the pages of *Sports Illustrated* one is stunned by a blue eyed, brown haired, well-built, tanned bodied man wearing nothing but bikini briefs. The man's briefs match his blue eyes and locker tile background. The blue color scheme for the layout promotes a sensuous image. The positioning of his hands direct the reader's eyes to the tight fitting underwear he is modeling. This advertisement suggest the style of a pin up poster by placing his signature across his chest. One might think that this advertisement is placed in the wrong magazine since it's sex appeal image would be attractive to women; however, the image appeals to men who wish to attract women by acquiring an image of a sexy man. The advertisement creates the illusion that a man who wears Just Jockey underwear will be as attractive to women as the male model, Jim Palmer.

5   The men who read *Sports Illustrated* are very knowledgable about sports figures: so the name Jim Palmer is well known as a Baseball Star and Sports Announcer/Analyst. The advertisement takes no chance that the reader will misjudge the model, Jim Palmer, as just a sexy body. The advertisers tell the reader in the top right corner of his credentials and in the bottom right corner, a small picture of him in a suit with announcer head-gear is displayed. This is to convince the audience that he is intelligent and that his statements concerning sports are considered a matter of importance. Do his statements in the advertisement deal with his expertise as a baseball star or sports analyst? No, it states "As far as I'm concerned, Jockey is the only underwear there is. Because no other underwear had that Jockey fit, that Jockey feel, that Jockey style. Just Jockey for all it's comforts." One might ask what makes Jim Palmer a better judge of underwear than the reader. One assumes the reader has just as much, and maybe more, experience with wearing underwear as Jim Palmer.

6   The wording of the quoate also deserves attention. Jim Palmer states that Just Jockey underwear has fit, feel, style, and comfort. All men's underwear manufacturers claim these qualities; so why buy Just Jockey? The advertisement does not state that this brand is better than another brand. It only states that the underwear won by Jim Palmer is Just Jockey. It implies that because it is Jockey it is better. This implication is based on the name Jockey which implies that a person is talented or better than others in sports. The name Jockey has great appeal to its audience for sports fans buy *Sports Illustrated*. The use of words in the Just Jockey advertisement promotes the image of the best since Jocks are the best in sports.

7   The advertisement for Just Jockey does not provide objective reasons for buying the merchandise. It is presented in a bold and unique way that will catch the eye of a reader. There is a thought in psychology

that to influence a person, reasoning and logic are not as important as getting the person to read and know the message. This advertisement certainly entices the reader to look at it's image that Just Jockey is the best underwear which produces a sexy, sports talented man. The argument does not need to make logical sense for the desires of a man who wishes these qualities may manipulate his mind to accept the image as presented. The Just Jockey advertisement is a good example of how advertisers use emotion and desire to sell a product or image.

Sharp!

1   I feel that most good advertisements have two basic criteria. A picture that captures the attention of the reader, and a positive and convincing wording in the advertisement which will persuade the consumer to purchase the product [Figure 7.3]. The function of the image and the wording are separate.

2   The image of the advertisement conveys a meaning that the advertisers are trying to convey to you the reader. The wording however expresses how this product is good for you and why you should purchase it.

3   When I glance though a magazine, I feel that most of the best advertisements are the ones that have both an image that captures my attention, and a convincing wording that explains the product. These types of advertisements are usually the ones that will persuade the consumer to purchase their product at the readers level without analyzing the ad.

4   The advertisement that I am analyzing is the new Miller non-alcoholic Sharps beer. This so called beer is actually a soda-pop. The Miller brewery is actually trying to sell their soda, by telling their audience that it is beer. This is where the picture and the placement of the ad come into play. The bottle of soda is in a bottle that is shaped like a beer bottle. The soda bottle is wrapped in a wrapper that has the same style of writing and the same color that would be found on real beer bottle. Behind the bottle of soda is a beer glass that has the soda inside. The bottle and the glass of soda look just like the advertisements for real beer. This visual layout is where the reader gets fooled with the pictures. The picture convinces the reader that the bottle of soda is actually almost beer. Once this image of a soda that tastes like beer is inside the reader head, the wording takes over.

5   In large dark letters at the top of the page there is a sentence that reads, ''Sharps Passes Bar Exam''. This phrase has a dual meaning that could impress our potential consumer in two ways. The first meaning is that their product passed a rigid exam, like the lawyers bar exam. Even though the beer didn't pass a bar exam in law, the product passed it in bars across the country. This dual meaning tells the reader that their prod-

SHARP'S PASSES BAR EXAM.

Miller Sharp's, the break-through <u>non-alcoholic brew</u>, is passing the ultimate test.

In bars across the country, beer drinkers are discovering that it delivers real beer taste.

The breakthrough lies in a unique new brewing process.

Most non-alcoholic malt beverages start out as regular beer, and then the alcohol is removed. Unfortunately, so is a good deal of the taste.

Sharp's, on the other hand, is the result of Miller's brewing breakthrough, Ever-Cool.™

During brewing, temperatures remain lower, so alcohol production is minimized. What <u>is</u> produced is the smooth, refreshing taste of real beer.

Try Miller Sharp's. The breakthrough taste that lets you <u>keep your edge</u>.™

Figure 7.3.
What did the writer miss or omit in his analysis of this advertisement? Why? (Reprinted by permission of Miller Brewing Company.)

uct is good enough to be served in bars across the country with real beer. This slogan gives the consumer a feeling that this soda will refresh a beer drinker, the same way a normal beer would. This could give the normal beer drinker the opportunity to enjoy a refreshing beverage in a situation that may not have been able to enjoy in, like the workplace or other places one wouldn't be allowed to consume beer.

6   I feel that this advertisement was directed towards the male in the blue collar workplace that has a taste for beer. Reasons for me picking this audience is the magazines that the ads where found in. For example *Sports Illustrated,* where I found this ad. The wording in this ad is directly targeted to this sort of reader. The ad tells the reader that he may be able to enjoy the taste of beer in a situation like the workplace where he could not have had beer. While still being able to "keep you edge". Reasons for the Miller brewery to pick this audience is the fact that there are a large portion of the population, mostly males that are in the blue collar workplace, that enjoy the taste of beer, but they cant drink it due to company policy or the dangerous nature of their work. This gives Miller brewery the chance to sell a product to the group of people in that situation, and take advantage of their situation.

7   The wording also has another job, it tries to impress the reader with bright yellow highlighted words. These highlighted words are sentences like "this beverage is an amazing breakthrough", and "we have the ability for you to keep your edge". These phrases convince the reader that the Miller brewery has an amazing breakthrough, and that they are working hard for the consumer. What they are actually doing is making a soda that tastes like beer, which really isn't very amazing at all. This kind of weasel wording gives the reader a false sense of security about the breweries capabilities.

8   From analyzing this advertisement, I learned that Miller was actually trying to sell the male consumer in the workplace soda that looked and tasted like beer. Miller did everything possible to give this soda the same identity as beer. The image of the soda in the bottle and the mug, made the soda look like beer. The wording tried to convince the reader that their soda was actually as good as real beer. From the wording and the image, Miller was trying to sell soda marketed as beer. By doing this taking advantage of a large target audience in the workplace, and persuade them to purchase their soda priced like beer.

Evaluating the Sample Essays

Meet in your groups to decide the merits of the two essays based on the evaluation criteria on page 108. After your group has agreed about which essay best fulfills the requirements of the assignment, choose one group member to act as spokesperson, reporting to the rest of the class your group's reasons for evaluating the essays as it did.

Revising Your Second Draft

Revise your second draft taking into account your group members' advice, the insight you gained from reviewing the sample essays, and the evaluation criteria on page 108. Remember, always ask to have a conference with your instructor if your questions about your essay are not resolved in class.

EDITING

Final-Draft Editing

If your instructor so requires, type your final version of this essay double-spaced. Proofread it carefully for any errors that your instructor has previously indicated you should correct.

In class exchange papers with a partner and proofread his or her paper for typos, spelling, punctuation, grammatical, or any other errors you can find. Draw an arrow above what you believe is an error, but do not correct it; that is the author's job.

When your partner returns your essay, correct any errors you think have been legitimately marked. If you are not sure whether the marked error is really an error or whether or not you have correctly fixed it, ask your partner first and then your instructor.

Postfinal-Draft Editing

Your teacher may have you revise a section of your essay or have you correct particular errors.

Expository Essay

WRITING ASSIGNMENT

The paper due at the end of this chapter is an essay about a topic of your choice. Because you will not do library research for this essay, you must pick a topic about which you have some knowledge and personal experience. You will need to make a point directed toward a specific audience, and develop that main point with supporting points and various kinds of evidence.

Why Write an Expository Essay?

The essays you wrote for Chapters 6 and 7 were **expository essays,** essays written to inform your audience of your opinion about a topic and developed by a logical sequence of related ideas. This chapter's expository essay assignment is different and challenging in that the topic and focus of the essay, the kinds of evidence generated, and the points made based upon that evidence are all up to you. As you write this essay, you will learn to focus, or narrow, a topic so that it is manageable; you will also add to what you know about various kinds of evidence, and you will make a major point and learn to make **subpoints,** or supporting points, based on your evidence. This is the kind of assignment you will most often write in college courses.

INVENTION: READING, WRITING, TALKING, AND ANALYZING FOR IDEAS

Various Kinds of Evidence

So far, you have written essays using descriptive details, anecdotes, personal experience, and examples as kinds of evidence to develop and support your points. There are also other kinds of evidence you can use to develop your points. You can develop paragraphs by defining; by using facts and statistics; by quoting authoritative sources; by using hypothetical, or invented, examples; and by using an analogy, comparing one idea or item to another. Study the following examples to become familiar with some, though not all, of the kinds of evidence you might use to illustrate or develop a paragraph's point in your essays.

1. Illustrate the point using **descriptive details.**

> The mockingbird took a single step into the air and dropped. His wings were still folded against his sides as though he were singing from a limb and not falling, accelerating thirty-two feet per second, through empty air. Just a breath before he would have been dashed to the ground, he unfurled his wings with exact, deliberate care, revealing the broad bars of white, spread his elegant, white-banded tail, and so floated onto the grass. I had just rounded a corner when his insouciant step caught my eye: there was no one else in sight. The fact of his free fall was like the old philosophical conundrum about the tree that falls in the forest. The answer must be, I think, that beauty and grace are performed whether or not we will or sense them. The least we can do is try to be there.
>
> Annie Dillard, *Pilgrim at Tinker Creek* (New York: Harper & Row, Publishers, 1974): 7.

2. Develop the point using an **anecdote.**

> I think, I ponder, I recall a hundred things—little things, foolish things that come to me without reason and fade again. . . .
>
> Kima the baboon, the big baboon that loved my father but hated me; Kima's grimaces, his threats, his chain in the courtyard; the morning he escaped to trap me against the wall of a hut, digging his teeth into my arm, clawing at my eyes, screaming his jealous hatred until, with childish courage born of terror I killed him dead, using a knobkerrie and frantic hands and sobbing fury—and ever afterward denied the guilt.
>
> Beryl Markham, *West with the Night* (San Francisco: North Point Press, 1983): 133, 134.

3. Develop a point by **defining.**

> A weasel word is "a word used in order to evade or retreat from a direct or forthright statement or position" (Webster). In other words, if we can't say it we'll weasel it. And, in fact, a weasel word has become more than just an evasion or retreat. We've trained our weasels. They can do anything. They can make you hear things that aren't being said, accept as truths things that have only been implied, and believe things that have only been suggested.
>
> Paul Stevens, "Weasel Words: God's Little Helpers," *I Can Sell You Anything* (New York: Ballantine/Del Rey/Fawcett Books, 1972): 91.

4. Develop a point with **examples.**

> The oat-bran action is happening on the upper cereal shelves, those at an adult's eye level. Meanwhile, down where kids can see (and grab), cereal makers are still packaging grain as candy. Old sugary favorites like *Trix* and *Frosted Flakes* have been joined by new sugary hopefuls like General Mill's *Cinnamon Toast Crunch* and Quaker's *Cap'n Crunch's*

Crunch Berries. General Mills, which specializes in the sweet, kid-oriented segment of the cereal market, has even managed to take oatmeal to new, sugary heights in Oatmeal Swirlers, with 4 1/2 teaspoons of sugar per serving. This cereal's gimmick: a squeeze-packet of a jamlike substance ("made with real fruit") for kids to decorate their mush.

"Cereal: Breakfast Food or Nutritional Supplement?" *Consumer Reports*, October 1989, 638.

5. Develop a point using an **analogy.**

Still a referee cannot be too rigid. Since league authorities rarely overrule his judgment, an official must also function as the sport's supreme court and thus deliberate if he, as the district judge, might have erred. Though never swayed by how loudly a fiery coach protests, a good official will change decisions when additional evidence appears.

Bill Surface, "Referee: Roughest Role in Sports," *Reader's Digest*, December 1976, 168–179.

6. Develop a point using **facts and statistics.**

In the 1980s, however, oil prices plunged, and Indian mineral revenues with them. So did federal expenditures for Indian programs, which under the Reagan Administration were cut by $1 billion a year. Funding for job training and technical-assistance projects declined 56 percent from 1980–1984 for example, and per-capita funding for the Indian Health Service, the U.S. Public Health Service agency that provides medical care to one million Indians, shrank by about half. The cuts had an immediate negative effect on Indian employment, because 44 percent of Indians' personal income comes from federal and tribal jobs (in contrast, public sector jobs provide 19 percent of salaries nationwide). Not surprisingly, overall Indian unemployment has in the past year climbed to 40 percent by the BIA's reckoning, which is widely regarded as conservative, from a low of 38 percent in 1987. The figure averages 75 percent on the ten largest reservations. "For practical purposes, there is no private-sector economy on many reservations," says Alan R. Parker, a Chippewa Cree who is the staff director of the Senate Indian Affairs Committee and a former president of the American Indian National Bank.

"Tribal Enterprise," *The Atlantic*, October 1989, 34.

7. Develop a point by **quoting or paraphrasing authoritative sources.**

Yet a more accurate picture of the American press immediately becomes clear when one considers how and where reporters find the news. Very few newspaper stories are the result of reporters digging through files; poring over documents; or interviewing experts, dissenters, or ordinary people. The overwhelming majority of stories are based on official sources—on information provided by members of Congress, presidential aides, and other political insiders. A media critic named Leon B. Sigal discovered as much after analyzing 2,850 news stories that appeared in the *New York Times* and the *Washington Post* between 1949 and 1969. Nearly four out of five of these stories, he found, involved official sources. The first fact of American journalism is its overwhelming dependence on sources, mostly official, usually powerful. "Sources supply the sense and substance of the day's news. Sources provide the arguments, the rebuttals, the explanations, the criticism," as Theodore L. Glasser, a professor of journalism at the University of Minnesota, wrote in a 1984 issue of *Quill,* a journalist's journal. Powerful people not only make news by their deeds but also tell reporters what to think of those deeds and the reporters then tell us. The dean of the *Washington Post,* columnist David Broder, notes that for many years the Associated Press covered the House of Representatives for scores of millions of Americans through daily chats with Rep. Howard W. Smith, a conservative Virginia Democrat who chaired the powerful Rules Committee.

Walter Karp, *Harper's Magazine,* reprinted in *Utne Reader,* November/December 1989, 60–61.

Exercise

1. For each of the seven samples of evidence, underline the point that the evidence supports.

2. Which of the seven samples have more than one kind of evidence supporting the point? List them and name the kinds of evidence used to support the point.

The Reading Process.

All of us bring to our reading previous experience, knowledge, beliefs, and assumptions about the topic an author addresses. Sometimes, the reading supports and extends what we already know; sometimes it creates an awareness and gives us knowledge we have never had before or clarifies vague half-thoughts we have had; and sometimes it flies in the face of what we believe, confusing our understanding of the topic.

These diverse responses to what we read should challenge us to read well, that is, as alertly, accurately, and fairly as we can. Reading well is especially important when we are reading difficult, unfamiliar material as happens, and *should* happen, in college. To read well is to be aware that essays contain material arranged **hierarchically,** that is, with less important or commonly known information subordinated to more important or less familiar material.

Hierarchical Structure of Essays

Traditionally an essay has three main sections.

1. An introduction, which provides

    a. **a context**—what "*most people think*" about the topic or the background necessary for a particular audience to understand the author's approach to the topic.

    b. **the main point**—the author's statement of opinion about the topic ("*But I assert . . .*"). The main point, often called the thesis, is usually found at the end of the introductory paragraph(s).

2. a body, which provides

   a. **subpoints**—opinions, or statements requiring proof, stated in each body paragraph or section that support the main point of the essay ("*Here is why . . .*"). Subpoints are often, though not always, found in the first sentence or so of the paragraph.

   b. **various kinds of evidence**—examples, anecdotes, quotes, facts and statistics, to name a few of those you have studied that support and develop the subpoint ("*Here is proof . . .*").

3. A conclusion, which provides

   a. statements reinforcing the significance of the main point.

   b. answers to the question "*So what*?" about the topic.

The italicized phrases provide an easy way to remember essay structure:

Most people think . . .
But I assert . . .

Here is why . . .
Here is proof . . .

So what?

Knowledge of essay structure should help you read any piece of writing more accurately; specifically, it will help you to pinpoint the logic behind the content and structure of the following essay, "Born to Run," which is more complex than the essays you have read so far. Finally, reading well will help you *write well* by providing techniques and subject matter to use in your own writing.

Prereading Suggestions

To read well is also to know what to look for in an essay before you actually begin to read it. This is known as **prereading.** Before you begin to read notice the essay's title. Based on the title, what do you expect the topic and point of the essay will be? Also, notice where the essay was originally published. What does this tell you about the essay's audience? How would you characterize the audience? As you read notice how the author tailors his approach to his topic based on his perception of his audience. Circle words whose meanings you are not sure you know. Finally, reread and label the different kinds of evidence the author uses.

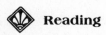

Reading

Born to Run

George Leonard

1   Running is one of the primal human acts, and the particular human form it takes, using a bipedal stride in a fully upright stance, has played an essential part in shaping our destiny. It was once believed that our hominid ancestors were rather pitiable creatures compared with the other animals of the jungles and savannas; lacking the fangs, claws, and specialized physical abilities of the predators, the hominids supposedly prevailed only because of their large brains and their ability to use tools. But there is now compelling evidence that our direct ancestors of some four million years ago had relatively small brains, only about a third the size of ours. What these hominids *did* have was a fully upright stance with the modern, doubly curved spine that enters the skull at the bottom rather than the back (as is the case with the apes). The upright stance increased the field of vision and freed the forelimbs for use in inspecting and manipulating objects, thus challenging the brain to increase its capacity through the process of natural selection. We can't specify the athletic ability of our four-million-year-old ancestors, but it was sufficient for the survival of the line, even without tools and high intelligence.

2   Much has been made of the blazing sprint speed of the cheetah, the prodigious high jumps of the kangaroo, the underwater skills of the dolphin, and the gymnastic prowess of the chimpanzee. But no animal can match the human animal in all-around athletic ability. If we were to hold a mammal decathlon with events in sprinting, endurance running, long jumping, highjumping, swimming, deep diving, gymnastics, striking, kicking, and burrowing, other animals would win most of the individual events. But a well-trained human would come up with the best overall score. And in one event—endurance running—the human would outperform all other animals of comparable size, as well as some quite a bit larger.

3   It is the extraordinary human capacity to run long and hard, even in the heat of day, that might well have made early man a formidable predator. In an article in a recent *Current Anthropology*, zoologist David Carrier of the University of Michigan points out that surviving primitive people, in pursuits lasting up to two days, have outrun many kinds of animals known for their great speed. "Bushmen are reported to run down duiker, steenbok, and gemsbok during the rainy season, and wildebeest and zebra during the hot dry season. Tarahumara Indians chase deer through the mountains of northern Mexico until the animals collapse from exhaustion, and then throttle them by hand. Paiutes and Navajo of the American Southwest are reported to have hunted pronghorn antelope (one of the fastest of all mammals) with this same technique. Furthermore,

aborigines of northwestern Australia are known to hunt kangaroo successfully in this way." (In the April 3, 1978, issue of *Sports Illustrated,* an Ashland, Oregon, runner named Michael Baughman described running down a deer. It turned out to be a surprisingly easy task. Even when the young buck stood trembling with its head hung low, so exhausted that its human pursuer could walk up and touch its flank, Baughman still felt "refreshed enough to be able to run for another half hour.")

4   This human dominance over animals known for their specialized running skills is even stranger than it might seem, for human running is not only relatively slow but also inefficient. Carrier notes that the energy cost of running (oxygen consumption per unit of body weight per unit of distance traveled) is about twice as high for humans as for most other mammals. This being the case, it would seem that a man wouldn't have a chance against a deer, but there are other factors that outweigh our energy inefficiency. Perhaps the most important is the human ability to dissipate the body heat built up during strenuous exertion. We possess the most efficient sweat glands in the animal kingdom; no other species sweats so copiously. Our evaporative cooling system works even better because of our unique nakedness, which may have evolved to make it possible for us to run long distances on hot days. Even the copious hair that remains on our heads serves this purpose, providing a shield for the head and shoulders when the sun is highest and its rays most destructive.

5   One thing is sure: when any animal reaches a certain core temperature, it can no longer run. At a blazing sixty-two miles an hour, the cheetah generates heat at a rate sixty times greater than while at rest. Overheating is what brings this swift animal to a halt; when its body temperature reaches 105, generally in less than three quarters of a mile, it simply stops. In a long chase, the first animal to overheat loses.

6   Our breathing system is also superior. In four-legged animals, breathing is tied into the motion and impact of the front feet and the bending motion of the body. Whether the animal is walking, trotting, or galloping, only one breath is possible for each locomotive cycle, which limits it to certain optimum speeds for each gait. Our upright stance, however, allows us to run with the same efficiency no matter what the speed: we spontaneously choose the breathing pattern (two strides per breath, three strides per breath, and so on) that is the most efficient for the speed. A marathoner, for instance, expends the same amount of energy whether he or she runs the distance in four hours or two and a half hours.

7   Even our large adrenal and thyroid glands predispose us toward running; they tend to increase the levels of those hormones that help the muscles use fatty acids and glucose efficiently. And our omnivorous diet itself, especially our capacity to load up on carbohydrates, gives us an edge over carnivores and most other animals in long-distance running.

8   All of this adds up to one simple fact: we are born to run, especially

to run great distances. Some observers, bemused by the runners who
have overflowed from tracks and trails to city sidewalks and streets, argue
that running is only a fad or even an addiction, a form of narcissim. But
to call running a fad makes as much sense as to call thinking a fad.
Endurance running is an essential human activity that preceded abstract
thought and indeed helped make it possible.

9   The recent debates on the value of running generally involve
immediate, practical matters: Does it help you lose weight? Is it good for
your heart? Will it help you live longer? These are important questions,
but they obscure the underlying motivation. People might start running
for any number of practical or self-serving reasons, but those who persist
experience something that entirely transcends the debate, something
deeply satisfying in and of itself: a reconnection with the roots of our
race, a reaffirmation of an ancient and noble pursuit.

10   Though we no longer run for food and survival, the importance of
this activity is still evident in the sports we most enjoy watching. Football,
basketball, baseball, and soccer, it might be said, are complicated
excuses for running. Tennis and other racket, net, and wall games
involve a series of short, dancing sprints. Pole vaulting, javelin throwing,
high jumping, long jumping, and triple jumping begin with and depend
upon running. Rugby, cricket, field hockey, team handball, hurdles,
steeplechase, various forms of tag, hide-and-seek, and capture-the-flag—
all are runners' games.

11   At the very least, running can give you all the aerobic conditioning
you need, with a minimum of specialized training or expenditure of time
and equipment. For those with busy schedules, in fact, running's time
demands are so modest as to make it almost irresistible. Walking might
well be the safest and surest way to aerobic health, but it takes about
three hours of brisk walking to give you the benefits of a one-hour run.
In his book *Running Without Fear,* Dr. Kenneth Cooper, creator of the
aerobics concept and one of the pioneers of the fitness movement,
recommends a minimum running distance of two miles three times a
week at an eight-to-ten-minute-a-mile pace, and a maximum of three
miles five times a week at the same pace. That adds up to forty-eight
minutes to an hour a week at the least, and two hours to two and a half
hours at the most. Anything more than that, according to Cooper, adds
little or nothing in the way of health benefits.

12   Cooper is among those who warn against the myth that running
gives certain protection against heart disease (though every large-scale
study has shown that vigorous exercise gives considerable protection).
He also argues strongly for coronary stress-testing prior to starting any
strenuous exercise program. Other experts, notably runner George
Sheehan, himself a cardiologist, question the accuracy of and need for
stress-testing. "If you listen to your body," Sheehan says, "running is

perfectly safe. No horse ever ran itself to death without a jockey on its back. If there's any disagreement between a machine and your body, listen to your body."

13   By and large, however, running experts have made a turn toward caution and moderation since the death of running guru Jim Fixx last summer. Joe Henderson, one of the most authoritative writers on the subject, sums it up in the December 1984 *Runner's World:* "Runners are more realistic in their thinking about what running can do for them. They take fewer risks in their approach to training and racing. They plan less for short-term success and more for long-term health and happiness."

14   All of this is to the good. Runners and would-be runners should be offered safe and sensible programs and warned against the dangers and pitfalls of their practice. And those who wish to run for specific, practical benefits—weight control, stress reduction, a healthier heart—must be given their due. But to limit the dialogue to these practical considerations is to demean the human spirit. Many people run not to lose weight but to loosen the chains of a mechanized culture, not to postpone death but to savor life. For these runners, the admonitions of the exercise critics are moot; they run quite consciously, as informed, consenting adults, to exceed their previous limits and to press the edges of the possible, whether this means completing their first circuit of a four-hundred-meter track without walking, or fighting for victory in a triathlon, as in this episode recounted in a recent issue of *American Medical News:*

15   Few moments in sports history have so poignantly captured the agony of defeat as when twenty-three-year-old Julie Moss was leading the women's division of the twenty-six-mile marathon of Hawaii's Iron-man Triathlon World Championship. *anecdote*

16   With only one hundred yards left between her and the finish, Moss fell to her knees. She then rose, ran a few more yards, and collapsed again. As TV cameras rolled, she lost control of her bodily functions. She got up again, ran, fell, and then started crawling. Passed by the second-place runner, she crawled across the finish line, stretched out her arm, and passed out.

17   Jim McKay of ABC Sports called it "heroic . . . one of the greatest moments in the history of televised sport." Gilbert Lang, M.D., an ortho-pedic surgeon at Roseville (California) Community Hospital and a long-time endurance runner, calls it "stupid—very nearly fatal."

18   Both Lang and McKay are right: it was stupid and it was heroic. Surely no runner should be encouraged to go so near the edge of death. But what kind of world would it be, how meager and pale, without such heroics? Perhaps there would be no human world at all, for there must have been countless times before the dawn of history when primitive hunters in pursuit of prey gave all of themselves in this

way so that members of their bands, our distant ancestors, could live. Athletes such as Julie Moss run for all of us, reaffirming our humanity, our very existence.

~ Journal Assignments

1. Write a journal page about your responses to this reading.
    a. What familiar ideas or information did you find in this essay?
    b. What unfamiliar ideas or information?
    c. Which parts of the essay seemed confusing? Why?
    d. Which parts seemed very clear? Why?
    e. What did you like or dislike about this essay? Why?
    f. What did you learn from this essay that most impressed you?

2. Make a list of vocabulary words from those you circled as you read this essay. Then, reread the essay and look up each vocabulary word as you come across it. Write down the definition of the word that fits the way it is used in the essay.

3. Brainstorm a list of topics you might care to write about. What topics, issues, problems with which you have some personal experience passionately interest or upset you? Some subject areas that might come to mind are *sports* (ways to become physically fit, the dangers related to getting physically fit, or the weaknesses and strengths of the NCAA's Propositions 42 and 48); *college life* (coping with study stress and your social life, advantages or disadvantages of going to school in the summer, or of being a commuter student, of living at home or in a dorm, of being a married or single student); *jobs* (the disadvantages or advantages of having to work while going to school or sexual harassment on the job); *music* (why some people want to censor the lyrics of some musical groups or why rapping is actually helping some kids stay off drugs); *movies, TV,* or *dance; animals* (animal rights); *grafitti* (their purpose); *hobbies* (the benefits of a particular one); *city life* or *country life* (the advantages of one of them); *"beauty"* (how it or the lack of it influences our lives); or *shopping* or *fashion* (some people's obsession with it or its therapeutic benefits).

4. Freewrite for at least one page about two of the topics on your list. You might begin by writing down what you know about the topic; why you find it interesting, important, entertaining, or any other adjective that applies to your topic; what other people know or should know about your topic; mistaken beliefs or attitudes about your topic; various parts or aspects of your topic; experiences you or others you know—or have heard about—have had with your topic. These ideas will get you started thinking about your topic.

Reading Questions

Content

1. George Leonard does not provide descriptions of any of his personal experiences in this reading, yet he forcefully and passionately projects his attachment to his subject. Find sentences from this reading that illustrate his strong personal attachment to his topic.

   a. Do you think Leonard is a runner? Upon what evidence from the reading do you base your answer?

   b. What kind of runner would Leonard be—one who runs for practical reasons, to maintain the health of his physical heart, or one who runs for metaphysical (look up this word!) reasons, to maintain the spirit of the heart? Upon what evidence from the text do you base your answer?

2. Readers who do not believe in evolution may be put off by the first paragraph of this essay.

   a. Do you think Leonard believes in evolution? Does he assume his audience believes in evolution? Cite evidence from the first paragraph to explain your answer.

   b. If your religious beliefs cause you to reject a belief in evolution, does that mean you must reject Leonard's thesis, or main point, that we are "born to run" and that running has played an important role in "shaping our destiny"? Must you reject all his supporting points or subpoints? With which of his subpoints do you agree? Disagree? (*Hint*: First identify the subpoints—secondary opinions supporting his main point—in paragraphs 2, 3, 9, 10, and 11. Then state what kind of evidence the author used to support each subpoint. For example, in paragraph 2 the author's subpoint is that "no animal can match the human animal in all-around athletic ability," and he uses a hypothetical illustration with examples of many kinds of athletic activities to support his subpoint.)

3. Leonard uses many kinds of evidence to develop and support the subpoints in his various paragraphs.

   a. In which paragraphs does he use quotes from authorities? What subpoints do they support?

   b. In which paragraphs does he use facts and statistics? What subpoints do they support?

   c. In which paragraphs does he use multiple examples? What subpoints do they support?

   d. In which paragraph does Leonard use an anecdote? What is the purpose of the anecdote?

Structure

1. This essay is organized into sections. How many sections are there? Briefly describe the contents of each and explain Leonard's reason for breaking his subject into these sections.

2. Because Leonard must clearly show the reader the relationship between his ideas, he has to use effective transitions between sections and between paragraphs, as well as within the paragraphs of his essay.

   a. We have already seen that the title helps us identify the author's main point. In which paragraph do we find the title repeated? What is the purpose of that paragraph; that is, how does it relate to the paragraphs before and after it? How does the phrase "All of this . . ." beginning that paragraph signal its purpose? In which other paragraph do you see that beginning phrase? How does that paragraph relate to those before and after it?

   b. In addition to transitional paragraphs connecting sections of the essay, Leonard writes transitional sentences, usually the last sentence of each paragraph, to set up a connection between paragraphs. Look at the final sentence in paragraph 2 and the first sentence of paragraph 3. How has Leonard created the transition between them?

   c. How has Leonard created the transition between paragraphs 3 and 4?

   d. Leonard also provides transitions within his paragraphs. In paragraph 2, for example, he provides a transition by narrowing his focus from all-around athletic ability to endurance running, one aspect of the athletic ability. More commonly, however, Leonard uses a variation of the organizing strategy "Most people think A, but I assert *B*" to provide a transition from more to less familiar information or to set up the relationship between apparently contradictory material. In which paragraphs does Leonard use this form? (*Hint:* Look for the word *but*. It usually indicates not only a shift in focus, from one aspect of a topic to another, but also flags a statement of opinion, which the author will go on to support with various kinds of evidence.)

In-Class Writing Assignment: Structural Analysis of an Expository Essay

To help you fix the structural elements of an expository essay in your mind you will write an essay analyzing the structure of "Born to Run." In this analysis you are concerned with *how* the writer makes the point, not what the writer says.

To get started on the right track, begin your analysis essay by copying the paragraph below, which will serve as the introductory paragraph for your essay.

> Most people do not really know what makes a good essay, but I can tell them that a good essay must state a point that is of significance to a particular audience and support it with subpoints and various kinds of evidence. ''Born to Run'' by George Leonard is a good example of an essay that does this.

In the body of your essay, tell your reader what Leonard's main point is and the audience for whom he is writing. Then discuss some of the kinds of evidence Leonard uses: examples, quoting authorities, facts and statistics, anecdotes, and so on. To do this name at least three kinds of evidence; give an example of each kind and identify the subpoint the evidence supports. (*Hint:* Note how to use the terms you have learned: Leonard makes the *subpoint* that ''. . . no animal can match the human animal in all-around athletic ability,'' and he uses an *example* about an animal decathalon, as *evidence* to support his *subpoint*.) End your essay with a concluding paragraph that tells your readers why it is important for them to know the structure of expository essays.

Before you begin to write this essay, you might want to organize your thoughts by taking some notes from the reading. Here is an example.

Subpoint	Kind of Evidence	Brief Description of Evidence
Our endurance running in comparison to other animals probably made us impressive hunters (paragraph 3)	Quotation from authority (a zoologist)	A zoologist said that surviving primitive peoples can outrun and thus successfully hunt animals known for their speed.
	Anecdote (a runner)	A runner from Oregon described how easy it was for him to outrun a deer.

 Writing Assignment: More Information

Exploring a Topic: The Six Journalistic Questions

After having discussed the typical essay form and Leonard's essay, and after having written an essay analyzing essay form, you might think that you should be able to sit down and draft your own essay, beginning with your main point, then subpoints, and finally, filling in the appropriate kinds of evidence to support all those points. Think again! Remember, most writers discover their point of view about a topic as they write. To begin with, you should be concerned with getting down on paper any information you can think of concerning your topic. So far you have brainstormed to list topics, issues, and problems that interest or concern you and with which you have some personal experience or knowledge, and you have done some directed freewriting in your journal about two of those topics.

To generate even more information about your topic, the next step is to answer the six standard journalistic questions about your topic: who? what? where? when? why? and how? Before doing this on your own, read and discuss the answers of one student, Joshua, to the six questions, which follow. Joshua's topic is alcoholism:

Who? *Who drinks too much?* People who are insecure, stressed, "party animals," lonely. *Who is affected by the alcoholic?* Family, friends, and victims of drunk drivers are affected by alcoholics. *Who should care about the problems caused by alcohol besides those already mentioned?* Educators—teachers, counselors, and physicians, and especially makers and advertisers of alcohol. *Who needs to know about this topic—who should be the audience for this paper?* Everybody! Mostly kids? It depends.

What? *What kind of alcohol is abused most?* Not sure, but kids usually drink beer (personal experience) and beer is the kind of alcohol usually advertised. *What causes alcoholism?* Maybe going to lots of social activities where people drink a lot—that's wanting to fit in—peer pressure, so people who are young and/or insecure are at risk. Advertising could promote alcoholism because advertisers make drinking seem fun, or glamorous, or relaxing (think of some specific commercials to illustrate this). *What are the effects of alcoholism?* For the drinker, bad health—maybe death (suicide), loss of job, money, family, home. For the drinker's victims—children and spouse might be abused, verbally and physically. Others might be victims of an accident caused by a drunk person. Society is a victim in that alcoholism causes a loss in human potential, so we all suffer. We all have to pay (money) for alcoholism too: consider insurance rates, prison costs, legal fees. . . .

When? Doesn't really apply to topic—*When to deal with the topic of educating against alcohol?* The sooner the better.

Where? Doesn't really apply either. *Where do people drink?* At home, at school, at play—Some people only drink at home, privately, some only publicly, but so what?

Why? *Why do people drink?* Answered this in **Who?** section. *Why do advertisers only show the positive side of drinking?* To make money obviously. *Why is drinking such a problem in this society?* Too much free time, too much pressure, so we need to relax and forget; too much of a tendency to rely on something besides ourselves to alter our moods, lives, feelings. . . .

How? *How do we stop alcohol abuse?* Education/prevention. More treatment programs. More truthful advertising. *How do we know when we or someone we know has a drinking problem?* Not sure, exactly—could find out.

Exercise Now, write out as many questions and answers to the six journalistic questions as you can for your own topic.

Focusing a Topic

After looking very carefully at Joshua's answers to the six journalistic questions you probably noticed that his topic, alcoholism, was very broad. Your class might ask and answer some further questions in order to narrow, or focus, the topic.

Questions to Help Narrow a Topic

1. Is this topic too broad to deal with in a short paper that will not include library research?
2. About what aspect of the topic could you gather enough evidence and become "an authority," without researching at the library?
3. How much information from the six journalistic questions is common knowledge?

Readers are not interested in reading about familiar information unless you can think of some way of interpreting what is good, bad, helpful, unhelpful, misleading, or incomplete about it.

One Student's Drafts

Read the following two drafts of Joshua's essays on alcoholism. Keep in mind the three questions for narrowing a topic as you read.

Draft 1   Alcohol: Families, Reasons

1   Alcohol is a very controversial subject which has had great impact on todays society. Most people believe that it is a stimulant or an upper, but compelling evidence has shown that is is a seditive or a downer. Many problems dealing with alcohol, however contrary to peoples beliefs, affect families drastically. (Alcohol referring to the using of alcohol to an extreme that overcomes your personality traits.) Alcohol is tearing families apart because the involved parties are to selfish to seek wise counsel. We can't specify what alcohol does to our bodies physically, but emotionally and mentally it is causing fatal effects, through suicide, divorce, and family child abuse. We start by educating the non users.

2   The social drinker starts his or her habit forming process with the first drink he or she takes. Peer pressure has caused many people to turn to casual drinking or social drinking, however not everyone is overcome by peer pressure it is still a dominating force. There was a motivational speaker who illistrated peer pressure through a story, he stated: There once was a bridge that collapsed between two shores, as cars approached the bridge they look at the car in front of them, not stopping, they sailed off the bridge without hesitation. We as individuals and society have an instinct to follow paths where others have crossed. We begin to take the role of followers.

3   Families are affected in various ways such as abuse, neglect, criminal problems, and suicide attempts. I once knew a young man that had been drinking very heavily. We had been at a freinds house when he decided that life wasn't worth living; he grabbed a knife and was about to stab himself when he was restrained by some of his friends. His family shocked and horrified of the event, that very well could have taken place and affected the rest of their lives. He later stated that he felt like he was not worthy to have life. Alcohol can affect you in several ways and could control your destiny.

4   Alcohol has a way of making us except other roles that are not our true nature. I have witnessed on occasion that shows an example of this. I went to a resturant last thursday night and I saw a family in the corner booth with two small children. There parents were so drunk that they could hardle manage to get up and leave. They finally managed to get up and leave and procede into a car. Children are hurt because of the parents naive attitudes and selfishness. Accidents can occur in one tenth of a second.

5   Divorce is one of the most socially acceptable things to do today. If marriage doesn't work they simply file for a divorce, nearly one out of three mariges in the United Sates will fail, not stated, however, is how many are possibly due to alcohol related reasons, well I now quite a few and I believe it is a problem in our society, however properly stated, alcohol abuse is not always the main related reason.

6   People do not only drink because of pressure from freinds, they also drink because it looks inticing and entertaining. Commercials have a big impact on the reasons for drinking they get pro-athletes, beautiful girls, and famous entertainers to promote their product. They also show bars where people are gathered together partying having a great time. So an ordinary man sitting in front of a football game is being lured into a pseudo cituation, however these commercials seem to leave out the thousands of lifes that are lost because of drunk driving. Or many more related to alcohol.

7   All of these stories help to illistrate and understand the effects of alcohol. Why? Why is there so many problems in society? Why don't parents and communities try to educate each other on the side effects of

alcohol? Some people are absolutely correct we are naive and passive. We don't understand alcohol, we can educate our children in order to keep our family units together.

Draft 2   *Advertising and Alcholism*

1   Alcoholism is a growing problem in todays society. We know the harmful effects of alcohol even though people tend to neglect them, however many of us are not aware of the effect of the inticing lures that are used to promote alcohol. The most influential example is television beer commercials, they have great impact on the reasons for using alcohol. Most people don't understand how realitive and parallel the effects of alcohol are in conjunction with these commercials.

2   Alcohol commercials use a variety of ways to influence the viewer. We view comedians, pro-athletes, movie stars and even in the case of the Bartyle and James commercial, we see older men who represent ordinary and simple people. For example in the Budweiser commercial they use a dog, called spuds (the party animal), to illistrate fun times and partying; there are people gathered around a pool, laughing dancing, and singing. People are socializing and being accepted. The viewer sees this as inticing and fun, sending messages to our mind that if you drink you will have fun and be accepted also, however this is not the case if you have ever gone to a party, they usually turn out quite differently. There are other commercials that display masculinity. Joe Piscipo plays the part of a muscle man, who shakes a guys hand so hard that his arm rips out of socket. This also sends a message to our subconsious minds, that it is funny and you wish you were are strong and rough as him. In the Bartyle and James commercials as stated before, appeal to us because they are viewed as being ordinary and common older men that are selling a great product. So you see that all these commercials have alot of things in common they are, funny, full of excitement, and showing that drinking is all fun and games, what they don't show is the thousands of people killed in accidents related to alcohol.

3   Another aspect of these commercials is the art of selling, they know when to interupt prime time T.V. with these enticing commercials. When was the last time that you watched a football game and didn't see a commercial on beer, probably never. These salesmen use advertising very ingeniously by delivering those commercials to an appropriate audience, for example, you don't see a lite beer commercial on prime time T.V. with the Cosby Show; this is because the viewers of this show are not not appropriate audiences.

4   We accept these commercials without thinking about the point they are implying, condoning alcohol abuse, while suicides and accidents sky rocket.

5   In a beautiful seen in Battle Creek, Michigan, on a wonderful lake men are fishing, sunbathing, and socializing. We enjoy the outdoors and love to be in them. The commercial focuses on this aspect and fun it would be to be there sipping a cold brew. A famous line comes from this commercial, "It doesn't get any better than this, that's Old Milwakuee Beer." There clever commercials and they hit you where you are the most vulnerable, you passions.

6   All of these commercials are inticing in one form or another, however, we don't view the suicides, divorce, family abuse, and death due to alcoholism. People know these aspects about alcohol and we tend to accept some of them, but we don't understand the adding implications of the commercials. So next time you view one of these commercials look and remember what goes on behind the scene.

Discussion: Joshua's Drafts

1. Which draft was written before Joshua had asked and answered the above three questions? How do you know?

2. What is the topic of draft 1? Of draft 2?

3. What is the logic behind the organization of draft 1? Of draft 2? (*Hint:* Look at the sentence that begins each paragraph and determine which are subpoints and which are subtopics.)

4. Which is the better draft? Why? (*Hint:* Consider audience, point, relationship of subpoints to main point, and supporting evidence.)

After Joshua had narrowed his topic and focused on the way in which beer ads influence TV viewers, he still did not sit down and simply list all the points he wanted to make. Instead he did what most writers need to do; he gathered evidence. He wrote answers to the six journalistic questions again, this time with television beer commercials as his topic; he watched the commercials, described them, classified them. Only then was he able to make points based on his interpretation of the evidence.

Exercises

1. As a class answer the six journalistic questions about a topic of your choice. Your instructor will act as scribe. Then answer the Questions to Help Narrow a Topic (p. 129).

2. Meet in your writing groups and answer the six journalistic questions about each others' topics. Act as scribe when your classmates are discussing your topic.

3. On your own, answer the Questions to Help Narrow a Topic in order to choose an aspect of the topic that you could develop into a successful essay. If you find that you are interpreting familiar in-

formation about your topic, keep in mind the "Most people think *A*, but I assert *B*" organizing strategy that George Leonard uses so successfully in his essay. Consider how your own views may differ from what most people think.

DRAFTING: WRITING, TALKING, REWRITING, AND EVALUATING

Freewriting and Drafting

The following steps will help you to freewrite and draft your essay.

1. **Freewrite:** After you have taken your topic through the six journalistic questions and then narrowed your topic, you should have focused on a manageable aspect, or part, of it. Now freewrite on this aspect of your topic; that is, write down everything you know and believe about this topic.

2. **Identify Opinions:** Next, read through your freewriting. Underline each statement that expresses your opinion about your topic. How did you arrive at these opinions? From interpreting your evidence— the examples, facts, anecdotes you recall about your topic? From having heard those opinions much of your life?

3. **Identify Main Point:** Carefully examine your opinions. Who (what audience) could benefit from knowing them? Which opinion is your main point? Your main point should cover *all* the opinions in your paper. Find or create the statement that does this. George Leonard's is a good example.

4. **Identify Subpoints:** Review the other opinions. Can you use them as subpoints; that is, do they support your main point? (Again, review Leonard's subpoints as illustration.) You may note that some of your opinions are repetitive. If so, combine them into one subpoint. Some of your opinions may not seem to have much to do with your main point. If you cannot find a way to show how they support your main point, delete them.

5. **Develop Evidence:** Now, consider your evidence. Find the evidence that most strongly develops each subpoint. What is left? If some evidence does not seem to support any of your subpoints, perhaps you have left out some explanation or have not quite accurately interpreted the meaning of the evidence. Try revising the subpoint first; the best-written papers are convincing because of their effective interpretation of the evidence. Perhaps your evidence could be strengthened. Can you think of any other kinds of evidence that might support your subpoint(s) more strongly?

6. **Outline:** Finally, outline your draft by following the typical expository essay format (you can leave out introductory background material—the context—as well as the conclusion for now):

State your main point.

State your *first* subpoint.

Support it with the evidence.

State your *second* subpoint.

Support it with the evidence.

State your *third* subpoint.

Support it with the evidence.

Your outline should show the subpoints for which you have the most and the least support, and thus which parts of your topic you have emphasized the most. You will then be able to decide if those are the parts you intended to emphasize and whether they support your main point, or purpose, in writing this essay.

7. **Order Subpoints:** Finally, look at the order of your subpoints. What is the logical relationship between them? What would happen if you changed their order? Can you write sentences of transition to illustrate the relationship between your subpoints?

Write the first draft.

First-Draft Activities

Bring copies of your first draft to class for group work. Exchange papers with your group members. Read through each member's draft and do the following:

1. Underline the main point. If you cannot find, or are not sure of, the main point, put a question mark in the margin next to the introductory paragraph(s).

2. Circle the audience for the paper if one is mentioned in the first paragraph(s); otherwise, write down who you think the audience is in the margin next to the introductory paragraph(s).

3. Underline the subpoint in each paragraph. If you cannot find a subpoint, put a question mark in the margin next to the paragraph. If you find a subpoint, but it does not support the main point, put parentheses around that sentence.

4. Once you have found the subpoint in the paragraph, read all the other sentences carefully. Are there any that do not support the subpoint? If so, put a question mark over the sentences that do not seem to belong.

When you have read all the drafts, discuss each writer's paper. Tell the writer what you found especially good about the essay and what you found confusing or difficult to understand. Then, give the draft copies back to their writers.

If your readers disagreed about which sentence stated the main point in your essay or were confused about who your audience was or what your subpoints were, you need to revise. If you are confused by your readers' responses, see your instructor!

Second-Draft Activities

Evaluation Criteria

An expository essay must:

1. begin with an introductory paragraph that
   a. provides a context for the essay: what most people (the audience) think about the topic
   b. states the main point about the topic in one focused sentence
2. include a body that presents at least three subpoints that support the main point
3. include various kinds of evidence to support each subpoint
4. end with a concluding paragraph that states the significance of the point to the audience

Sample Student Essays

Following are two students' expository essays. Read them carefully and rate them according to the criteria above.

Single Parent Students

1   The decision to go back to college as a non-traditional student can pose as a frightening experience, but for the single parent it presents additional problems. The odds are against them financially, emotionally, and socially: A non-traditional student is one who has been away from the scholastic environment for at least seven years. Generally wanting or needing a change to their marketability; for the single parent additional problems have made it necessary, but to some, and unrealistic challenge. Many barriers must be fought, and the road to a degree is met with many unsupportive and disbelieving relations to contend with.

2   The single parent must be resourceful. Many programs are designed to assist them, but are not of general knowledge. The more resourceful

the parent the better the odds are for their success. Within the proper effort, they will find many options are available to them which will remove many roadblocks. They first should visit with their academic counselor who has been trained to work with single parents, which will begin their climb towards success. Each additional step-up the ladder will bring them closer to their goal, increasing self-esteem, and will map their goal appropriately. The odds are against Freshmen with an average of 60% not finishing the first year. A single parent has added responsibilities of family, home, and work to contend with, while the traditional freshmen student has very limited worries. Single parents may find this average even more frightening, but with the will to succeed comes SUCCESS! A stick-to-it attitude is needed to finish school. Single parents must be very focused, more so than most students if they are to succeed in college.

3   The resourceful single parent will find many programs available to them often free services which will eliminate many roadblocks which may stand in their way. Day-care is often provided for a low fee and in most cases free. Many Federal and State grants are obtainable which cover the majority of financial responsibilities, even through graduate school. The PELL Grant is the most popular covering tuition, books and fees, which is held by the Financial Aid office in account form. This office pays all school costs and sends remaining money to the student's home to cover any additional costs which may arise. Family Housing is designed to help the parent through stressful periods of schooling by offering a community center for the children in their housing project with volunteers who design activities for the children and allow parents time to study during mid-terms and finals. The Women's Resources Center on campus provides counseling to eliminate the stress which is inevitable. Social functions are also offered through the Center which provides recreation designed to eliminate the stress factor by providing a very supportive, relaxing atmosphere. The parent also meets others faced with the same academic status as they are experiencing making strong friendships which may eliminate the lonely battle. Support groups are formed, which has been proven through extensive psychological experiments to be the best way to elevate personal and social problems through group discussion based on specific topics. The parent is able to work through specific problems with others who may have dealt with the same problem in the past.

4   The single parent will be faced with authority that gives very little emotional support to their endeavors. I have encountered family members that feel the four year academic commitment is unfair to my children. My employer found the return to college as a threat to the position I held which made it impossible for me to continue working. State agencies are designed to help the single parent succeed, but their apprehension is apparent and even frightening when they produce even more fail-

ure statistics. Clear communication and determination will demonstrate the ability to finish college and beat the odds. This determination makes the will to succeed and even stronger driving force.

5   With proper scheduling and time management the single parent will have even greater chances of succeeding. Children, job, classes, and studying will be handled with proper time given to each. Universities offer classes in study habits which are designed for student who have been away from school for many years. Scheduling and time management are offered in this course along with stress management, concentration techniques, proper note taking, memory techniques, and test preparation. These skills eliminate much wasted time, giving the student extra scheduled time to children and other important functions they must attend to.

6   The long term results are evident. Sacrifice brings the single parent the much due respect from their peers and unbelieving authority which makes for a strong self-esteem. The odds do meet with a few single parents which find the years of academic battle an unreachable goal. But for the single parent sticking to their strong will for success find happiness, a positive self-esteem, and the respect of their public. As for their children, what better example of love, than succeeding at this endeavor to make for them, a chance for a brighter future with a parent educated and able to financially meet their needs. They've watched their parent's determination and their approving cheer at graduation brings the single parent a joyous pride which will last them a life time.

Getting the Most from Your College Job

1   Most people are disdainful of night work. There is a stereotype about night jobs being menial, dead end and low paying. A common term for night work is graveyard shift which comes from the archetypical night job, digging graves. But that prejudice creates job opportunities for others because the jobs have to be filled. More money and benefits will be offered by employers to get people in those jobs. I believe that, if a student must work, the graveyard shift has the most to offer.

2   It is comparatively fast and easy for a student to get a job at night. A person who wants night work will compete with fewer people for available jobs. A high turnover rate relative to day shifts also contributes to ease in getting night employment. People moonlighting to earn extra money will often quit their night jobs when they have satisfied their goals. People who learned a job at night are often promoted to day shifts as a reward for good work. And some people find they don't like working nights and quit to go back to day work. All of this adds up to a higher turnover rate and more available jobs. I have been working nights and

attending college off and on for six years. I have had ten different grave-yard jobs and have never spent more than three to five days finding a good job. I have expended less effort finding a night job than a compara-ble job during the day. College bulletin boards, the Sunday paper and the state job service always have night positions listed and employers are eager to get them filled.

3   Students can earn more money working nights. For example, a clerk earns $5.50 per hour during the day. The same clerk working nights would earn $6.00 per hour. The reason for this wage differential is supply and demand. For reasons already discussed, most people prefer not to work nights. Demand for workers therefore exceeds the supply of people willing to work. To entice more people into night jobs more money is offered. In my experience more money is a certainty. When I compare wages with friends and co-workers from the day shifts, I find I am making ten to fifteen percent more for equivalent jobs.

4   Students who work nights usually have time to study on the job. I have found that after learning a night job I can usually perform it in less than half the time expected by my supervisor. The time remaining is my own to do with as I choose. I have learned to juggle, play the guitar, read novels and written English papers while at work. Co-workers and friends who work nights have related similar experiences from their night jobs. One reason for the free time is the small amount of work assigned. Super-visors rarely work the night shift and are unfamiliar with the time required to complete assigned duties. In addition, many managers would rather assign less work and not run the risk of losing hard to replace employees. There are far fewer interruptions at night and work goes much faster. Also most night work is rote and not very complicated which leads to quicker completion. All of this adds up to a student being paid to study.

5   A student who has to work while attending college is at a disadvan-tage relative to those students who don't have to work. A job on the graveyard shift offers benefits that counteract that disadvantage to some extent.

Evaluating the Sample Essays

After you have rated the essays using the evaluation criteria on page 135, meet in groups and compare your ratings. Discuss reasons for your agreement or disagreement and report to the class for a discussion of the rating.

Revising Your Second Draft

Evaluate your second draft according to the same criteria you used for the student samples. Which criteria have you met? Which have you not? Revise your draft to meet the criteria.

EDITING

Final-Draft Editing

Exchange your essay with a partner. Proofread your partner's essay carefully, looking for typographical, spelling, and mechanical errors. Pencil a check mark above the errors, but do not fix them. Return the essay.

Correct the errors your partner marked if you agree they are errors. If you are not sure, ask your partner. If you both have questions about possible errors, ask your teacher.

Final-Draft Analysis: Writing a Structural Analysis of Your Own Expository Essay

As a final assignment for this chapter, write an analysis of your own expository essay just as you did for George Leonard's essay, "Born to Run." Start your essay with the following paragraph:

> Most people do not really know what makes a good essay, but I can tell them that a good essay must state a point that has significance for a particular audience and support it with subpoints and various kinds of evidence. My essay (add Your Title) is a good example of an essay that does this.

In the body of your essay, tell your reader your main point, the audience you are writing for, and the significance of your point for your audience. Then discuss some of the kinds of evidence you have used. Give a brief description of each kind of evidence you name and identify the subpoint it supports. End your essay with a concluding paragraph that tells your readers why it is important for them as writers to know about expository essay structure.

Summary Writing

WRITING ASSIGNMENT

Rather than writing one paper for this chapter, you will write three summaries. The first summary will be a collaborative effort: your writing group will produce one final draft as a group project. The second summary will be a collaborative effort only in the prewriting stages; each group member will turn in an independent final summary. The third summary will be written entirely independently.

Why Write a Summary?

Summary writing has many uses both for you personally and as part of college writing assignments. The personal benefit of summarizing material is that it helps you both to remember what you have read and to understand it better.

Summaries have many uses in college writing. Professors often require summaries to check whether you remember and understand assigned material. For instance, identification questions in exams ask, in essence, for very short summaries, and essay questions usually require summarizing for at least part of the answer. Longer papers call for summarizing the evidence or opinions of others in support of your own conclusions. College assignments seldom require summaries alone, but they frequently require you to incorporate summaries into larger pieces of writing.

You are probably familiar with the idea of summarizing, but writing a good summary is more difficult than it sounds. The processes you practice in this chapter will help you to become much more proficient at the task.

THE BASICS OF SUMMARIZING

As you work with your writing group members, you will learn how to select the information that is important enough to include in a summary. You will also learn to write that information into summary form.

Reading

It is important to know where a piece of writing was originally published to read and summarize effectively. This is true for several reasons: first, different publications appeal to different audiences; second, different kinds, or **genres,** of writing have different purposes; and third, different genres call for different patterns of organization. The latter means that a newspaper article, for instance, is organized differently from a short story, which is organized differently from a textbook or a scientific report. Recognizing these differences will help you distinguish important points from supporting evidence for summary writing.

In this unit, the readings represent three different genres: newspaper feature writing, textbook writing, and scholarly writing. The selection you are about to read, an example of newspaper feature writing, originally appeared in the *New York Times*. You will note, when you read the next two selections in this chapter, that content and organization vary greatly from genre to genre.

 ## Grouping Students by Ability Comes Under Fire

William J. Warren

1   By the time they reach high school, the vast majority of American students have been categorized by their teachers and counselors into classes for fast, average or slow learners. Now an increasing number of education experts are saying that this practice is psychologically damaging to children and of little or no educational value.

2   Defenders acknowledge failings of the system but maintain that it allows teachers to address the particular needs of students who have widely diverse aptitudes and levels of achievement. Ideally, they say, this spares less able students from intimidation by brighter ones and permits faster learners to excel. They say most of the problems with placing students of differing ability on different study tracks stem from how individual educators use it, not from the tracking system itself.

3   Education experts say more than 90 percent of ninth graders are grouped in classes according to their ability. The grouping may involve just one course, like remedial English or honors mathematics, or a student may be placed in an entire series of courses geared to presumed academic potential and goals.

4   This sorting begins as early as the first grade, when students are placed in ability groups within classes for instruction in reading or mathematics. Then, as they proceed through the elementary grades, more and more of their courses are divided into separate classes, with placement based on performance, standardized tests or teacher recommendations. By the time they reach high school they may have

entered college-bound or non-college-bound tracks that determine which courses they take.

5   "We're making real big decisions about real little kids," said Robert Slavin, director of elementary school programs at Johns Hopkins University's Center for Research on Elementary and Middle Schools. "These early decisions about kids can have long-term consequences."

6   Critics say some students' potential is stifled because early differences in achievement and motivation can become set, as if in concrete, when children are placed in tracks. "In a basic track, you find students who are remedial and students who are very bright but not motivated," said Carolyn Anderson, assistant superintendent of Niles Township High Schools in Skokie, Ill. "We tend to confuse potential with performance."

7   "These decisions can be self-fulfilling prophecies," said Theodore Sizer, a professor of education at Brown University. "If people believe in us, we can do things we never believed possible. Tracking puts kids into boxes that determine what they do in school and what's expected of them."

8   Jeannie Oakes, a social scientist at the Rand Corporation, has written a book that is highly critical of tracking, which she says does not help high achievers and may hurt average and slow learners.

9   Many educators agree with Dr. Oakes. "One's expectations immediately drop when dealing with low-track kids," said Paula Evans, a former high school teacher who is director of the teacher training program at Brown. Children in the low tracks need high-achieving students as role models, she said. "Kids do better when they're in classes with kids who do better."

10   Without the example set by high-achieving students, Ms. Anderson said, "a peer value system develops in which learning and studying are not of great value."

11   The results are poor academic performance and increased disciplinary problems. "Low-track students are less likely to graduate high school and more likely to be involved in delinquency," said Dr. Slavin.

12   Tracking is rooted in the development of public secondary education at the turn of the century. Grouping students by ability was a way of coping with a flood of southern and eastern European immigrants, who spoke in foreign tongues and had different cultural norms. Now, despite the mounting criticism of tracking, it has become entrenched.

13   The people who are in a position to change the system benefit most from it, says Dr. Slavin. "The most powerful teachers, " he said, "have an investment in the system because they have worked their way up through it."

14   Further, education researchers note that parents whose children are

in programs for talented students are generally pleased with the education they receive and fear they will be held back if mixed with less able students.

15   "Parents of the higher achievement kids want to perpetuate the system," said Dr. Slavin.

16   Education experts also note that these parents tend to be affluent and to be more influential and involved in local educational affairs than the lower-income parents, whose children less often benefit from enhanced programs.

17   Mary Futrell, president of the National Education Association, the nation's largest teachers' union, is concerned that in some schools children on the low tracks "do not get a solid academic education."

18   "Kids at the top are reading Socrates, and kids at the bottom are reading Superman," she said. "For kids at the top, the emphasis is on creativity. For kids at the bottom, the emphasis is on discipline and conformity."

19   Dr. Oakes asserts that children on the low tracks are cheated out of a good education for a reason hardly surprising. "The lion's share of a school's resources go to classes for gifted and talented students," she said. "They have access to the best teachers and an enriched curriculum. All kids would do a whole lot better with those advantages."

20   The dividing of students into ability groups is of special concern because a disproportionate number of minority and poor children wind up in the lower tracks. "How do we explain that when you walk into a school, there are no minorities in academic college-bound programs?" said Mrs. Futrell.

21   Government studies show that children from wealthier homes start school with an advantage. They are more likely to already know the alphabet or even how to read. "Tracking is racially and socioeconomically divisive," said Adam Gamoran, a University of Wisconsin sociologist who is studying the practice. "But the schools are not creating the division, they're reflecting it."

22   While parents and teachers of high-track students almost invariably support ability grouping, they are not its only defenders. Some say the system can also help students who might otherwise be left behind by allowing good teachers to tailor instruction to their needs.

23   "The real criticism is the way tracking has been handled," said Bonnie Dana, curriculum coordinator for the Weyauwega-Fremont school district in Wisconsin. "The strongest teachers should be working with the weakest students."

24   Ms. Dana, who taught low-track high school students for 10 years, says that she "challenged the children to the maximum" and the low-track children do not need more advanced children as role models.

25   "I should be the example," she said, "not some honor roll

student." She said children in her classes felt more comfortable being segregated from advanced students. "They would say to me, 'If I raised my hand in a mixed group, they would call me a geek.'"

26   Mrs. Futrell said that while the N.E.A. was concerned about "the ways tracking has been abused and misused, we are not saying throw the baby out with the bath water."

27   "Tracking has its good points," she added, "when it's focused on areas where the child is weak."

28   Reba Page, a professor of education at the University of California at Riverside, says, "Tracking is a red herring." She argues that the real issue is the degree to which society is committed to educating all children, not merely the most promising.

29   "I don't believe we'll ever get rid of tracking," said Ms. Anderson, "so we'd better clean up how we do it."

✎ Journal Assignment

Write a journal page in which you discuss your own experience with school tracking. You might simply describe your experience, or you can answer the following questions:

1. Were students in your school(s) grouped either by ability level or vocational expectations (college prep, business, arts, mechanics)?

2. Do you think tracking is fair? Beneficial to students?

3. Do you agree with the critics or with the supporters of tracking? Why?

Reading Questions

Content

1. The introductory paragraph is only two sentences long. Which sentence provides the background information, or context, of the article? Which states the main point? What is the main point?

2. Does paragraph 2 describe the views of people who agree or disagree with the main point? What arguments do these people make to support their view?

3. What is the purpose of paragraphs 3 and 4?

4. Robert Slavin does not state directly in paragraph 5 whether he is a critic or a proponent of tracking. Which side do you think he is on? What clues does he give?

5. In the next few paragraphs, the views of at least five different educational experts are quoted. Do these views support the main point of the article or argue against it? In your own words, rephrase the arguments that each of these experts makes.

6. Paragraphs 12 through 16 do not really argue for or against tracking. What do they do instead?

7. Paragraph 17 returns to arguments against tracking. What further arguments are made?

8. In which paragraph does the writer return to the proponents' views of tracking? What additional arguments are made to support tracking?

9. What is the conclusion of the article? Do you agree with it?

Structure

1. How would you describe a newspaper's audience? (*Hint:* Think about people reading newspapers. When do they read them? What are they looking for? How much time do they spend on the newspaper?)

2. One of the characteristics of newspaper articles is very short paragraphs, usually two to three sentences long at the most. In addition, every quotation is printed as a paragraph by itself. Why do you think newspaper articles use such short paragraphs?

3. Newspaper reporters are expected to present information impartially, giving both sides of a controversial issue. What does William Warren do to maintain the appearance of impartiality in this article?

4. You know from your own newspaper reading that the writer's name is included with some articles but not with others. A reporter who writes an unsigned article (one without his or her name) is expected to be completely objective, including no personal opinion at all. (Whether this is possible or not is another question.) However, when the article is signed, as this one is, the writer is allowed to include some personal opinion. The following questions will help you recognize clues to Warren's personal opinion about the issue of tracking:

   a. Newspaper stories are organized to move from the most important to the least important information (because hurried readers might not read all the way to the end of the article). Look at the order in which the evidence opposing and supporting ability grouping is given. Where does most of the opposing information appear? the supporting information? What does this tell you about the writer's real opinion concerning this topic?

   b. Newspaper writers typically rely heavily on quotations from experts to convey various points of view about an issue. Warren is no exception. However, if readers are to be convinced, they must believe that the people quoted really are experts on the subject. What information does Warren give us about each person quoted to convince us that he or she is an expert?

   c. How many expert witnesses are quoted in opposition to tracking? In support of it? Note the qualifications of the experts who
oppose tracking and those who support it. Do the supporters or
the critics have more impressive qualifications? Why would
Warren quote more and better-qualified witnesses to support one
side of an argument than the other?

   d. What other clues are there to Warren's personal opinion?

Writing Summaries

What You Already Know

You probably know the major rules about summaries from your past
writing experience:

1. A summary includes only the views expressed in the source, not
   the writer's own views.

2. A summary includes only the most important information from the
   source, that is, the main point and subpoints. So a summary is much
   shorter than the source, usually no more than one quarter its length.

3. A summary is written in the summary writer's words, not the original author's words.

4. A summary is written so that a reader who has not read the source
   can understand what it said.

These general rules provide the starting point for summary writing. But
they are not as easy to apply as they sound. To begin with, it is difficult to
keep your own opinion out of a summary, especially if you disagree with
the writer. Another difficulty is figuring out what is really the most important
information in the original source and what can be omitted from the summary. In addition, putting another writer's ideas into your own words can
be a real challenge. As you work through the rest of this chapter, you will
learn techniques to help you do these difficult tasks well.

Paraphrasing

Paraphrasing is a way to include an author's complete idea in your summary. To paraphrase means to put someone else's words or ideas into your
own words. Remember, you paraphrase an idea only when it is so important
that you want the complete idea to appear in your summary.

    Another way to include a complete idea in the summary is simply to
quote it word for word, but writers paraphrase rather than quote an idea for
several reasons. One is that they can sometimes make the idea clearer by
putting it in their own language. Another reason is specific to college writing:
students prove to their professors that they understand an idea when they

put it in their own words. A third reason is that sometimes a paraphrase fits more smoothly into the summary than a quotation.

For the summary assignments in this unit, you must paraphrase rather than quote important ideas. This is to ensure that you understand the ideas in the source and to give you practice paraphrasing.

To paraphrase, that is, to put an idea from the source into your own words, follow these guidelines:

1. Take out all the words in the original that you never use yourself (unless they are key words essential to the meaning of the idea), and *substitute words from your own vocabulary*. If you do not know what a word in the original means, look it up in the dictionary. Find the meaning that fits the sentence in the source. Reread the original sentence. Its meaning should be much clearer to you now.

2. Use no phrase of three words or more in the same order that they appear in the original.

3. Change the order of phrases or ideas in the original.

Here is an example of paraphrasing from William J. Warren's article.

Original
"We're making real big decisions about real little kids," said Robert Slavin, director of elementary school programs at Johns Hopkins University's Center for Research on Elementary and Middle Schools. "These early decisions about kids can have long-term effects."

Paraphrase
Robert Slavin, an expert on elementary education, believes that educators should not make important decisions that might shape children's futures when children are very young.

Note that except for a few key words, Slavin's words have been replaced by the paraphrase writer's words; the order of information has been rearranged in the paraphrase, and the meaning has been clarified by explicitly stating what was only inferred in the original: important decisions about children *should not* be made at an early age.

Exercise Paraphrase the following excerpts from the William L. Warren article:

1. Now an increasing number of education experts are saying that this practice is psychologically damaging to children and of little or no educational value.

2. Critics say some students' potential is stifled because early differences in achievement and motivation can become set, as if in concrete, when children are placed in tracks.

3. The dividing of students into ability groups is of special concern

because a disproportionate number of minority and poor children wind up in the lower tracks.

4. Mrs. Futrell said that while the N.E.A. was concerned about the ways tracking has been abused and misused, we are not saying throw the baby out with the bath water.

As you know, when you write a summary you do not paraphrase all of the information in the source. You leave some out entirely, such as the evidence supporting subpoints, and you find ways to condense other information—more about that later.

Writing Assignment 1: Writing a Summary as a Group

Your first essay assignment in this chapter is to summarize "Grouping Students by Ability Comes Under Fire" by William J. Warren. It will be a group project. First read the information below. It explains how to write a summary of this article and demonstrates some of the steps. Then get together with your writing group to complete the steps and write the summary. You will write one summary as a group to hand in to your teacher.

Recognizing Important Information: Deciding What to Include in the Summary

Step 1 in deciding what to include in your summary is to divide the article into sections by subtopics. You have probably already done this in your class discussion of the article. Review the sections with your group.

Label the subtopic of each section. Paragraphs 3 and 4 might be labeled "Explanation of tracking," and paragraphs 5 though 11 might be labeled "Critics' views of tracking."

Reread the article to be sure your labels are accurate.

Step 2 in deciding what to include in the summary is to read each section separately and, as a group, compose a sentence that summarizes the main idea of each section. Have your scribe write down each sentence. Here is how you go about it.

Sometimes the main idea of a section is stated explicitly somewhere in the section. When this is so, paraphrase the idea.

At other times, the main idea may be strung throughout the section. This is so in paragraphs 5 through 11, which recount arguments against tracking. Your job, then, is to separate the important information from the less important information. *For summary writing, you can usually define the less important information as the evidence used to support the subpoints.* You know from working with expository writing what evidence looks like: quotations, statistics, examples, various kinds of details, and anecdotes. Cross out the evidence in the source paragraphs.

We will use paragraphs 5 through 11 as an example of how to do this. We have crossed out the evidence.

~~"We're making real big decisions about real little kids," said Robert Slavin, director of elementary school programs at Johns Hopkins University's Center for Research on Elementary and Middle Schools. "These early decisions about kids can have long-term consequences."~~ 5

Critics say some students' potential is stifled because early differences in achievement and motivation can become set, as if in concrete, when children are placed in tracks. ~~"In a basic track, you find students who are remedial and students who are very bright but not motivated," said Carolyn Anderson, assistant superintendent of Niles Township High Schools in Skokie, Ill. "We tend to confuse potential with performance."~~ 6

~~"These decisions can be self-fulfilling prophecies," said Theodore Sizer, a professor of education at Brown University. "If people believe in us, we can do things we never believed possible. Tracking puts kids into boxes that determine what they do in school and what's expected of them."~~ 7

Jeannie Oakes, ~~a social scientist at the Rand Corporation, has written a book that~~ is highly critical of tracking, which she says does not help high achievers and may hurt average and slow learners. 8

~~Many educators agree with Dr. Oakes.~~ "One's expectations immediately drop when dealing with low-track kids," ~~said Paula Evans, a former high school teacher who is director of the teacher training program at Brown.~~ Children in the low tracks need high-achieving students as role models, ~~she said. "Kids do better when they're in classes with kids who do better."~~ 9

~~Without the examples set by high-achieving students, Ms. Anderson said, "a peer value system develops in which learning and studying are not of great value."~~ 10

The results are poor academic performance and increased disciplinary problems. ~~"Low track students are less likely to graduate high school and more likely to be involved in delinquency," said Dr. Slavin.~~ 11

Note that some quoted information has not been crossed out. Usually, authors restate quoted information in their own words. In fact, when you quote information in college papers, you *must* restate the quoted point in your own words. Then the quotation becomes evidence for the point you make in your own words. But sometimes, especially in newspaper articles, the writer does not restate the information quoted from experts. If this information is important to the article, you must include it in your summary.

Once you cross out the evidence, what you have left are subpoints. In paragraphs 5 through 11 there are five subpoints left. Now you can write a sentence containing each subpoint. At this stage you may begin to paraphrase, but you can use some of the author's words as well.

> Tracking stifles students' potential because low tracks reinforce low motivation and low achievement. (from paragraph 6)
> Tracking does not help fast learners and hurts average and slow learners. (from paragraph 8)
> Teachers have low expectations for children in lower tracks. Children in low tracks need high-achieving students in their classes as role models. (from paragraph 9)
> Students in lower tracks have low academic performance and poor discipline. (from paragraph 11)

Step 3 is to connect the subpoint sentences in the section. Try to rewrite your subpoints into one or two summary sentences for the section. The four sentences above might be combined as follows:

> Critics argue that tracking can smother students' potential by lowering teachers' expectations for them. They claim that it does not benefit fast learners and can hurt slower learners by preventing lower track students from exposure to positive role models, and creating discipline problems.

Repeat the process above to write summary sentences for the rest of the sections.

Writing the Main Point

Review your summary sentences for each section and reread the introductory paragraph of the article to decide what the main point is. The pitfalls of writing the main point are making it either too broad or too narrow. Look at the example below, in which the main point is italicized. It is too broad. Can you explain why?

> In an article published in the December 21, 1988 issue of the *New York Times,* William J. Warren asserts *that there are many problems in today's education system.*

The next one is too narrow. Again, can you explain why?

> In an article published in the December 21, 1988 issue of the *New York Times,* William J. Warren asserts *that students placed in lower tracks in school are less likely to graduate from high school and more likely to cause trouble.*

The first sentence of your summary must contain the title and author of the source as well as the main point. There are some standard ways to write the first sentence of a summary. We recommend the following form for the summary of a newspaper article:

In an article appearing in the December 21, 1988, issue of the New York Times, William J. Warren states that . . . (main point).

Note the identifying information included for a newspaper article:

Date
Name of newspaper
Name of writer (if known)

Now compose your own sentence to state the main point of the article. Be sure that the scope of your main point sentence matches the scope of the article.

Writing the First Draft

The summary should be in the form of a single paragraph. It is a good idea to write the first draft on every other line of your paper so that you can make revisions easily.

Begin your summary with your main point statement, including the title and author. The rest of your summary is made up of the summarizing sentences that you wrote for each section of the article. As you copy your summarizing statements into your summary paragraph, consider how the ideas are related to each other. Make the sentences read like a coherent paragraph by adding appropriate transitional words.

Reread your summary and consider the following:

1. Does it include the main point and important subpoints of the article?
2. Does it omit details, statistics, and other kinds of supporting evidence?
3. Are the sentences clearly stated in your own words?
4. Are the ideas linked by transitions so that the summary sounds like a coherent paragraph?

Make whatever revisions your group feels are necessary and recopy the paragraph.

USING THE BASICS

Reading

The following reading, excerpted from a college textbook in sociology, discusses the same subject as the previous article. Although the two readings share the same topic, general purpose (to inform), and much the same point of view, they are very different from each other.

As you read this selection, you need to be aware that sociologists commonly agree that one purpose of the American educational system is to "sort and select," as the authors put it, which students are capable of going on to higher education and leadership roles in society, and which students will fulfill roles as workers and followers. According to sociologists, standardized achievement tests, college entrance tests like the SAT and ACT, and ability grouping and tracking within the schools are some of the means used to sort and select students for these various roles.

 ## Ability Grouping and Tracking

Daniel U. Levine and Robert J. Havinghurst

1   Sorting and selecting for further success in the educational system take place in part through ability grouping and tracking. At both the elementary and secondary levels, many schools use ability grouping (or homogeneous grouping) in attempting to facilitate teaching and learning (Passow 1988). Students with high academic performance are placed in a class of high achievers or in a subgroup of high achievers within the classroom; those with low performance are placed in low-achieving classes or subgroups; and those in between are placed in average groups. In many schools, the high, average, and low levels are further subdivided according to previous achievement.

2   Tracking refers to the practice in high schools of enrolling students in college preparatory classes (usually high-achieving students), or general, business, or vocational tracks for lower achievers or students not intending to go to college or preferring to pursue less academic subjects. (The general curriculum usually includes little mathematics and no advanced science or foreign language courses.)

3   Ability grouping or tracking in schools enrolling a socially diverse population tends to be correlated with social class and racial/ethnic status. Partly because economically and socially disadvantaged students have lower average achievement scores than do middle-class students and nonminority students . . ., they are found disproportionately in low-achieving classes and nonacademic tracks, while middle-class students are disproportionately represented in higher-achieving classes and college preparatory courses and tracks. In addition, social class has an independent effect on track placement beyond its association with achievement. In 1982, 80 percent of high-achieving seniors high in socioeconomic status were in an academic track, compared with only 52 percent of seniors who were high in achievement but low in status (Vanfossen, Jones, and Spade 1987).

4   The pattern of grouping varies from community to community and school to school. In some schools, ability groups are formed only in

particular subject-matter areas, as when those children in a grade who are poor in reading, or those who are particularly good in science, are given special instruction as a group. In such schools, the child may spend only one period a day with a special group; the rest of the time, with his or her regular group. This modification of homogeneous grouping tends to counteract the possible social-class biases that may otherwise operate.

5   To take another example, schools in homogeneous parts of a large city, where the school population is drawn from one or two social classes, may use a scheme of sectioning by ability that brings together those children with the most motivation for education. The children who consistently work hard often seem to teachers to be the abler ones and will tend to be grouped together.

6   Ability grouping has been severely criticized since about 1965 on the basis of the double-barrelled argument that (1) the ability tests as they now exist tend to favor middle-class children and (2) the tests now in use tend to segregate students by social class and by race. In some places, ability grouping has been ruled illegal by the courts, and school boards in some of the larger cities have abandoned or reduced the extent of ability grouping. This trend became widespread after the Supreme Court's 1967 ruling in *Hobson v. Hansen,* which stated that separation of Washington, D.C., students into fast and slow tracks resulted in unconstitutional segregation of minority and nonminority students. After 1967, the courts and the federal government frequently required desegragating [*sic*] school districts to reduce or eliminate grouping of students based on ability test scores, previous achievement, or other measures that might reflect a student's disadvantaged background rather than his or her true academic potential.

7   Although ability grouping usually has been introduced in order to facilitate teaching and learning, much research indicates that it generally has not improved student achievement. Reviews of research on this topic have most often concluded that ability grouping has little or no consistent effect (Good and Marshall 1984). Some studies, however, indicate that homogeneous grouping promotes better performance among high achievers (Kulik and Kulik 1987) and/or further depresses the performance of low achieving students (Dar and Resh 1986; Soørensen and Hallinan 1986). Instances in which ability grouping appears to be harmful to the performance of low achievers are thought to occur because teachers have low expectations for students and thus pace instruction at a very slow rate (Gamoran 1986a), because students are stigmatized and thus not motivated by being placed in slow classes or groups, and also because low achievers frequently reinforce each other's negative attitudes and behaviors.

8   Detrimental phenomena associated with ability grouping and tracking have been documented by Jeannie Oakes in a study of the school experiences of students in more than 1,000 classrooms. Using

data collected as part of a study of schooling in thirty-eight nationally representative districts including both elementary and secondary schools, Oakes found that students in high-ability classes generally had more challenging instruction than did those in low-ability classes, which tended to emphasize "simple memory tasks" and literal comprehension. Oakes concluded that the rudimentary curriculum content in low-ability classes "was such that it would be likely to lock students into that track level . . . [by omitting topics] that constitute prerequisite knowledge and skills for access to classes in . . . higher track levels" (Oakes 1985, 77–78).

9   Oakes also found that students in high-ability classes were significantly more "involved" in their learning than were those in low-ability classes. The latter students, she concluded, "reported that they were far less concerned about completing classroom tasks . . . [and] also reported far greater degrees of apathy—not caring about what goes on in class or even concerned about failing"(Oakes 1985, 130). One of her overall conclusions was that given the correlation between economically and socially disadvantaged background on the one hand and low-track placement on the other, ability grouping and tracking frequently constitute "in-school barriers to upward mobility for capable poor and minority students. . . . [Once placed in low-level classes, their] achievements seem to be further inhibited by the type of knowledge they are exposed to and the quality of learning opportunities they are afforded" (Oakes 1985, 134).

10   Ability grouping and tracking thus frequently seem to reinforce the low performance of disadvantaged students as part of the educational system's general arrangements for sorting and selecting meritorious students who are likely to be successful at the next level. Tracking at the high-school level also operates to depress further low-status students' self-esteem, contact with highly motivated peers, participation in extracurricular activities, and subsequent enrollment in postsecondary education (Vanfossen, Jones, and Spade 1987). Therefore, what begins as an attempt to ensure that instruction is appropriate for students given their previous performance (Nevi 1987) may be harmful for low achievers who might achieve more in heterogeneous classes with more challenging instruction.

11   This problem in the sorting and selecting process raises a number of complicated and difficult questions for which there are no simple answers. For example, how can the pace of instruction in heterogeneous classes be maintained at a level that challenges high achievers without frustrating low achievers? How might instruction in low-ability classes be improved to avoid the detrimental effects frequently associated with homogeneous grouping of low achievers? How can high expectations be maintained in low-level classes so that grouping and tracking function to provide remediation and special assistance for selected students rather

than increasing the gap between high and low achievers? We return to these types of questions elsewhere in this book, particularly in Chapters 8 and 13.

Vocabulary

Look up the definitions for each of the following words from ''Ability Grouping and Tracking.'' You may find many definitions for the same word. Write down the word and *the definition that fits its use in the text.* You are doing this because one of the best ways to learn new vocabulary is to study the meanings of words as they are used in context.

homogeneous (paragraph 1)
facilitate (paragraph 1)
academic (paragraph 1)
diverse (paragraph 3)
correlate (paragraph 3)
disproportionately (paragraph 3)
modification (paragraph 4)
counteract (paragraph 4)
depress (paragraph 7)
pace (verb, paragraph 7)
stigmatized (paragraph 7)
reinforce (paragraph 7)
detrimental (paragraph 8)
phenomenon (paragraph 8)

document (verb, paragraph 8)
literal (paragraph 8)
rudimentary (paragraph 8)
access (paragraph 8)
apathy (paragraph 9)
constitute (paragraph 9)
inhibited (paragraph 9)
afforded (paragraph 9)
meritorious (paragraph 10)
postsecondary (paragraph 10)
ensure (paragraph 10)
heterogeneous (paragraph 10)
function (verb, paragraph 11)
remediation (paragraph 11)

✎ Journal Assignment

Write a journal entry responding to this reading. You might write about several different aspects of it: What more did you learn about the issue of tracking? How is the writing different from the newspaper article? Why is the writing in textbooks so different from newspaper writing?

Reading Questions

As you were reading, you noted many differences between textbook writing and newspaper writing. These are two different genres of writing whose audiences, purposes, and patterns of organization differ from each other in many ways. The first difference you probably noticed was that the textbook is much more difficult to understand. For that reason, the first set of questions below is designed to help you understand the content. The second set will help you understand both the reasons for the differences between the two kinds of writing and how textbook chapters are typically organized.

Content

1. According to paragraphs 1 and 2, what is the difference between ability grouping and tracking?

2. In paragraph 3 what is meant by social class? By "economically and socially disadvantaged students"?

3. According to paragraph 3, which social class is usually found in lower tracks? Why? High-achieving students do come from both higher and lower social classes. Are all high-achieving students in the academic tracks? What difference does social class make in whether high-achieving students are in academic tracks?

4. Why did the Supreme Court find tracking in Washington, D.C., schools unconstitutional?

5. Paragraph 7 discusses research about the effects of ability grouping. Have the results of the research been consistent?

6. What detrimental effects of ability grouping did Jeannie Oakes discover in her research? What are the causes?

Structure

1. Who is the audience for this reading? For the previous reading? In what ways does the newspaper audience differ from the textbook audience? Think of as many differences as you can. How do you think these differences affect the writing?

2. We said above that the two readings share the same general purpose, but that is an oversimplification. Though they both do inform, how do the purposes of the two differ?

3. What information is given in paragraphs 1 and 2 of the selection? Why did the authors put this information first?

4. Compare the kinds of evidence used in the textbook excerpt to the kinds used in the newspaper article. How do they differ?

5. Reread paragraph 3. It is very difficult to understand. We will analyze it in detail.

   a. Which sentence contains the subpoint?
   b. What two correlations between social class and ability grouping do the writers identify? What transition words in the text link the two correlations to each other?
   c. Which sentence contains an example?

6. Compare paragraph 3 to any paragraph in the newspaper article. Discuss the ways in which they differ. What conclusions can you draw about the organization of textbook paragraphs?

7. Reread paragraph 8.

   a. Which sentence contains the subpoint?

    b. According to this paragraph, why are ability grouping and tracking detrimental?

    c. Reread paragraph 9. Does it add more information about the topic sentence in paragraph 8 or begin a new topic? How can you tell?

8. What kinds of evidence do you find in paragraphs 8 and 9?

9. What do you think is the authors' point of view about ability grouping and tracking? How can you tell?

10. On the basis of what you know about the differences between newspaper articles and textbook writing, how would you advise readers to approach reading a newspaper article? What parts of it should they pay most attention to? How would you advise readers to approach textbook reading? Where will they find the most important information?

Paraphrasing

Exercise   Paraphrase the sentences below from "Ability Grouping and Tracking."

Some of them are sentences you may eventually want to include in your summaries. Others are difficult sentences that paraphrasing will help to clarify.

1. Ability grouping or tracking in schools enrolling a socially diverse population tends to be correlated with social class and racial/ethnic status.

2. Partly because economically and socially disadvantaged students have lower average achievement scores than do middle-class students and nonminority students, they are found disproportionately in low-achieving classes and nonacademic tracks, while middle-class students are disproportionately represented in higher-achieving classes and college preparatory courses and tracks.

3. Oakes concluded that the rudimentary curriculum content in low-ability classes was such that it would be likely to lock students into that track level . . . [by omitting topics] that constitute prerequisite knowledge and skills for access to classes in . . . higher track levels (Oakes 1985, 77–88).

Your class might discuss what the various punctuation marks mean. What do the three dots mean? the brackets? the parentheses?

Review of the Summary Process

Below is an outline of the process for writing a summary. The outline extracts the main steps from the directions you followed to summarize "Ability Grouping Comes Under Fire.'' These steps will work for any summary writing you do.

1. After reading the source once, read it again. On the second time through, divide it into sections by subtopics. (If the source is not a library book, you can draw a line between sections on the source page).

2. Read each section. Decide what the subtopic of the section is and label it in the margin if the source is not a library book. If it is, write your labels on your own piece of paper.

3. Read each section again. Compose a sentence that summarizes the main idea of the section. To decide what the main idea is
   a. Identify which sentences are evidence. Cross them out.
   b. Reread what you have left. You will not automatically include everything that you have left in your summary.
      (1) You may decide that part of what is left is an unimportant subpoint that does not belong in a summary. Ignore it.
      (2) You may find that what you have left is important but can be condensed. Write a sentence that shortens the information into fewer words.
      (3) If you find that everything left is very important, paraphrase it for the summary.

4. Review the sentences you have written for each section and reread the introductory paragraph(s) of the source. Write an introductory sentence that names the author, the source, and states the main point of the source. (In some cases this may require two sentences.)

5. Write the first draft of your summary in paragraph format. Write on every other line of your paper so that you can go back and revise easily. Your first draft is made up of your introductory statement and summary sentences for each section of the source, plus transitional or relational words and phrases to connect the ideas.

6. Reread both the source and your draft. Check to make sure that the draft
   a. names the author and title of the source
   b. states the main point of the source in the first or second sentence
   c. omits supporting evidence such as descriptive details, quotations, anecdotes, and other less important information
   d. states the author's important subpoints clearly

7. Revise your draft. If it does not meet one or more of the requirements in step 6 above, rewrite it to meet them. Then write in any additional transitional or relational words or phrases needed to link the ideas in your summary closely together.

Writing Assignment 2: Collaborative Drafting and Independent Composition

Write a summary of "Ability Grouping and Tracking." This time do the beginning steps of the summary in your writing groups, but do all of the drafting and composing independently.

Meet in your writing groups to do steps 1 and 2 of the Summary Process, above.

Write the rest of the summary (steps 3–7) independently as homework. Check your draft against the evaluation criteria below. Then revise, making whatever changes are necessary to meet the criteria.

Evaluation Criteria

For readings as short as the ones in this chapter, your summary should be only one paragraph long. When the source is longer than the readings in this chapter, a summary might be more than one paragraph. In your paragraph you should do the following:

1. Name the title and author of the source in the first sentence of the summary.

2. State the main point (the topic of the essay plus the author's opinion about the topic) in your own words in one focused sentence. You should be able to put this into the first sentence of the summary along with the author's name and title, but it must come no later than the second sentence. The scope of this sentence should match the scope of the essay.

3. State each subpoint from each major section in the essay in one sentence or two at the most. Do not include evidence.

4. Use your own words. The summary should have no quoted information and no phrases of three or more words lifted from the original.

5. Include transitions to link the ideas together to make the paragraph read as a coherent unit.

6. End with a concluding sentence. It should reflect the conclusion of the source or restate the main point.

APPLYING WHAT YOU HAVE LEARNED

Reading

The following reading is from one of the leading experts on ability grouping in American schools, Jeannie Oakes. She was quoted in both of the preceding readings. This selection is excerpted from her book on the subject, *Keeping Track: How Schools Structure Inequality.*

◈ **Keeping Track**
_____

Jeannie Oakes

1   . . . Tracking is the process whereby students are divided into categories so that they can be assigned in groups to various kinds of classes. Sometimes students are classified as fast, average, or slow learners and placed into fast, average, or slow classes on the basis of their scores on achievement or ability tests. Often teachers' estimates of what students have already learned or their potential for learning more determine how students are identified and placed. Sometimes students are classified according to what seems most appropriate to their future lives. Sometimes, but rarely in any genuine sense, students themselves choose to be in "vocational," "general," or "academic" programs. In some schools students are classified and placed separately for each academic subject they take—fast in math, average in science; in other schools a single decision determines a student's program of classes for the entire day, semester, year, and perhaps even six years of secondary schooling. However it's done, tracking, in essence, is sorting—a sorting of students that has certain predictable characteristics.

2   First, students are identified in a rather public way as to their intellectual capabilities and accomplishments and separated into a hierarchical system of groups for instruction. Second, these groups are labeled quite openly and characterized in the minds of teachers and others as being of a certain type—high ability, low achieving, slow, average, and so on. Clearly these groups are not equally valued in the school; occasional defensive responses and appearances of special privilege—i.e., small classes, programmed learning, and the like for slower students—rarely mask the essential fact that they are less preferred. Third, individual students in these groups come to be defined by others—both adults and their peers—in terms of these group types. In other words, a student in a high-achieving group is seen as a high-achieving *person*, bright, smart, quick, and in the eyes of many, *good*. And those in the low-achieving groups come to be called slow, below average, and—often when people are being less careful—dummies, sweathogs, or yahoos. Fourth, on the basis of these sorting decisions, the groupings of students that result, and the way educators see the students in these groups, teenagers are treated by and experience schools very differently.

3   Tracking is [a] taken-for-granted school practice. It is so much a part of how instruction is organized in secondary schools—and has been for as long as most of us can remember—that we seldom question it. We *assume* that it is best for students. But we don't very often look behind this assumption to the evidence and beliefs on which it rests.

4   I don't mean to imply by this that no one is concerned about grouping students. I think, in fact, that the contrary is true. School people

usually spend a great deal of thought deciding what group students should be placed in. They want to make sure that placements are appropriate and fair. And further, what appear to be incorrect placements are often brought to the attention of teachers and counselors, usually with a great deal of concern. Adjustments sometimes need to be made. This is something we seem to want to be very responsible about. But this very concern over correct and fair placements underscores my point. In some way, we all know that what group or track a student is in makes a very real difference in his education. So at some level, we know that grouping is a very serious business. What we don't seem to question very much, however, is whether the practice of grouping students itself helps us achieve what we intend in schools.

LEARNING BEYOND CONTENT

QUESTION:

What are the five most critical things you want the students in your class to learn this year? By learn, we mean everything that the student should have upon leaving the class that (s)he did not have upon entering.

5   We asked this question of each of the teachers during our interviews with them. Among their responses, teachers of high-track classes typically included the following kinds of answers.

RESPONSES:

Interpreting and identifying. Evaluation, investigating power.

> *High-track Science—junior high*

Deal with thinking activities—Think for basic answers—essay-type questions.

> *High-track English—junior high*

Ability to reason logically in all subject areas.

> *High-track math—senior high*

The art of research.

> *High-track English—senior high*

Learn how to test and prove ideas. Use and work with scientific equipment. Learning basic scientific facts and principles.

> *High-track Science—junior high*

Scientific reasoning and logic.

> *High-track Science—senior high*

Investigating technology, investigating values.

> *High-track Social Science—junior high*

Self-reliance, taking on responsibilites themselves.

> *High-track Science—junior high*

To learn values and morals—to make own personal decisions.

> *High-track English—junior high*

To think critically—to analyze, ask questions.
> *High-track Social Science—junior high*

Individual interpretation of materials covered.
> *High-track English—senior high*

Logical thought processes. Analysis of given information. Ability to understand exactly what is asked in a question. Ability to perceive the relationship between information that is given in a problem or a statement and what is asked.
> *High-track Science—senior high*

Love and respect for math—want them to stay curious, excited and to keep believing they can do it.
> *High-track Math—junior high*

To realize that all people are entitled to certain inalienable rights.
> *High-track Social Science—junior high*

To think critically (analyzing).
> *High-track English—senior high*

How to think critically—analyze data, convert word problems into numerical order.
> *High-track Math—senior high*

To be creative—able to express oneself.
> *High-track English—senior high*

The most important thing—think more logically when they leave.
> *High-track Math—senior high*

Ability to think and use information. Concept development.
> *High-track Science—senior high*

Ability to think for themselves.
> *High-track Science—senior high*

How to evaluate—think objectively. To think logically and with clarity and to put it on paper. To be able to appreciate a variety of authors' works and opinions without judging them by their own personal standards.
> *High-track English—senior high*

Confidence in their own thoughts.
> *High-track English—senior high*

Able to collect and organize information. Able to think critically.
> *High-track Social Science—junior high*

Determine best approach to problem solving. Recognize different approaches.
> *High-track Math—senior high*

That their own talents and thoughts are important. Development of imagination. Critical thinking.
> *High-track English—senior high*

Problem-solving situations—made to think for themselves. Realizing importance of their education and use of time. Easy way is not always the best way.   *High-track Science—senior high*

Better feeling for their own abilities and sense of what it's like in a college course.

> *High-track Math—senior high*

To gain some interpretive skills.

> *High-track English—senior high*

6   Teachers of low-track classes said the following kinds of learning were essential for their students:

Develop more self-discipline—better use of time.

> *Low-track English—junior high*

Respect for each other.

> *Low-track Math—junior high*

I want them to respect my position—if they'll get this, I'll be happy.

> *Low-track Math—junior high*

That they know that their paychecks will be correct when they receive them. Punctuality, self-discipline and honesty will make them successful in their job. They must begin and end each day with a smile. To be able to figure their own income tax (at the) end of the year. Properly planning to insure favorable performances.

> *Low-track Math—senior high*

Self-discipline, cooperativeness, and responsibility.

> *Low-track Science—junior high*

I teach personal hygiene—to try to get the students to at least be aware of how to keep themselves clean.

> *Low-track Vocational Education—junior high*

Independence—start and complete a task on their own.

> *Low-track English—senior high*

Responsibility of working with people without standing over them.

> *Low-track Science—senior high*

Ability to use reading as a tool—e.g., how to fill out forms, write a check, get a job.

> *Low-track English—junior high*

How to fill out insurance forms. Income tax returns.

> *Low-track Math—senior high*

Understanding the basic words to survive in a job. Being able to take care of their own finances—e.g., banking, income tax, etc. Being able to prepare for, seek, and maintain a job. To associate words with a particular job.

> *Low-track English—senior high*

To be able to work with other students. To be able to work alone. To be able to follow directions.

> *Low-track English—junior high*

Socialization—retarded in social skills.

> *Low-track English—junior high*

How to cope with frustration.
                                    Low-track English—junior high
Business-oriented skills—how to fill out a job application.
                                    Low-track English—junior high
More mature behavior (less outspoken).
                                    Low-track Science—junior high
Respect for their fellow man (students and teachers).
                                    Low-track Science—junior high
Learn to work independently—use a sense of responsibility.
                                    Low-track Science—senior high
Content—minimal. Realistic about goals. Develop ones they can achieve.
                                    Low-track Science—senior high
Practical math skills for everyday living. A sense of responsibility.
                                    Low-track Math—senior high
To learn how to follow one set of directions at a time, take a directive order and act upon it.
                                    Low-track Social Science—junior high
Life skills. Work with checking account.
                                    Low-track Math—junior high

Good work habits.
                                    Low-track Math—junior high

Respect. Growth in maturity.

                                    Low-track Math—junior high

QUESTION:
What is the most important thing you have learned or done so far in this class?

7   High-track students named the following kinds of things:

RESPONSES:
I have learned to form my own opinions on situations. I have also learned to not be swayed so much by another person's opinion but to look at both opinions with an open mind. I know now that to have a good solid opinion on a subject I must have facts to support my opinion. Decisions in later life will probably be made easier because of this.
                                    High-track English—senior high
I've learned to study completely, and to know everything there is to know.
                                    High-track English—senior high
I have learned to speak in front of a group of people, and not be scared to death of everyone.
                                    High-track English—senior high

To know how to communicate with my teachers like friends and as teachers at the same time. To have confidence in myself other than my skills and class work.

> *High-track English—junior high*

I have learned to be creative and free in doing things.

> *High-track English—senior high*

I have learned how to make hard problems easier to solve.

> *High-track Math—senior high*

The most important thing I have learned in this class this quarter is how to express my feelings.

> *High-track English—senior high*

How to organize myself and present an argument.

> *High-track English—senior high*

I'm learning how to communicate with large groups of people.

> *High-track English—senior high*

The most important thing I have learned or done in this class is I now have the ability to be able to speak in front of a crowd without being petrified, as I was before taking this class.

> *High-track English—senior high*

I want to be a lawyer and debate has taught me to dig for answers and get involved. I can express myself.

> *High-track English—senior high*

The most important thing I have learned is how to speak in front of a group of people with confidence.

> *High-track English—senior high*

I have learned how to argue in a calm and collected way.

> *High-track English—senior high*

How to express myself through writing and being able to compose the different thoughts in a logical manner; this is also a class where I may express my creativity.

> *High-track English—senior high*

Learned to think things out. Like in a book I learned to try and understand what the author is really saying to find the author's true thoughts.

> *High-track English—senior high*

I've learned to look into depth of certain things and express my thoughts on paper.

> *High-track English—senior high*

The most important thing I have learned in this class is to loosen up my mind when it comes to writing. I have learned to be more imaginative.

> *High-track English—senior high*

How to present myself orally and how to listen and to think quick.

> *High-track English—senior high*

To understand concepts and ideas and experiment with them. Also, to work independently.

High-track Science—senior high

My instructor has opened a whole new world for me in this class, I truly enjoy this class. He has given me the drive to search and find out answers to questions. If there is one thing that I have learned from this class it would have to be the want for learning.

High-track Social Studies—senior high

It taught us how to think in a logical way to work things out with a process of elimination.

High-track Math—senior high

I have learned that in high school the English classes treat you more like an adult.

High-track English—senior high

I have proved to myself that I have the discipline to take a difficult class just for the knowledge, even though it has nothing to do with my career plans.

High-track Math—senior high

I have learned that I have a wider span of imagination than I thought. I have also learned to put how I feel and what I feel into words and explain them better.

High-track English—senior high

Many times in this class I get wrong answers, but in this class you learn to learn from your mistakes, also that even if you do have a wrong answer you should keep trying and striving for that correct answer. This, along with the subject I have learned from this class, and I think it's very important.

High-track Math—senior high

How to think and reason logically and scientifically.

High-track Math—senior high

I think the most important thing I've done in this class is exercise my brain. To work out problems logically so I can learn to work out problems later in life logically.

High-track Math—senior high

Brains work faster and faster.

High-track Math—senior high

Learning about how others respond and act—what makes them do the things they do—talking about relations, and how happenings in earlier life can affect children when they are growing up. The class discussions make it really interesting and the teacher startles us sometimes because he can really understand things from our point of view.

High-track Social Science—senior high

The most important thing that I have learned in this class is the benefit of logical and organized thinking, learning is made much easier *when the simple processes of organizing thoughts have been grasped.*

> *High-track Math—senior high*

8   Low-track students were more likely to give answers like these:

Behave in class.

> *Low-track English—junior high*

I have learned that I should do my questions for the book when he asks me to.

> *Low-track Science—senior high*

Self-control.

> *Low-track Social Studies—junior high*

Manners.

> *Low-track English—junior high*

How to shut up.

> *Low-track Vocational Education—junior high*

The most important thing I have learned in this class is to always have your homework in and have materials ready whenever she is ready.

> *Low-track Vocational Education—senior high*

Write and getting my homework done.

> *Low-track English—junior high*

Working on my Ps and Qs.

> *Low-track English—junior high*

I think the most important is coming into class and getting our folders and going to work.

> *Low-track Math—junior high*

I have learned about many things like having manners, respecting other people, not talking when the teacher is talking.

> *Low-track English—junior high*

Learned to work myself.

> *Low-track Math—junior high*

I learned about being quiet when the teacher is talking.

> *Low-track Social Studies—junior high*

To learn how to listen and follow the directions of the teacher.

> *Low-track Math—senior high*

I learn to respect the teacher.

> *Low-track Vocational Education—junior high*

Learn to get along with the students and the teacher.

> *Low-track English—junior high*

How to go through a cart and find a folder by myself.

> *Low-track Math—junior high*

To be a better listener in class.

> *Low-track English—senior high*

In this class, I have learned manners.

> *Low-track English—junior high*

Reading Questions

There are no questions about content or structure for this essay because part of your job when you write summaries independently is to figure out the meaning and structure for yourself. However, there is one question you may want to discuss as a class.

> A large portion of this excerpt is made up of quoted material. Why does Oakes include so much quotation? What points are implied, but not stated explicitly in the quoted material? How should the quoted material be handled in the summary?

 Writing Assignment 3: Writing a Summary Independently

Write a summary of Oakes's article. Assume that the person who reads your summary has not read the source.

EDITING

Final-Draft Editing

1. Exchange your summary with a partner. Proofread your partner's essay carefully looking for typographical, spelling, and mechanical errors. Put a pencilled check mark above the errors, but do not fix them. Return the essay.

2. Correct the errors your partner marked if you agree they are errors. If you are not sure, ask your partner. If you both have questions about possible errors, ask your teacher.

Postfinal-Draft Editing

Your teacher may have you revise a section of your essay or have you correct particular errors.

Documented Expository Essay

WRITING ASSIGNMENT

The paper due at the end of this chapter is a three- to five-page expository essay in which you assert a point about an issue and support your point, with evidence from both research and your own experience. You will use the periodicals in your library for sources, citing at least three different articles in your paper.

Why Write a Documented Expository Essay?

This assignment represents the culmination of all you have learned throughout the course. Besides incorporating what you know about descriptive, narrative, and expository writing, you will use your paraphrasing and summarizing skills to integrate knowledge from other sources into your own paper. All three of the major elements of this assignment, asserting a point, researching the topic, and considering the topic in the light of your own experience, are important.

The research requirement is not intended to introduce you to every resource the library offers, but to help you master the use of one resource, **periodicals.** The word in this sense means anything published at regular intervals— daily (a newspaper), weekly (*Time Magazine*), monthly (*Car and Driver*), or at any other regular interval.

The assignment limits your research to periodicals for several reasons. First, you probably have less experience locating periodicals in your library than locating books, so this assignment will help you learn how to use a new source of information. Second, periodicals provide the most up-to-date information (after computer networks) of any form of publication. Third, different periodicals are aimed at different audiences, so scanning a variety of periodicals for information on a single topic will give you a broad range of information. Finally, articles in periodicals are, obviously, much shorter than books, so you will have time to read, evaluate, and synthesize several different sources of information about your topic.

The assignment requires you to pick a topic with which you have had personal experience because your experience grants a certain degree of authority to what you say. You learned that this is true when you wrote your personal narrative essay. This is not to say that personal experience with a problem like divorce, poverty, ability grouping in schools, or drugs means that you know all there is to know about it. What it does mean is that you have a uniquely individual perspective that allows you some insights not available to others. Doing research about the topic gives you the opportunity to find out what other people think and have learned about the issue, so you can understand it better yourself. When you write about the topic, you add your own voice to the written conversation about the issue. This is at the heart of academic writing.

The personal-experience requirement gives you another advantage. Since you already know something about the topic, you do not have to start from scratch, as you would if you picked a topic like nuclear power. Your background knowledge gives you a sense of what questions to ask and can probably help you to focus your topic.

You can see that this assignment does not merely require you to write a report on a topic. It requires you to think about issues related to your topic, focus on one such issue, make your own judgment (state your point) about the issue, and support your point with evidence from your research and personal experience.

INVENTION: READING, WRITING, TALKING, AND RESEARCHING FOR IDEAS

Finding a Topic

Below are a variety of things to do, both individually and as a class, to find a topic for this assignment.

Individual Activities

1. Review your own journal and past writing assignments for possible essay topics.

    a. Did you write your personal narrative or expository paper about a subject that you would like to know more about? If so, this might be your opportunity to explore it further.

    b. As you wrote journal entries about possible topics for other papers, did you discard some because you felt you did not know enough to write a good paper about them? This might be your chance to find out more.

   c. You have all had experience with advertising and education, two topics of previous chapters, and you might decide to investigate further some issue connected with either of these topics. Education, and tracking specifically, is the topic that will be used throughout this chapter to illustrate research methods.

2. If your review yields no likely topics, brainstorm or freewrite for a topic.

   a. To brainstorm, list every topic you can think of. Just begin writing at the top of your journal page and try to fill the page with topics. Do not eliminate anything that comes to mind. Then review your list to see which topics really interest you.

   b. To freewrite, time yourself for fifteen minutes and write without pausing for the full fifteen minutes. Write down any topic you can think of and anything that comes to mind about the topic.

3. Review what you have written. What aspects of the topic does your writing show you to be most interested in? What would you like to know more about?

Class Activities

Meet in writing groups in order to brainstorm. Pick a scribe. Instruct the scribe to write down every topic, no matter how dumb or impossible it seems.

1. Spend ten minutes brainstorming as many topics as you can think of.

2. Discuss whether your topics fit the assignment's requirements. Could a student have had experience with this topic? (The personal experience requirement generally eliminates such topics as capital punishment or the destruction of rain forests in Brazil, important as these topics are.) Is it a topic of public interest or controversy? If so, you will be able to find articles about it in periodicals. Cross topics off your list if you must answer no to either of these questions.

3. Meet together as a class, and let the scribes read to the class the topics remaining on your lists. Your instructor will write them on the board.

4. You may want to take down the class's entire list in your own notebook. If not, look it over carefully and take down topics that interest you.

The topics on your list are probably too broad for a three- to five-page paper. You will need to *narrow* your topic. The best way to focus, or narrow, a topic is, paradoxically, first to expand it by thinking about every possible angle from which it can be viewed. Doing this will help you find the best angle of approach for your own paper. The following exercises give you a variety of ways to probe a topic. You will practice them first as a class and then use them individually on your own topics.

1. Review the process for using the six journalistic questions in Chapter 8. Then pick one of the topics from your class's brainstorming list and ask the six questions of it. Remember that the point is not simply to ask the questions; it is to come up with as many different answers for each question as you can. You might find a focused topic for your paper among the answers to the questions.

2. Many other questions can help you focus on a particular aspect of a larger topic. Some of them are listed below. As a class, pick one of the topics from your list and come up with as many answers to each question as you can. You might find the focus for your paper among your answers.

   a. Into what parts can your topic be divided? That is, what subcategories does your topic contain? (For instance, one subcategory of the broad topic of education is tracking. Others include grading and standardized tests. Can you think of more?) You might decide to write about one of the subcategories.
   b. What is the purpose of the topic?
   c. What are some examples of your topic?
   d. What are the causes of your topic?
   e. What are the results of your topic?
   f. Of what rules, laws, or regulations about your topic are you aware?
   g. What are the economic, psychological, or emotional costs of your topic?
   h. How would you define your topic?

Beginning the Research

When you have decided on a narrowed topic, you are ready to begin your research, but do not stop thinking about your focus. As you do your research, you may have to shift your focus because you find abundant material on a different aspect of your topic or because you find yourself changing your opinion about the topic on the basis of the evidence you find. If this happens, do not worry. It is all part of learning. You must be flexible enough to change your focus as your research demands.

Periodicals

Because the only sources you may use for this assignment are periodicals, a few more words about them are in order. There are two different types of periodicals, usually called popular and professional or scholarly. **Popular periodicals** are intended for a general audience, that is, people with a high-school or college education. **Professional** or **scholarly periodicals** are intended for experts in a particular field.

To give you an idea of how the two types differ, popular and professional or scholarly publications may, for instance, each contain an article on a new medical breakthrough. The article in the popular magazine—*Newsweek,* for example—will be written in language any literate person can understand and will discuss why the discovery is important to ordinary people. The article in the professional or scholarly journal—say the *New England Journal of Medicine*—is likely to use more technical terms and to include information about procedures and other matters of interest to specialists.

The Library

Libraries, as you know, are wondrously rich sources of information. The student's problem is figuring out how to get the information needed at the moment. Over the years librarians have developed various systems for classifying and indexing library holdings. **Holdings** refer to all the resources the library has in any form: books, periodicals, maps, videotapes, microfilms, and so on.

There is no single **index,** or alphabetical listing, of every item in the library. You know that the catalog, usually computerized now, is an index of *books* in the library. However, for this assignment you will not use the book catalog because it contains *only* books. You will use periodical indexes instead. Your library probably has periodical indexes in two different forms, or **formats** as they are called: bound (meaning put together like a book with hard covers) and on computers.

Your librarian is your first resource in the library, but librarians will not do the research for you. They only tell you how to get started and then help when you get stuck. You need to be able to tell your librarian two things when you ask for help getting started: your topic and the type of source you need (in this case, periodicals). The first question to ask is where the indexes are for your type of source. (In this case, "Where are the indexes for periodicals?") Your librarian will direct you to either the shelves containing the bound indexes or the computer terminal with periodical indexes.

Bound Indexes Two important bound indexes for undergraduate students are the *Readers' Guide to Periodical Literature* and the *New York Times Index.* The *Readers' Guide* lists all of the articles published in popular magazines, while the *New York Times Index* lists every article published in the *New York Times* (kind of amazing, when you think about it). Both indexes are organized by year. You will find a separate bound volume for every year prior to the current one. The current year's listings to date are in smaller paperback booklets.

As an example of how to find information in periodicals, we will use our own research from Chapter 9 to locate an article about the disadvantages of tracking.

First, we tried the *Readers' Guide* for 1988, just because 1988 was the most recent volume. Within each volume, magazine articles are listed alphabetically by topic. We looked up tracking but did not find it. So we returned to the larger topic of which it is a subcategory, education. This is an important strategy: *If you do not find the specific heading you are looking for, think of a larger category that might contain it.* Figure 10.1 (p. 175) reprints a photocopy of the page that lists education.

Under the heading "EDUCATION" are several subcategories. We spotted "Ability Grouping in Education," a synonym for tracking. This is another important strategy: *Look for synonyms for the term you have in mind.* We then turned to the A's and found the page reprinted in Figure 10.2 (p. 176).

Sure enough, there was "ABILITY GROUPING IN EDUCATION" in the second column. What do the phrases and symbols in the citation mean? Look at Figure 10.2 again. The first entry under Ability Grouping gives the following information:

1. title of article (Avoiding damaging labels)

2. author (F. Roberts)

3. illustrations (*il* means the article includes illustrations. If there were no *il*, it would mean the article is not illustrated.)

4. name of periodical *(Parents)*

5. volume and page number of article (63:49, meaning volume 63, page 49)

6. date (O '88)

All indexes provide help for understanding their own information, and this help is usually found at the beginning of the volume. The helpful pages in the *Readers' Guide* include

1. "Abbreviations of Periodicals Indexed": a list of the full name of all abbreviated periodical titles.

2. "Periodicals Indexed": additional information about the periodicals listed. Use this page if you are unfamiliar with the periodical and want more information about it.

Figure 10.1.

Page 638 from *Readers' Guide to Periodical Literature 1988.* (Reprinted by permission of H. W. Wilson Co.)

EDMONTON (ALTA.)
Crime
A Getty family crisis [Alberta premier's son D. Getty arrested
on cocaine trafficking charges] J. Howse. *Maclean's* 101:21
Ag 29 '88
Police
Police-force scandals. P. Kaihla. il *Maclean's* 101:28 My 9
'88
Politics and government
The politics of put-downs [feud between Premier D. Getty
and Edmonton Mayor L. Decore] P. Kaihla. il pors
Maclean's 101:16 Ap 18 '88
Stores
The bizarre bazaar [West Edmonton Mall] J. Queenan. il
Gentlemen's Quarterly 58:308-11+ N '88
EDMUNDS, JOHN FRANCIS W. *See* Edmonds, Francis
William, 1806-1863
EDMUNDSON, MARK
A will to cultural power: deconstructing the de Man scandal.
Harper's 277:67-71 Jl '88
EDPER ENTERPRISES
The Brascan ring [excerpt from The brass ring] P. Best and
A. Shortell. il *Maclean's* 101:26+ O 3 '88
EDSALL, RANDY
about
The wintertime scramble for big-time talent. G. Witkin. il
pors *U.S. News & World Report* 104:66-7 Ja 25 '88
EDSALL, THOMAS BYRNE
Race in politics. *The New York Review of Books* 35:23-4
D 22 '88
The return of inequality. il *The Atlantic* 261:86-90+ Je '88
EDTA *See* Ethylenediamine tetraacetic acid
EDUARDO IGLESIAS AUTO MUSEUM *See* Museo del
Automóvril Eduardo Iglesias
EDUCATION
See also
> Ability grouping in education
> Acceleration (Education)
> Accountability (Education)
> Adult education
> Aesthetic education
> Aged—Education
> Alcohol education
> Art teachers—Education
> Arts teachers—Education
> Asian Americans—Education
> Athletes—Education
> Bilingual education
> Black athletes—Education
> Black celebrities—Education
> Black women—Education
> Blacks—Education
> Blind—Education
> Business and education
> Catholic schools
> Children—Education
> Children, Gifted—Education
> Children of immigrants—Education
> Children of migrant laborers—Education
> Chinese Americans—Education
> Church and education
> Citizenship education
> Clergy—Education
> Coeducation
> College education
> Colleges and universities
> Communication in education
> Communications satellites—Educational use
> Communism and education
> Community and junior colleges
> Community education
> Comparative education
> Computers—Educational use
> Correlation (Education)
> Drug education
> Economics and education
> Educators
> mary education

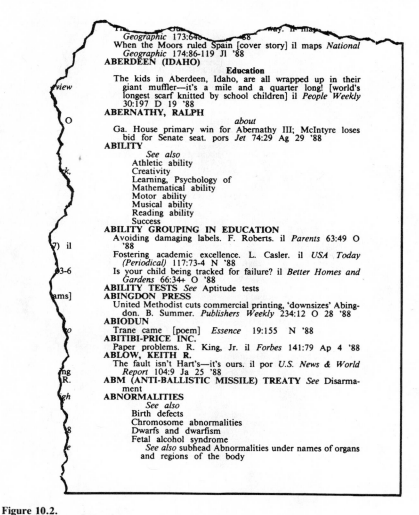

Geographic 173:6 ... 68
When the Moors ruled Spain [cover story] il maps *National Geographic* 174:86-119 Jl '88
ABERDEEN (IDAHO)
                  Education
   The kids in Aberdeen, Idaho, are all wrapped up in their giant muffler—it's a mile and a quarter long! [world's longest scarf knitted by school children] il *People Weekly* 30:197 D 19 '88
ABERNATHY, RALPH
                about
   Ga. House primary win for Abernathy III; McIntyre loses bid for Senate seat. pors *Jet* 74:29 Ag 29 '88
ABILITY
      See also
      Athletic ability
      Creativity
      Learning, Psychology of
      Mathematical ability
      Motor ability
      Musical ability
      Reading ability
      Success
ABILITY GROUPING IN EDUCATION
   Avoiding damaging labels. F. Roberts. il *Parents* 63:49 O '88
   Fostering academic excellence. L. Casler. il *USA Today (Periodical)* 117:73-4 N '88
   Is your child being tracked for failure? il *Better Homes and Gardens* 66:34+ O '88
ABILITY TESTS *See* Aptitude tests
ABINGDON PRESS
   United Methodist cuts commercial printing, 'downsizes' Abingdon. B. Summer. *Publishers Weekly* 234:12 O 28 '88
ABIODUN
   Trane came [poem] *Essence* 19:155 N '88
ABITIBI-PRICE INC.
   Paper problems. R. King, Jr. il *Forbes* 141:79 Ap 4 '88
ABLOW, KEITH R.
   The fault isn't Hart's—it's ours. il por *U.S. News & World Report* 104:9 Ja 25 '88
ABM (ANTI-BALLISTIC MISSILE) TREATY *See* Disarmament
ABNORMALITIES
      See also
      Birth defects
      Chromosome abnormalities
      Dwarfs and dwarfism
      Fetal alcohol syndrome
         See also subhead Abnormalities under names of organs and regions of the body

Figure 10.2.
Page 2 from *Readers' Guide to Periodical Literature 1988.* (Reprinted by permission of H. W. Wilson Co.)

3. ''Abbreviations'': If you find other abbreviations that you do not understand—for instance, the O in the citation above—turn to this page. It lists all of the abbreviations used in the index except magazine titles. You would learn that O stands for October.

Write down the entire citation of any articles that seem appropriate for your paper. Keep this information even after you find the article, because you might want to go back to it later, and you will also need the information for your List of References (bibliography). We wrote down the three citations from the 1988 *Readers' Guide* and continued to look through previous years' indexes for more articles.

None of the articles we found was quite satisfactory for our purposes, so we decided to try the *New York Times*. Newspapers are not indexed in the *Readers' Guide,* but major newspapers like the *New York Times*, the *Washington Post*, and the *Wall Street Journal* publish their own indexes. You will see as you read the page reprinted in Figure 10.3 (p. 178) that the *New York Times Index* is quite different from the *Readers' Guide*. Articles are still listed alphabetically, by topic, but within each topic the articles are listed in chronological order according to the date they appeared. Another major difference between the *New York Times Index* and the *Readers' Guide* is that the *New York Times Index* includes **abstracts,** or very short summaries, of all its articles rather than just titles. The abstracts are very handy because they often provide enough information to enable you to decide whether you can use the article.

We found the William J. Warren article reprinted in Chapter 9 in the *New York Times Index* for 1988. You will find the abstract towards the bottom of the third column. (You might compare this summary to your own. Did this writer get the main points? Is it as clearly written as yours? How are the purposes for this summary different from yours?)

Once again, you need to figure out what the citation means. Information is given in the following order:

1. Abstract
2. Type of illustrations (photos)
3. Length of article (M for medium)
4. Date (D 21: December 21)
5. Newspaper section (II)
6. Page and column (8:3)

The *New York Times Index* provides help for its users on the page titled "How to Use the New York Times Index" in the front of the book.

The Warren article on tracking is stored on a microfiche in our library. Our library, and probably yours, has a machine for making paper copies from microfiche. Ask your librarian about it.

Computerized Indexes If your library has computerized indexes for periodicals, your research process will be quite different. Because indexed computer systems vary a good deal, your librarian will be your major source of help. However, you need the same two basic pieces of information to begin your research: a topic and the kind of publication (book, periodical, or other) that you want to use.

Yugoslavia, D 31

Pres-elect Bush, citing 'enormous problems, particularly in our own hemisphere,' asserts that American policy toward world's debtor countries needs 'a whole new look' (M), D 20,II,10:4

Organization of Economic Cooperation and Development predicts that strong economic growth in industrialized world will slow next year as several nations work to keep inflation in check (M), D 21,IV, 6:1

Conference Board says global economic expansion should continue at a healthy pace, led by industrial nations of Pacific region; says world's 10 leading industrial nations are expected to have 4% annual rate of growth (M), D 29,II,18:4

ECONOMIC COOPERATION AND DEVELOPMENT, ORGANIZATION FOR (OECD).
See also
Economic Conditions and Trends, D 21
ECONOMIC EDUCATION, JOINT COUNCIL ON.
See also
Economics, D 29
ECONOMICS

National survey finds more than half of all high school students in United States cannot define basic economic terms; William B Walstad, author of study, calls level of economic knowledge among students 'shocking'; more than 8,000 high school students took his mulitple-choice test last spring; study was conducted for Joint Council on Economic Education; excerpted questions from test (M), D 29,I,1:2

EDBERG, STEFAN. See also
Tennis, D 17,18
EDELMAN, ASHER B. See also
Storehouse Plc, D 28
EDGEMONT (SD)

Edgemont, SD, fails in all efforts to fill the hole left in its economy when Army closed ammunition depot there in 1967; map (M), D 28,II,5:1

EDISON (NJ). See also
New York Times, D 16
EDITORIALS. See also
Agriculture, D 17
Airlines and Airplanes, D 17,24,26,27,30
Apparel, D 30
Aral Sea (USSR), D 27
Blacks (in US), D 17,22
Children and Youth, D 18,26
Christmas, D 20,22,24,25
Courts, D 28
Credit, D 22
Crossword Puzzles, D 21
Dictionaries, D 23
Drug Addiction and Abuse, D 25
Education and Schools, D 16
Environment, D 26
Environmental Protection Agency (Epa), D 26
Fish and Other Marine Life, D 21
Forests and Forestry, D 21
Health and Human Services, Department of, D 23
Homeless Persons, D 25
Housing, D 31
Housing and Urban Development, Department of, D 21
Humidifiers, D 25
Immigration and Emigration, D 19
Interior, Department of the, D 26
International Trade and World Market, D 28,31
Israel, State of, D 21

o..ted from con-
f..ays educational
..f district's children
w..rd members;
p..
..nstruction reform
b..ork City
s..
..ves measure
c..hority for New
Y..e on Legislature
t..asure is second
m..pass in
D..expected success
is..re created by
re..ools and
pe..l labor leaders
(M..
..request for state
c..in city's school
s..Counsel to
d..ght conduct its
o..that he will meet
w..16,II,4:1
..Guarriaci, 23-
ye..on cot behind
b..Brooklyn, NY
(S..
..ity displays
le..s public school
tea..public school system
do..ublic will
re..as it does to
le..s 60-year-old
Op..als say items
re..red basic
eq..red by school's
$5..1,29:2
..ol Board District
12..ting match as
b..lves against
a..d district funds;
p..
..of inspector
g..pened
in..ork City's 32
lo..D 17,I,30:4
C..imes Magazine
ab..llor Richard R
G..ld executive
re..
..ty school boards
in..I City have
sp..y Gov Cuomo
to..-controlled New
Y..d to kill bills;
ph
..ltimore, Md, bars
st..eather or fur
co..l senior high
sc..school violence
(S..
..ensions of the
K..Samuel M
E..rnds that even
su..rs are being
ma..; says trend
pr..outs and for New
Y..ol

program has become so popular additional pupils are eager to join; photo (M), D 18,XXIII,6:5

Op-Ed article by Libertarian party leader John Chodes suggests tax-supported public education has failed and should be replaced by private system such as that run by Joseph Lancaster in slums of London in early 19th century (S), D 19,I,17:1

Students at Catholic boys high school in Morristown, New Jersey, work to bring Christmas gifts of donated toys, food and clothing to more than 700 needy families in eastern Kentucky; photo (M), D 19,II,1:2

Clifford Burr, who is retarded and blind, receives what his parents say is best possible 21st birthday present possible: chance for complete education; parents, Kenneth and Betty Burr, say gift came when US Appeals Court for Second Circuit ruled on December 12 that New York State must provide 18 months of 'compensatory education' for him to make up for school time he lost in 1984, 1985 and 1986, when state and school officials argued over what school he would attend; case discussed (M), D 19,II, 3:2

New York City Council Pres Andrew J Stein assails Education Board pres Robert F Wagner Jr, asserting that Wagner is ultimately responsible for any corruption that might be found in local school boards (S), D 19,II,4:3

Hundred homeless children in three Queens shelters will be given training in such subjects as music, visual arts, theater and science in pilot project announced by New York City officials; project will bus children to after-school and Saturday sessions at such institutions in Queens as Queens Museum, American Museum of Moving Image and city's Hall of Science (M), D 20,II,1:2

Mayor Koch says he will name commission to investigate allegations of corruption in local school districts by week's end but denies that panel was intended to help dismantle decentralization (M), D 20,II,3:1

Photo of Gov Mario Cuomo at ceremony in Harlem where he signs three bills intended to improve school system; bills provide for agency to handle building and renovation, commission to review decentralization and barring of politicians and school employees from serving on school boards, D 21,II,4:4

Boston Private Industry Council demands structural changes in way Boston public schools are run before it renews Boston Compact, 1982 agreement by which private businesses guarantee jobs for high-school graduates if school system improves test scores and lowers dropout rate; first change is new pupil assignment plan that would give parents some choice in which public schools their children attend; second is to decentralize decision-making by giving principals more authority in their own buildings but also requiring that they share this with teachers; drawings (M), D 21,II,8:1

Increasing number of educators attack policy in place in vast majority of American school systems under which students are categorized by their teachers and counselors into classes for fast, average or slow learners; say such 'tracking' is psychologically damaging to children and of little or no educational value; defenders acknowledge failings but maintain that it allows teachers to address particular needs of students who have widely diverse aptitudes and levels of achievement; photos (M), D 21,II,8:3

Figure 10.3.

Page 31 from *New York Times Index 1988*. (Copyright © 1988 by The New York Times Company. Reprinted by permission.)

If you have never used a computer before, sit down in front of the terminal for a few minutes before asking your librarian for help. Read any directions provided for the computer. Then study the keys on the computer, the numbered and named keys as well as the letter keys, locating all of the keys mentioned in the directions. This might provide you with enough information to get started. If it does, see how far you can get by following the computer's directions. If it does not, ask your librarian for help. If you miss anything because the librarian is talking too fast or not giving you all the information you need, ask for a repetition of the step(s) you missed. It is probably not your fault that you do not understand. The librarian does not intend to confuse you, but people who are familiar with computers tend to skip directions that are obvious to themselves but new to beginners.

There are some outstanding advantages to computerized indexes. First, you can find articles in them faster than in bound indexes because they contain several years of citations in one program. For instance, Infotrac, an index widely available in libraries now, carries listings for the past three years. Second, computerized indexes are likely to include abstracts of articles. Third, some of them contain a wider range of materials than any single printed index. For instance, Infotrac contains the most current 60 days of articles of the *New York Times* and the *Wall Street Journal,* as well as indexes for over 1,100 popular and professional periodicals. Fourth, you can usually print the citations for your topic on a printer located near the computer terminal. This saves you the time of copying them down by hand.

The procedure for locating your topic is a little different on the computer than when using a bound index. Most computer programs use what is called the **keyword procedure** for locating articles about a topic. First type in your major topic heading, which is the keyword. For our search, that was "education." Then, when the computer screen asks for it, type in other words or phrases that limit your topic to your specific area. Our second was "ability grouping." Then hit the key that starts the search. If no titles appear under the specific area, go back to the subject screen and try a synonym. We tried "tracking" as a synonym. If none of your synonyms produce any citations, you might, at this point, ask your librarian to think of any other headings you can use to find your specific topic. If that fails, then your only choice is to return to the larger topic (education) and scan all of its citations (there may be hundreds).

Part of the printout from our computer search for articles on tracking is reproduced in Figure 10.4 (pp. 180–181). You can see that the information is quite clear. The order of the information is author, title, name of periodical, volume number, page number, and date.

Some libraries also offer an additional service with their computer systems. They store all of the articles indexed in the computer

6 RGA
Nevi, Charles
In defense of tracking
The Education Digest v53 p50-2 September '87

SUBJECTS COVERED:
Ability grouping in education

ABSTRACT: Condensed from an article in the March 1987 issue of Educational
Leadership. As education has become more complex, content more broad, and
the student population more heterogeneous, tracking has become a more
viable method of accommodating these differences in the classroom. Critics
of tracking assert that lower-level tracked classes are taught by
unmotivated teachers and do not challenge students. Treating all students
in the same way, however, does not lead to equity or excellence.
Appropriate tracking offers the best possible match between the student and
the instructional environment.

7 RGA
Bracey, Gerald W.
The social impact of ability grouping (research by Linda Grant and James
Rothenberg)
Phi Delta Kappan v68 p701-2 May '87
il

SUBJECTS COVERED:
School children/Social and economic status
Ability grouping in education

ABSTRACT: Following a study of seven first-grade classrooms and one
second-grade classroom in three midwestern school districts, Linda Grant of
the University of Georgia and James Rothenberg of Amherst College expressed
skepticism concerning the effectiveness of grouping reading students
according to their ability. The study also revealed that students in
classrooms located in white-collar neighborhoods engaged in more
self-directed activities than students in classrooms located in blue-collar
neighborhoods and that low-ability students in white-collar neighborhoods
were able to perform individual reading exercises, while low-ability
students from blue-collar neighborhoods were barely able to read. Grant
and Rothenberg called for a more vigorous search for workable alternatives,
such as individualized reading programs, heterogeneous ability grouping,
and various types of peer tutoring.

8 RGA
Roberts, Francis
Should kids be grouped by ability?
Parents v62 p59 June '87
il

SUBJECTS COVERED:
Ability grouping in education

ABSTRACT: Most children do not perform equally in all school subjects, so
grouping children by assumed ability is a naive educational arrangement.
Daylong ability grouping is a subjective and inaccurate process that may
lead to long-term stereotyping. It almost inevitably results in lower
expectations and lower performance from the allegedly less able groups.

Figure 10.4.

Computer printout page from *Readers' Guide Abstracts,* an on-disc reference. (Reprinted by permission of H. W. Wilson Co.)

9 RGA
Oakes, Jeannie
Keeping track, part 2: curriculum inequality and school reform (tracking)
Phi Delta Kappan v68 p148-54 October '86
il

SUBJECTS COVERED:
Ability grouping in education
Educational equalization

ABSTRACT: Tracking began in the days of dramatically increased immigration to the United States, developing along lines of race and class as an acceptable solution to considerable social disequilibrium. The practice became so ingrained that it was extended to schools with largely homogenous populations. Tracking and ability grouping, however, begin a cycle of restricted opportunities for lower-track and vocational students. Neither program overcomes student deficiencies or provides students with access to high-quality learning opportunities. Schools must instead promote heterogeneity, reconstruct curricula, and restructure classroom instruction while rethinking their views on the purpose of education. Only then will U.S. schools become humane, equitable, and truly educational places.

10 RGA
Bracey, Gerald W.
Ability grouping and student achievement in elementary schools
Phi Delta Kappan v68 p76-7 September '86

SUBJECTS COVERED:
Ability grouping in education
Student achievements

ABSTRACT: Two studies using much of the same data came to different conclusions about the effects of ability grouping on student achievement. Chen-Lin and James Kulik used meta-analysis of 28 studies and concluded that students in grouped classes gained somewhat more than those in ungrouped classes. Robert Slavin used a best-evidence synthesis and reached the opposite conclusion. If studies of gifted students are dropped from the Kuliks' study, however, the Kuliks' reported improvement in grouped classes disappears.

11 RGA
Oakes, Jeannie
Keeping track, part 1: the policy and practice of curriculum inequality
Phi Delta Kappan v68 p12-17 September '86
bibl f il

SUBJECTS COVERED:
Ability grouping in education
Educational equalization

ABSTRACT: Tracking, the division of students into separate classes according to achievement abilities, widens rather than narrows the gap between students at different levels. The bulk of the evidence does not support the assumption that students will perform better in groups containing only those with roughly equal capabilities. Nor does tracking appear to improve students' attitudes about themselves or school. One study of 38 U.S. schools shows important discrepancies between higher and lower tracks in student access to knowledge, classroom instructional opportunities, and classroom learning environments. Unfortunately, poor and minority students are most likely to be placed in lower-track curricula. Thus, tracking achieves neither excellence nor equality.

in a special section of the library on microfilm, microfiche, or an electronic (computer) format. If your library offers this service, the computer citation will include a code number that will direct you straight to the source you are looking for. Ask your librarian if your library subscribes to such a service. Infotrac provides two of these services, Magazine Collection (for popular periodicals) and Business Collection (for periodicals on business subjects).

Finding the Periodical   If your library does not subscribe to the Magazine Collection or Business Collection service, the next step is to find out whether your library subscribes to the periodicals you need. Ask your librarian how to find out what periodicals your library carries. Once you know that the library subscribes to your periodicals, you must locate them. Either check the posted building diagram or ask your librarian where the periodical section is.

When you get to the periodical section, show your librarian your citations and ask whether past issues of these periodicals are bound in volumes or available on microfilm or microfiche. If they are in bound volumes, you will find the periodicals themselves bound together in hardcover books. If they are on microfilm or microfiche, which is very likely for popular magazines, you will need to ask your librarian how to use the viewing machines. Microfilm looks like a roll of film. Microfiche comes on flat film cards. The advantage to libraries of both is that they greatly reduce the size of the printed material, so they take up much less storage space. Do not let the viewing machines intimidate you. They are very easy to use once you know how.

Research Assignment 1: Gathering Sources

Find and take down (either by hand or computer printer) the complete citations for fifteen articles relating to your topic. Make a photocopy of your list to hand in to your teacher. Keep the original for your own use.

Research Assignment 2: Taking Notes

Find the five articles from your list that seem most useful. Read and take notes on them. Follow your teacher's recommendations for how to take notes.

You know how to find important information in your articles from reading and writing expository essays and writing your summaries. However, you are not looking for exactly the same kind of information now as you were when you wrote summaries. You want to spot information you can use in your paper. To do so, proceed as follows for each article:

1. Decide whether the main point or any of the subpoints are pertinent to your topic. If they are, make note of them.

2. Check the author's evidence. Would this evidence help support your topic? If so, take it down in your notes, too. You may either copy, paraphrase, or summarize any evidence that might be useful.

DRAFTING: WRITING, TALKING, REWRITING, AND EVALUATING

Controlling Your Information

At this point, if all has gone well, you should be very confused. In fact, we have developed a diagram (Figure 10.5) to illustrate how the research and writing process usually works. You can see that chaos is a natural phase on the way to a final draft of your essay. Now you must learn how to move on from this phase.

Besides your own knowledge, gained from your experience with the topic, you now have a welter of information from other writers. You need to gain control over it. Here are some ways to do that.

Reading Your Notes

To gain control over your information, first read your notes. Then answer the following questions about your five articles:

1. Do they all deal with the same aspect of your topic? (With tracking, we might have found that all of the articles discussed the problem of stigmatization of lower-track students, or we might have found that one article discussed stigmatization, another achievement, and another the actions the parents can take to move their children from one track to another.)

2. Do your authors agree or disagree? (Again, with tracking, we might find that two authors who discussed student achievement disagree on the effects of tracking: one might say it promotes high achievement, and another might say it leads to failure.)

Now group your articles by topic and agreement. First, put together the articles (or your notes on them) that discuss the same aspects of the topic. Within those groups, put together the authors who agree with each other.

Freewriting

Put your notes aside, and freewrite about your topic in your journal. (This should take from half an hour to an hour.) You might write about the following ideas:

1. What aspects of this topic do I find most interesting?

2. About which aspects have I found the most information?

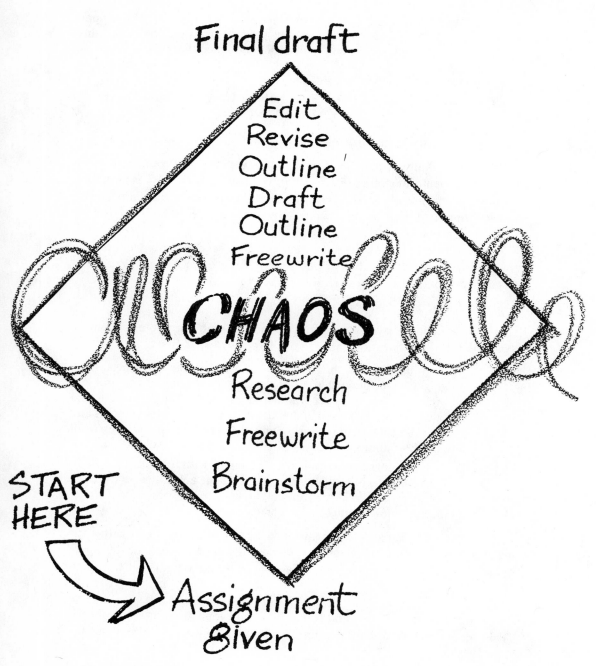

Final draft

Edit
Revise
Outline
Draft
Outline
Freewrite

CHAOS

Research

Freewrite

Brainstorm

START
HERE

Assignment
Given

Figure 10.5.
The writing process.

3. What have I learned that I did not know before?

4. What is my own experience in regard to this topic?

5. How have my opinions changed about the topic?

6. What new questions do I have about the topic?

Clustering

Put your notes aside and try to visualize the relationships between the various pieces of information you have so far. This procedure is called **clustering.** You begin by putting your main topic in the middle of a blank sheet of paper and circling it. Then extend branches from the main idea to subordinate ideas, circling each new idea you think of. Include related ideas on the same branch. Figure 10.6 is an example of clustering for a paper on tracking in education.

Examine your clusters. Which branches are longest? Which do you find most interesting? You might play with the relationships between ideas by making several more cluster diagrams, shifting around the branches and circles as you see new connections between ideas.

Stating Your Main Point

You are ready to decide on the main point of your paper. Remember that your main point must state both your topic and the opinion you will support about that topic. For instance, on the basis of what we discovered about our interests and information from the clustering diagram in Figure 10.6, the main point of our paper about this topic would be

Labeling in schools is harmful to students.

What is our topic? What is our opinion about it?

Your main point will further limit the focus of your topic. You probably will not write about everything included in your cluster diagram. You now need to review your freewrite and your clustering to decide which areas to focus on and which to eliminate.

Make a new cluster diagram, putting your main point in the middle. Include all of the circles from your first diagram *relating to your main point*. Also add new information that you think of relating to the main point. Leave out all the circles from the original diagram that are no longer pertinent. Figure 10.7 shows our new cluster diagram.

Deciding on Your Audience

At this point you need to think about audience. Who needs to know about your topic? Who needs to be convinced of your opinion? Thinking about audience helps you to understand your own purpose in writing.

We all know that the real audience for school papers is the instructor

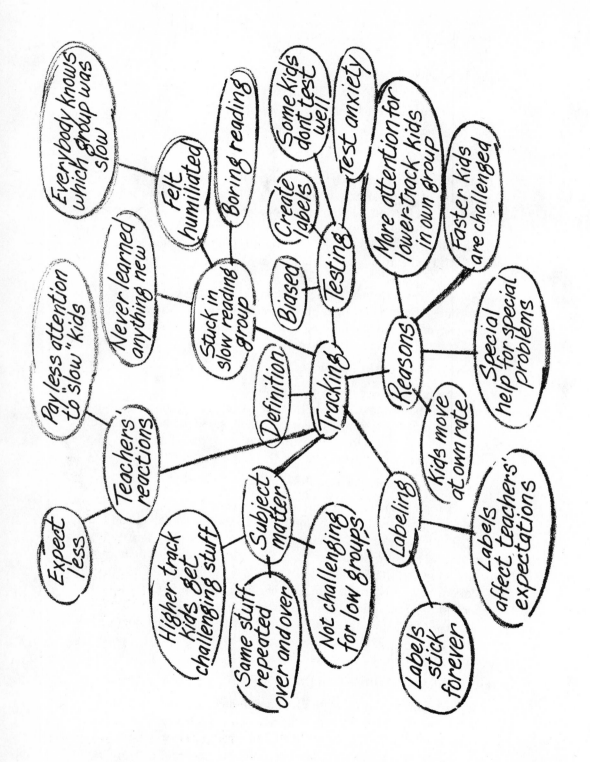

Everybody knows which group was slow

Felt humiliated

Boring reading

Some kids don't test well

Test anxiety

Create labels

More attention for lower-track kids in own group

Faster kids are challenged

Never learned anything new

Stuck in slow reading group

Biased

Testing

Pay less attention to "slow" kids

Definition

Tracking

Reasons

Special help for special problems

Teachers' reactions

Kids move at own rate

Labeling

Expect less

Higher track kids get challenging stuff

Subject matter

Not challenging for low groups

Labels affect teachers' expectations

Same stuff repeated over and over

Labels stick forever

186

and classmates. However, in most writing situations outside of school, you know ahead of time that a particular audience will be reading your writing. Remember, for instance, how carefully advertisers plan their writing for particular audiences. Imagining an audience for this paper other than the teacher and students gives you practice in adjusting your writing to the needs of your readers.

The audience for our paper on labeling, then, would be school officials and parents. School officials have the power to make the changes, so they need to be convinced of our point of view. Parents also need to be aware of the arguments against labeling, so that they can support their own children in school and join with other parents to force school officials to address the problem.

Thinking about audience will help you organize your paper. What does your particular audience need to know about your topic in order to understand the points you want to make? You will need to be sure to include such information in your paper.

Identifying Your Subpoints

You should be ready to make an outline of your paper, including your main point, and each of your subpoints. Your subpoints will come from the circles on your cluster diagram. *The purpose of this outline is to order your information for the paper.* You are deciding what needs to come first, what should come second, and so on. Our outline appears below. This outline just lists the subpoints. and indicates the source of the evidence to support them. The evidence itself must still be added.

I. Labeling in schools is harmful to students.
    A. Definition of labeling.
    B. The most important tool for labeling students is the standardized test.
        1. Tests are inaccurate.
            a. Culturally biased (evidence from research).
            b. Test anxiety (evidence from research and personal experience).
            c. Kids do not realize how serious they are.
                (1) My friend's experience: screwed up a test on purpose (anecdote).
    C. Labels stick all through school.
        1. (Reasons from research.)
    D. Labels affect teachers' expectations for students' performance.
        1. Studies show kids' performances are affected by teachers' expectations (summarize studies).
        2. Teachers expect less of kids labeled as slow (quote studies).

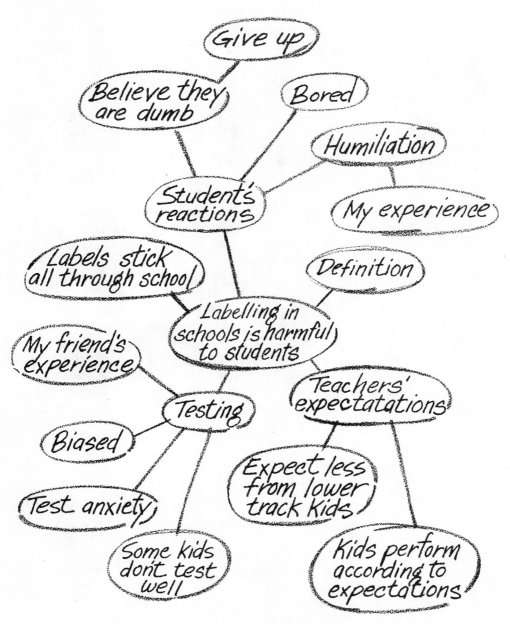

Figure 10.7.
Revised cluster map for an essay on tracking in education.

    E. Labels lower kids' self-esteem.
      1. My experience in slow-track reading group (anecdote).
      2. Effects of experience: humiliation (evidence from personal experience).

Assessing the Need for More Research

Now review your notes, together with your freewriting and clustering. Do you have enough information to support your main point and subpoints? Are there gaps in your information? If so, now is the time to return to the library for more information.

Begin by using the original list of fifteen articles you compiled. Do any of them seem to offer the information you need? If so, find the articles. If not, return to the indexes to locate more information.

Documenting Your Information

You are almost ready to write your first draft, but there is one more thing you need to know first. When using information from other sources in your own writing, you must give credit to the original author. As you have worked through this text, you have learned three ways to include material from outside sources: quoting, paraphrasing, and summarizing. Using other authors' ideas without acknowledging them amounts to stealing their ideas and is illegal as well as unethical. So you must be careful to name the author of all new material you learned from other writers. Giving credit is so important among writers that elaborate systems have been developed to do it.

The two groups whose systems for acknowledging sources are most widely used are the American Psychological Association (APA) and the Modern Language Associate (MLA). Each of these organizations publishes a book describing in great detail how to **document,** or give credit for, information found in various kinds of publications. Social studies fields, such as political science and psychology, use the APA system, while humanities areas, such as English and philosophy, use the MLA system. (Various sciences have their own systems, the most widely used one being that published by the American Chemical Society.)

APA Rules for Crediting Sources

Neither the APA nor the MLA uses footnotes to document sources anymore. Both require that you include enough information in the text of your paper to refer the reader to the correct citation in the bibliography, or **list of references,** at the end of the paper. (We will discuss the bibliography or list of references later in this chapter.)

The APA requires that in the paragraph with the borrowed information you give the author's last name, the year of publication for the article, and the page number on which the information appeared. However, you have some latitude about exactly how to include this data.

We will use a quotation from ''Ability Grouping and Tracking'' in Chapter 9 as an example. The information to be included is

> Ability grouping or tracking in schools enrolling a socially diverse population tends to be correlated with social class and racial/ethnic status.

One way to include this information is *quotation:*

> Levine and Havighurst (1989) state, ''Ability grouping or tracking in schools enrolling a socially diverse population tends to be correlated with social class and racial/ethnic status'' (p. 48).

Note the information that must be included:

Authors' last names
Date of publication of the source
Page number of the quotation

Note, too, the punctuation that is used for each of these pieces of information: parentheses for the date and page number. And, finally, note where the information is located in relation to the quotation: the page number is at the end of the quotation, but the authors' names and the date appear at the beginning as part of our sentence.

Another way to include the information is *paraphrase*. The information from the original text can be paraphrased as follows:

> When the student population of a school is ethnically and economically mixed, the ability groups tend to divide along race and class lines (Levine and Havighurst, 1989, p. 48).

Even though we have paraphrased the material rather than quoted it, we must tell our readers that the idea came from someone else. We did not invent it, and it was not part of our own background knowledge. We do this by giving the same information as for quoted material in parentheses at the end of the idea.

The important things to remember about following the APA system for crediting sources are the following:

1. You must include the author's last name, the date of publication, and the page number.
2. The author's name can be part of your own sentence, or it can be included in the parentheses at the end of the quotation, paraphrase, or summary.

3. If the author's name is part of your own sentence, the date of publication of the source is put in parentheses after the author's name.

MLA Rules For Crediting Sources

Here is what the MLA Handbook says about documenting sources:

"You must indicate exactly what you have derived from each source and exactly where in that work you found the material. The most practical way to supply this information is to insert brief parenthetical acknowledgments in your paper wherever you incorporate another's words, facts, or ideas. Usually, the author's last name and a page reference are enough to identify the source and the specific location from which you have borrowed material" (Gibaldi and Achtert, 136).

We have documented the quotation from the MLA handbook in the way that MLA prescribes in the quotation. Note these features:

The MLA system does not require the date of publication of the source.

The MLA system does not require the *p.* before the page number.

Like the APA, the MLA system does put the quotation marks at the end of the last word quoted, the parentheses after the quotation marks, and the period outside of the last parentheses mark.

If the idea were paraphrased rather than quoted, the quotation marks would not be used, the parentheses would come directly after the last word of the borrowed idea, and the period would still follow the parentheses.

Assignment: Write Your First Draft

You are now ready to write your first draft. Follow the order you set up in your outline. Remember that your outline included only subpoints. You will probably develop each subpoint in your outline into an entire paragraph. You will use the information from your research and your own experience to develop each paragraph. Even in your first draft, be sure to document all of the information that came from research.

This paper is an expository paper, like the one you wrote in Chapter 8, so you may want to review the information about the hierarchical structure of essays on pages 118–119. This structure does not apply just to the writing of professionals. Your own writing should follow the same organizational pattern. Reread carefully what should be included in each of the paper's sections: the introduction, the body, and the conclusion. This time, *you* are the author. The sections of your own paper should include the same kind of information.

First-Draft Activities

Responding to the First Draft

Make copies of your draft for group work. Read each group member's draft and do the following:

1. Underline the main point. If you cannot find, or are not sure of, the main point, put a question mark next to the introductory paragraph(s).

2. Circle the audience for the paper if one is mentioned in the first paragraph(s); otherwise, write down who you think the audience is in the margin next to the introductory paragraph(s).

3. Underline the subpoint in each paragraph. If you cannot find a subpoint, put a question mark in the margin next to the paragraph. If you find a subpoint, but it does not support the main point, put parentheses around that sentence.

4. Once you have found the subpoint in the paragraph, read all the other sentences carefully. Are there any that do not support the subpoint? If so, put a question mark over the sentences that do not seem to belong.

Outlining to Revise

Write an outline of your first draft as it is now. You are doing this to help you follow the organization of your own draft.

1. Write your main point in a single sentence at the top of your paper. Review the content of each paragraph. In a word or a phrase, what is each paragraph about? Write each word or phrase as a subtopic in your outline.

2. Read your outline carefully. Did you actually follow the original outline you wrote before writing the draft? If not, why did you change? Did you add more information? Do you think your subpoints are now in a logical order?

3. Review your writing group's comments. Could they find a subpoint in each paragraph? If not, it means that you did not make the point of the paragraph clear to your readers. Did they find a different subpoint from what you considered it to be? Again, if this is the case, you have not made the point of the paragraph clear.

4. Did your group suggest a different order for your information? Do you agree that their organization would be an improvement?

    Now write another outline. This time your purpose is to write out the organizational pattern that you *want to follow for your final paper*. Make any changes in subpoints or order that you think will make your paper easier for a reader to follow.

Assignment: Write Your Second Draft

Follow your second outline as you write your second draft. It may require you to make some major shifts in the order or emphasis of information. Part of good writing is the ability to evaluate your drafts and make major revisions when necessary.

Second-Draft Activities

Evaluation Criteria

A documented expository essay should do all of the following:

1. Include an introductory paragraph or section that
   a. establishes the context for the essay—what most people think about this topic or background information concerning the topic
   b. introduces the topic and main point of the essay in one focused sentence
2. Include a body in which
   a. each paragraph develops the main point of the paper
   b. each paragraph includes a subpoint and supporting evidence
   c. evidence comes from the student's own experience and citations from at least three articles
   d. transitions show how one idea relates to the next
3. Include a conclusion that reminds your audience of the significance of your topic and point
4. Document the cited information according to either the APA or the MLA system
5. Follow either the APA or the MLA system for the list of works cited
6. Accord with the conventions of standard English in spelling, punctuation, and grammatical structure.

Sample Student Essay

Read the following student essay.

Daycare: Do Kids Suffer or Prosper?

1   Most parents and child experts would agree that a stay-at-home parent is the ideal primary caretaker in most situations; however, economics and various other reasons are making this situation a novelty. Organizations involved with child care services project that by 1995 approximately two-thirds of all preschool children in the United States will have

mothers in the work force (Brower, 1987, p. 54). As more mothers enter the work force, we, as parents, begin to question the effects that day care has on our children at various stages of development.

2   Some experts feel that daycare interrupts the bond between mother and infant. They also believe that it produces insecurity in children as well. These conclusions were derived from the Strange Situation Test which was developed in the 1960's by Mary Ainsworth, Ph.D.. This test consists of seven, three minute episodes: (1) the mother and infant are placed in a room and the mother puts the child down to play; (2) a stranger then comes in and attempts to play with the child; (3) the mother leaves; (4) the mother reenters the room and the stranger leaves; (5) the child remains alone as the mother leaves; (6) the stranger returns to the room; (7) finally the mother returns and picks the baby up. This test is videotaped and evaluations of the baby take place. The experts base their evaluations on the reaction of the baby in the last episode where the mother picks the baby up. The infants' reaction is then placed into one of three groups: Secure: the infants distress is reduced by the mother returning and the baby returns to playing, Insecure/Avoidant: the baby ignores and avoids the mother, Insecure/Resistant: the baby isn't comforted by the mothers presence. A study, using this test, by Jay Belsky Ph.D., and Michael J. Rovine found a substantial but small group of children who were cared for outside the home to be insecure. (Galinsky and Phillips, 1988, p. 112).

3   Many experts believe this test has inaccurate conclusions because it was originally intended to measure the infant/mother attachment in a decade when most infants were raised at home by a parent. Alison Clarke-Stewart, Ph.D., (1988) states that after compiling sixteen studies, which assess attachment, there were 29 percent of children with twenty hours or less spent in daycare that were classified as insecure. Of the children who spent more than twenty hours in a daycare situation per week, thirty eight percent were evaluated as insecure. In her opinion, this is not a large enough difference to conclude that infants with working mothers are in danger. Dr. Clarke-Stewart suggests that the behavior of the "child care" infants in the Strange Situation test actually signals greater maturity, not insecurity (p. 114). Experts also contend that this test does not include important factors such as: the child's temperament, the family situation or the quality of the child care (Galinsky and Phillips, 1988, p. 114–115).

4   Although the experts have conflicting views on the effects of day care on infants, many experts and parents agree that preschool is a benefit for two to five year olds. Day care not only prepares preschoolers academically, it also provides them with important social skills. In this age group, peer relationships become an important part of development; however, these relationships can be alternately combative and pleasant (Frank and Lang, 1987, p. 61). It is important for children to have both

types of skills when entering Kindergarten. Through experience, I have found that if these skills are acquired before starting formal school, the child often has a successful and positive career in school. My daughter, who attended preschool for three years, began elementary school with advanced academic and social skills. Although she is in the first grade, she reads on a third grade level. I feel that because she was prepared for school, Christi was able to concentrate on building the skills she already possessed rather than trying to acquire academic skills as well as adapting to a foreign environment. Once children begin school, they become very independent but they still need supervision after school.

5   Working parents of school-age children do not always realize this fact and many children are left home in empty houses for at least two hours daily. This is usually not a safe situation and it is better for young school-age children to attend an after school setting where they can have time to do homework or play games with supervision. While supervision is important, it is also important for it not to be too structured or academic. After all, they have usually already spent seven hours concentrating on academics in a structured environment. Community programs such as the Y.M.C.A. and 4-H are good examples of after school care. These programs offer informal sports and non-academic creative projects. (Frank and Lang, 1987, p.59).

6   Although the experts have differing opinions on the effects of day care, many will agree that there are certain qualities to look for when searching for a "good" day care. Parents need to look for small group sizes and good child/staff ratios. This allows more time for individualized attention. It is important to also find a care center that encourages parent participation in their programs. Care centers which encourage parents' input usually have better communication with parents (Mitchell, 1989, p. 669)

7   Through research and personal experience, I have come to the conclusion that day care is not detrimental to child development and in some areas it may be beneficial, provided that parents use common sense and useful guidelines when choosing their day care.

LIST OF REFERENCES

Bower, B. 1987, July 25. Quality day-care and social growth. *Science News*, 132. 54–55.

Galinsky, E. and Phillips, D. 1988, November. Day-care debate. Parents, 63. 112–15.

Frank, M. and Lang, M. 1987, May. Day care dilemma: from infants to pre-teens. USA Today, 115, 59–62.

Mitchell, A.W. 1989, May. Guiding principles, *Phi Delta Kappan,* 10, 669.

Evaluating the Sample Essay

In your writing group, evaluate the student essay according to the criteria above. Does it meet each of the criteria? Once you have done this, check your own second draft according to the criteria. Have you met them? If not, revise your paper to meet them.

Preparing the List of References or List of Works Cited

The term *bibliography* is no longer used by either the APA or the MLA to refer to the sources of information used in a paper. Instead, the list is called either List of References (APA) or List of Works Cited (MLA).

The List of References or Works Cited comes on a separate page at the very end of your paper. List your sources in alphabetical order by the last name of the author. Below are examples of the APA and MLA formats for listing newspaper and periodical articles. (In the future when you write papers for other courses, you will probably need to cite other kinds of sources. When that time comes, ask your professor whether you should use the APA or the MLA documentation system, and then go to the library to get a copy of the proper handbook. It will tell you how to list books and every other kind of source you can think of, including interviews, TV programs, and movies.)

APA Format

Oakes, J. (1986, October). Keeping track, part 2: curriculum inequality and school reform. *Phi Delta Kappan, 68,* 148–54.
Warren, W.J. (1988, December 21). Grouping students by ability comes under fire. *New York Times.* p. 8.

If the author of the source is not named, as is often the case with newspaper articles, move the title of the article to the first position in the citation. Everything else remains in the same position. Alphabetize by the first word of the title, not counting *A, An* or *The.* Keep in mind the following guidelines as you prepare your list of references:

1. List authors last name first, followed by initials.
2. Place the date of publication after the author's name, year first, then month, and for newspapers, date.
3. Capitalize only the first word of the title of the article.
4. Capitalize the initial letter of all the words in the title of the publica-

tion (except for articles, such as *a* or *the*, and prepositions), and underline it.

5. Include *p.* before page numbers in newspapers and magazines but not in journals. (The reason for this rule stumps us!)

6. Watch every comma and period. Make sure you put commas and periods in exactly the same places in your citations. Consistency is important.

MLA Format

The same two articles cited above by APA format are given below using the MLA format.

> Oakes, Jeannie. "Keeping Track, Part 2: Curriculum Inequality and School Reform." *Phi Delta Kappan* 68 (1986): 148–154.
> Warren, William J. "Grouping Students by Ability Comes Under Fire." *New York Times* 21 December 1988: II8.

Exercise A   As a class, play detective: see how many differences you can find between the APA system and the MLA system for listing periodicals and newspapers.

Exercise B   Correct the punctuation on the List of References at the end of the documented essay on page 195, according to APA rules.

EDITING

Final-Draft Editing

1. Exchange your essay with a partner. Proofread your partner's essay carefully looking for typographical, spelling, and mechanical errors. Put a pencilled check mark above the errors, but do not fix them. Return the essay.

2. Correct the errors your partner marked if you agree they are errors. If you are not sure, ask your partner. If you both have questions about possible errors, ask your teacher.

Postfinal-Draft Editing

Your teacher may have you revise a section of your essay or have you correct particular errors.

Handbook

I Grammar

WHY STUDY GRAMMAR?

Educated readers have certain expectations about how English sentences should look and sound based on grammatical conventions that they think are correct. When sentences do not meet these expectations, readers are often confused or annoyed. Writers who want such a reader to pay attention to their message must know and abide by these conventions. This is the major reason for knowing the fundamentals of standard English grammar. Another important reason is to give you and your teacher a common language in which to talk about sentences and style. Once you understand these fundamentals, they will become tools to use in order to spot problems and to edit your own sentences.

USING THIS HANDBOOK

This short handbook is not intended as a review of all English grammar. Rather, it is designed to teach some fundamentals that apply to your own writing. It begins with the basic grammatical structure of English sentences and then moves to more complex variations and to some problems that tend to arise as your writing becomes more sophisticated. You will be asked not only to do exercises that illustrate the points under discussion, but also to return to your own essays to look for the same problems and make corrections and revisions. In this way you will focus on those problems occurring in your own writing and will learn how conventional grammar contributes to the coherence of your writing.

I.1 VERBS AND SUBJECTS

It may seem that, like snowflakes, no two English sentences are exactly the same. Every sentence, unless the speaker or writer is purposely repeating exactly what someone else has said, is made up of different words in different arrangements from every other sentence. However, all English sentences are based on seven or eight underlying patterns that make them more alike than they appear on the surface. The most common of these is the **subject-verb pattern.** In all sentences in this pattern, the subject precedes the verb. This is the only pattern dealt with in depth in this handbook, not only because it is by far the most often-used pattern in writing, but also because it serves as the framework for much more sophisticated sentences.

The first thing you need to do to work with the subject-verb pattern is to be able to identify subjects and verbs in sentences. Since the verb is the heart of a sentence, we will begin with **verbs.**

Verbs

The Old Reliables

We will begin with a group of words that you can *always* count on being verbs, so we will call them the Old Reliables. Every time you see one of these words in a sentence, you can be sure that it is either the main verb or part of a verb phrase (these terms will be defined in more detail later). The list is short but is so important that you should memorize it.

am	is	are	was	were
has		had		
does		did		

Exercise A

Circle the verb in each of the following sentences:

*Some Rock History: Trivia and Otherwise**

1. Chuck Berry's only number one pop single was "Maybellene."

2. In spite of this, he is perhaps the most influential songwriter and guitarist in rock music.

3. James Brown's home town was Macon, Georgia.

4. Macon, Georgia, is also Little Richard's home town.

5. James Brown never had a number one record on the pop charts.

6. However, he had many hits at the top of the R&B and Soul charts.

7. Little Richard's last name is Penniman.

8. Marvin Gaye's last hit single was "Sexual Healing."

9. "Tutti Frutti," "Long Tall Sally," "Reddy Teddy," and "Rip It Up" were all originally Little Richard's songs.

10. The Beatles had two drummers before Ringo Starr.

11. They were Pete Best and Tommy Moore.

12. "Penny Lane," "Strawberry Fields," and "Abbey Road," all Beatles' titles, are all real places in Britain.

13. Influenced by Chuck Berry and other American rock greats, The Beatles did much to change the face of rock music.

14. Their musical innovations were the topic of discussion of classical as well as popular music critics.

15. Reggae artist Bob Marley's group was The Wailers.

16. Bob Marley and the Wailers did backup for Sly and the Family Stone on tour in the early seventies.

*Based on Editors of Consumers' Guide, *Rock 'n' Roll Trivia* (New York: Beekman House, 1985).

Exercise B

Fill in the blanks in the following sentences with the appropriate word from the list of Old Reliables:

1. "(I Can't Get No) Satisfaction" _____ the Rolling Stones' first hit in America.
2. "It's All Over Now" _____ their first British hit.
3. The Quarrymen, Johnny and the Moondogs, and The Silver Beatles _____ all former names of the Beatles.
4. Quincy Jones _____ more than 30 Grammys and Oscars to his name.
5. Frank Sinatra, Johnny Mathis, Ray Charles, and Michael Jackson _____ among the artists with whom Jones has worked.
6. Janis Joplin _____ a meteoric career.
7. Her trademark _____ the raw energy of her music.
8. Unfortunately, drugs _____ her downfall.
9. An overdose of heroin _____ the cause of her death in 1970.
10. Once considered the music of the young, rock now _____ loyal fans across the generations.

Action Verbs

You have often heard that verbs name an action. The next group of verbs you will study are **action verbs.** Since English has so many action verbs that you could not possibly memorize them all, you need to be able to recognize them by their three common characteristics.

1. The most obvious characteristic of action verbs is that **they state an action.**

The cow *jumped* over the moon.

It is easy to visualize the action of jumping, so it is clear that *jumped* is the verb in this sentence.

Some actions are more subtle.

Anna *smiled* ruefully at his joke.

Still, we can visualize a smile as an action that lips do, so we can understand why *smiled* is considered an action verb.

Some so-called actions cannot be seen at all.

The witness *considered* her response carefully.

It helps to think of verbs like *consider* as a *mental* action: something the brain is doing even through we cannot actually see the brain cells at work. Here are a couple more examples.

Cheryl *dreams* about a career as an astronaut.
Alex *thinks* about Maria day and night.

2. Another characteristic unique to verbs is that **their form or spelling can change to indicate changes in the time that an action occurred.**

Let us look again at the two sentences above as examples.

Cheryl *dreams* about a career as an astronaut.

We can change *dreams* to the past tense by changing the final letters of the word.

Cheryl *dreamed* about a career as an astronaut.

The action of dreaming happened sometime in the past. We call this form the **past tense** of the verb.

In like manner, *thinks* in the second sentence is in the *present tense*.

Alex *thinks* about Maria day and night.

The form *thinks* indicates that the thinking is happening right now, in the present. We call this form the **present tense** of the verb. We can change the spelling of the word to indicate that the thinking happened at sometime in the past.

Alex *thought* about Maria day and night.

Verbs change from present to past tense in two different ways. The first way is to change the verb ending to *-ed*. Verbs that form their past tense this way are called **regular verbs.** Here are a few examples:

walks	walked
plays	played
watches	watched
turns	turned
types	typed

The second way to change from present to past tense, illustrated by *thinks/ thought,* is a change in the spelling of the word. Verbs that change from present to past tense by changing spelling are called **irregular verbs.** Many common verbs are irregular. Here are a few examples, just to give you the idea.

teaches	taught
rides	rode
catches	caught
eats	ate
drinks	drank
runs	ran
shoots	shot
throws	threw
drives	drove

You can think of many more.

The simple present and past tenses described above are only two of the many kinds of changes that verbs can make to indicate the time that an action happens. Others will be discussed in more detail later.

You can use this information to test whether a word in a sentence is a verb. Try to change its form to a different tense. If you cannot make such a change, the word is not a verb. Try changing to the past tense any of the words in the sentence "Cheryl dreams about a career as an astronaut," and you will find that *dreams* is the only word that has a past tense form.

Verbs can take other endings besides the present tense -*s* or -*es* and the past tense -*ed*. They are -*es*, -*ing*, and -*en*. You need to know these endings because they help you spot verbs, but they are not foolproof signs of verbs. They can be used only as clues along with the other tests for verbs. Here are all of the verb endings:

-s   walk*s*
-es   wish*es*
-ing   walk*ing*
-ed   walk*ed*
-en   driv*en*

3. Another characteristic of verbs is that **they make sense if they are placed after the words he or they in a sentence.** Here is an example to show you how this feature can help you to identify a verb. The task is to find the verb in the following sentence:

In 1989 the Polish people elected their first non-Communist government in 44 years.

Put each word after *he* or *they*, one at a time:

They _____
(They *in*, They *1989*, They *the* . . .)

Whichever word makes sense when placed in the blank after *they* is the verb of the sentence.

You should study these characteristics of verbs until you know them very well. None of the three characteristics can by itself identify every verb, but used together, they should make it much easier for you to find most verbs in sentences.

Exercise

Circle the verb in each of the following sentences. If the verb is in the present tense, write *present* in the blank at the end of the sentence. If it is in the past tense, write *past* in the blank.

A Short History of Sports*

1. The ancient Greeks valued a sound body and mind. _____
2. Many of their myths tell tales of athletic prowess. _____
3. The Greeks invented the Olympic games. _____
4. At the height of the Greek Olympics, as many as 50,000 spectators watched the games. _____
5. The Greeks banned women from competition in sporting events. _____

*Based on Arthur R. Ashe, Jr., *A Hard Road to Glory*. (New York: Warner Books, 1988).

6. Many of the early Greek events still play an important part in modern Olympic games. _____

7. These include such events as boxing, wrestling, and foot races. _____

8. Another event, chariot racing, no longer exists as an Olympic event, for obvious reasons. _____

9. However, several events on horseback remain in the modern Olympics. _____

10. The original Olympics lasted for over 1,000 years, from 776 B.C. until A.D. 265. _____

Verb Phrases

So far all of the verbs you have identified have been single-word verbs. Now the task becomes even more complicated. Frequently, the verb in English sentences is made up of more than one word. Such multiple word verbs are called **verb phrases.**

The main job of a verb phrase is to pin down the time of the action more precisely than a single-word verb can. We will return to two familiar sentences for examples:

Alex *has been thinking* about Maria day and night ever since she broke up with him.

The verb phrase *has been thinking* tells us that the action of thinking started sometime in the past and is still going on now.

Cheryl *had dreamed* of becoming an astronaut for years before she submitted her application for space flight training.

The verb phrase *had dreamed* indicates that the action of dreaming both began and ended in the past.

Verb phrases are made of up two parts: **helping verbs** and a **main verb.** The helping verbs, which are the first words in the verb phrase, include all those in the list of Old Reliables plus a few more with which you will soon become familiar. The main verb can be either an action verb or one of the verbs on the Old Reliables list.

Students often have trouble deciding what is the last word of the verb phrase. Unfortunately, no hard and fast rules exist to tell you this, but here are some useful clues.

1. If there is an action word in the verb phrase, it is the last word of the phrase.

Charles <u>has been singing</u> in the church choir for twenty-five years.
            vp

2. If a verb in a verb phrase ends with *-ed* or *-en* (except *been*), it is the final verb of the phrase.

McEnroe and Lendl <u>have played</u> many tennis matches against each other.
            vp

Mel <u>had been bored</u> silly until Renee arrived.
        vp

The bird's cage <u>was cleaned</u> three times that day.
               vp

The Beatles <u>have been acclaimed</u> for their musical versatility.
              vp

All hope <u>was given</u> up for his safe return.
         vp

Karen <u>has eaten</u> two pizzas in the last hour.
      vp

3. Frequently, the last word of a verb phrase is separated from another word that looks like a verb by the little word *to*.

Florence <u>expected</u> *to* win the tournament.
         v

She <u>has expected</u> *to* win every tournament.
      vp

She <u>hoped</u> *to* score early in the match.
    v

Win and *score* are obviously action words, and they often are the main verb in a sequence. However, *when such a verb is directly preceded by* to, *it is never the main verb of the sentence.* It is a different kind of grammatical unit, called an **infinitive.** You do not need to remember the term *infinitive;* you just need to remember that an action word directly preceded by the word *to* is never the main verb of the sentence.

Exercise A

All of the sentences below contain verb phrases. Remember that any word on the Old Reliables list is part of the verb phrase. The sentences also include some additional helping verbs, which have been italicized to help you become familiar with them. Underline the entire verb phrase including any italicized helping verbs.

1. We had been waiting for Dick for three hours.
2. He was driving a 1965 Volkswagen Bug.
3. My mother had driven that car for twenty-five years.
4. Finally, Dick did arrive, safe and sound.
5. However, the Bug's engine was choking as if on its last breath.
6. At long last, Jerry has found a job.
7. He had *been* looking for at least three months.
8. He had lost hope more than once.
9. He *will be* working ten-hour shifts four days a week.
10. His four workdays *will be* followed by three days off.
11. He *will be* making good money.
12. I am expecting a phone call from my grandmother.
13. She is arriving from Memphis today.

14. She is planning to stay at least two weeks.

15. She has flown only once before in her life.

16. My doctor has advised me to diet.

17. She says I *have* gained too much weight.

18. So I am eating nothing but rabbit food.

19. I *have been* dreaming of steaks and chocolate cake every night for a week.

20. So far I *have* lost three pounds.

Exercise B

To become more familiar with helping verbs that are not on the Old Reliables list, copy down each of the italicized words in the sentences above.

Helping Verbs

Here is a fairly complete list of helping verbs, including the Old Reliables and some others.

Forms of to be

am   is   are   was   were   being   been   be

Forms of to have

has   have   had   having

Forms of to do

does   do   did   doing   done

Most of the verbs in the list above can serve as either helping verbs or the main verb in the sentence. Verbs in the *following* list will almost always be helping verbs. When you see one of these verbs in a sentence, you can be pretty sure that it is only the first word of a verb phrase. In order to identify the whole verb phrase, you need to keep looking for the main verb.

can	could
may	might
must	ought
shall	should
will	would

Exercise A

The following sentences might contain any of the kinds of verbs we have discussed so far. Underline the verb or verb phrase. If you have trouble spotting the verb, review all the information about verbs above and apply what you know to each sentence.

More Sports History

1. The Romans turned sports into something other than a mere game.

2. Athletes no longer competed for symbolic prizes like an olive wreath.

3. Instead, rich patrons would train slaves as gladiators.

4. The gladiators fought to the death as entertainment for the crowds.

5. From the fall of the Roman Empire to the 1800s, Europeans have had ambivalent emotions about sports.

6. Some religious groups have been convinced that they are sinful. (*Hint:* there is both a verb phrase and a single-word verb in this sentence.)

7. According to these groups, sports contributed to idleness.

8. Most Africans, on the other hand, never have had such ambivalent emotions about sports.

9. Traditionally, Africans have considered sports necessary to both physical and mental well-being.

10. Sports were important both as physical training for survival and as entertainment.

11. Sports also played a part in religious rituals.

12. Wrestling has always been very popular in Africa as well as Europe. (*Hint: Always* is not a verb. Try applying the tests for verbs to *always,* and you will find that it does not meet them. You will frequently find words that are not verbs inserted in the middle of a verb phrase—just one more thing to watch out for.)

13. Foot races, gymnastics, and other sports taught speed, endurance, and strength.

14. Archery was also used as part of a warrior's training.

Exercise B

Underline the verb or verb phrase.

Some More Rock History and Trivia

1. Marvin Gaye first recorded "I Heard it Through the Grapevine" in the 1960s.

2. It became a hit again in the 1980s in the film *The Big Chill.*

3. The generation of the 1980s also heard it on telephone and raisin commercials on TV.

4. Before her success as a vocalist, Roberta Flack had earned degrees in music and education from Howard University.

5. The Everly Brothers, popular in the late 1950s and early 1960s, were best known for their harmonizing.

6. Their style influenced several groups of the 1960s, including the Beatles, the Beach Boys, and Simon and Garfunkel.

7. Tina Turner has experienced many ups and downs in her career.

8. Her first hits were recorded with her then-husband Ike Turner.

9. Everyone thought that Ike had all the talent. (*Hint:* Did you catch two single-word verbs in this sentence?)

10. No one thought that Tina could be successful on her own. (*Hint:* This sentence has a single-word verb and a verb phrase.)

11. But through the mid-1980s Tina staged an impressive comeback.

12. Now over 50 years old, she is still recording successfully.

13. And her live performances still stun audiences.

14. She is doing very well on her own.

15. Her perseverance can serve as an example to others.

16. Robert Plant of Led Zeppelin has experienced much personal tragedy.

17. First, he was injured in a car crash in Greece in 1975.

18. Then, in 1977 his young son died of a viral infection.

19. Regardless of these events, Plant has continued to perform, both with the band and after the band's dissolution, solo.

20. Led Zeppelin's phenomenal hit "Stairway to Heaven" was never released as a single.

21. Though Pink Floyd is a British group, it took its name from two American blues artists, Pink Anderson and Floyd Council. (*Hint:* Did you spot two single-word verbs?)

22. Pink Floyd combined bleak lyrics with outstanding sound production.

23. Its live performances were spectacular light and sound shows.

Subjects

Identifying the Subject

The verb is half of the core of the subject-verb sentence pattern. The other half is, obviously, the **subject.** Every action, or verb, must have someone or something performing the action. The underlying logic is that an action does not happen by itself. Somebody or something performs the action. The subject of the sentence is the person or thing performing the action of the verb.

Let us return to our two overworked examples.

Alex thought about Maria day and night.

We know the verb is *thought.* Who is doing the thinking? The answer is Alex, so *Alex* is the subject of the verb *thought.*

Cheryl dreams about a career as an astronaut.

Who is doing the dreaming? Cheryl. So *Cheryl* is the subject of the verb *dreams.* Now let us look at an example of a *thing* as the subject of a verb.

Temperatures have climbed over 100 degrees for the past five days.

What is the verb phrase in this sentence? If you answered *have climbed,* you are right. What has climbed over 100 degrees? Temperatures. So *temperatures* is the subject of the verb phrase *have climbed.*

Here are some important steps for finding the subject of the verb:

1. Find the verb in the sentence.

2. Put the question words *who* or *what* before the verb.

Who thought?

Who dreams?

What has climbed?

3. The answer is the subject of the verb.

One more important clue for finding the subject: *In most English sentences the subject comes before the verb.* We will glance at a couple of exceptions below and then return to this common subject-verb pattern.

Question and "There" Sentence Patterns

At this point, you need to become aware of two common English sentence patterns besides the subject-verb pattern. The first is the **question pattern:**

Do **you** like licorice?
V S V

What is your favorite TV **program?**
    V   S

The second is the **"there" pattern,** which begins with *there.*

There are 50 **states** in the United States.
    V   S

There are 300 students in my chemistry lecture.
    V   S

In both of these patterns, the subject comes either between the verbs in a verb phrase or after the verb, not before the verb. We mention these patterns to point out that the subject-verb pattern is not the *only* English sentence pattern. However, students seldom run into trouble in their writing with either of these patterns, so we will virtually ignore them in this text. You simply need to know that if you do run into one of these patterns, you will not find the subject before the verb. Now let us return to the subject-verb pattern.

Nouns and Pronouns as Subjects

Two types of words that can serve as subjects are **nouns** and **pronouns.** Nouns, as you recall, are words that name persons, places, things, or ideas. Pronouns substitute for nouns. There are many different kinds of pronouns. We will consider only two of them here: **subject pronouns** and **demonstrative pronouns.** It is not important to know the terms *subjective* and *demonstrative,* but it is important to recognize the pronouns themselves. Here they are.

Subjective Pronouns

I   we
you
he, she, it   they

Demonstrative Pronouns

this   that
these   those

These words are very short and very common, so you might tend to overlook them. Remember, however, they may be playing the important role of subject in a sentence.

Exercise

Find the verbs in the following sentences. Underline them and label them with a *v.* Then find the subject. Circle it.

The Edmund Fitzgerald*

1. The *Edmund Fitzgerald* is legendary on the Great Lakes.

2. The ship sank almost without warning on November 10, 1975.

3. It was making its last voyage of the season. (*Hint:* What is the only word in the sentence that precedes the verb phrase?)

4. It left Superior, Wisconsin, on November 9 under threatening skies.

5. By the next day, the storm had blown into gale-force winds.

6. The captain radioed to another freighter on the lake.

7. However, he expressed no concern about immediate danger to ship or crew.

8. Only a few minutes later, the *Edmund Fitzgerald* disappeared from radar screens.

9. It was only 15 miles from Whitefish Bay, a safe harbor.

10. No one even received a distress call.

11. All 29 men of the crew were lost.

12. No bodies were ever recovered.

13. Searchers found very little wreckage.

14. Later, underwater divers discovered the wreckage.

15. The hull had broken in two.

16. Some terrific force must have caused the ship to break in two.

17. The second freighter made it safely to port.

*Based on Paige St. John (AP), "Grieving parents stare at film of shipwreck" p. A3, col. 5. *Salt Lake Tribune,* August 28, 1989, p. 3.

18. Fourteen years later, in 1989, technology provided a new way to study the wreck.

19. Researchers sent a robot submarine into the cold, murky depths of Lake Michigan.

20. It took the first clear pictures of the wreckage.

21. Scientists are hoping to learn the cause of the wreck from these pictures.

22. Canadian singer Gordon Lightfoot immortalized the wreck in a ballad.

23. The ballad was appropriately called "The Wreck of the *Edmund Fitzgerald*."

Multiple Subjects and Verbs in a Single Sentence

Most of the sentences in the exercises so far have had just one subject and one verb or verb phrase. However, it is common for a verb to have two or more subjects, for a subject to have two or more verbs, and for a single sentence to have two or more pairs of subjects and verbs. Here are some examples.

One Subject and Two Verbs

Alicia <u>had read</u> the drivers' manual and <u>had practiced</u> behind the wheel for hours.
   s   vp   vp

Two Subjects and One Verb

She and her **mother** <u>drove</u> to the drivers' testing center.
  s   s   v

Two Subject-Verb Pairs

After **Alicia** *took* the written test, **she** <u>climbed</u> into the pickup for the road test.
      s   v   s   v

Exercise

The sentences below might have just one subject and verb, or any combination of subjects and verbs. Underline the verbs or verb phrases and label them *v* or *vp*. Circle the subjects.

1. Sports historians generally agree that American football and rugby were born in England at the same time. (*Hint:* Do not quit looking after just one subject and one verb.)

2. It happened during a soccer game at Rugby School.

3. In the last minutes of the game, a frustrated player picked up the ball and ran across the goal line with it.

4. This move was, of course, completely illegal in soccer.

5. However, people liked it, so they invented a new game and called it Rugby.

6. In Rugby, players can run with the ball legally.

7. Rugby is the forerunner of American football.

8. The first American football game was probably played between Princeton and Rutgers on November 6, 1869.

9. Rutgers won.

10. Rutgers would not beat Princeton again in football for 69 years.

11. This early game looked very little like modern football.

12. For instance, a successful kick scored one "goal," and a touchdown scored no points.

13. A touchdown only gave the offense the opportunity for a kick.

14. Downs and yard lines did not exist.

15. Therefore, if the offense was willing to go scoreless, it could hold onto the ball for its entire half.

16. In 1881, Yale and Princeton did exactly this.

17. Both teams were undefeated when they met for the final game of the season.

18. Neither team wanted to give up their claim to the championship, so each team was happy with a 0–0 tie.

19. However, fans and many players were unhappy with this strategy.

20. Walter Camp came to the rescue.

21. He is known as the father of American football because he invented so many of its rules.

22. He proposed the concept of "downs."

23. Originally, teams were allowed three downs to advance the ball five yards.

24. From 1880 to 1900, Yale and Princeton had the best records in college football.

25. In those years, both schools won nearly 200 games and lost under 20.

26. Football reached the Midwest in the 1890s, and the rest is history.

Subject-Verb Agreement

Recognizing a Singular or Plural Subject

So far, we have described some of the basic features of English sentences. You are now ready to study some of the grammatical problems sentences cause for students. The first of these is subject-verb agreement. Various dialects of English have different rules about subject-verb agreement. To write acceptably in college, you need to know the rules of the dialect called Standard English.

When we first discussed verbs, we mentioned that -s and -es are two of the typical verb endings. They have a very special use. They go with a **singular subject.** A singular subject means that only one person or thing is doing the action. Look at these examples.

Lori *drives* too fast in school zones.
People usually *drive* too fast in school zones.
That copy machine *breaks* down daily.
Copy machines *break* down often.
Samuel *works* the morning shift.

Samuel and Anna *work* different shifts.
Samuel *watches* the children in the evening.
The children usually *watch* TV after homework.

When the subject is only one person or thing, the *-s* or *-es* ending is added to the verb. When the subject includes two or more people or things, the *-s* or *-es* is omitted. When we add or delete the *-s* or *-es* to the verb, depending on whether the subject is singular or plural, we are making the subject and verb **agree.**

Exercise

The first verb in each of the following sentences has a plural subject. In the second sentence, a singular subject is given. Complete the second sentence by changing the verb to the singular form and copying the rest of the sentence.

Examples

Bears hibernate in the winter.

A bear *hibernates in the winter.*

Children play hard from sunup to sundown.

Eddie *plays hard from sunup to sundown.*

1. Many musicians play several different instruments.
   Sting _____ .

2. Students often write as many as seven or eight long papers a semester in writing classes.
   Joanna _____ .

3. High-pitched tones hurt dogs' ears.
   A shrill whistle _____ .

4. Many modern painters use bright, clear colors.
   David Hockney _____ .

5. Some sports cause serious physical injuries.
   Football _____ .

6. Modern conveniences make life easier.
   A dishwasher _____ .

7. Physical activities strengthen muscles.
   Body conditioning _____ .

8. Sports provide a road to riches for a few good athletes.
   Basketball _____ .

9. Faucets leak.
   My kitchen faucet _____ .

10. Tenants talk to neighbors on the porch steps every evening.
    My mom _____ .

Is and Are

The present-tense forms of the very irregular verb *to be* can cause special problems. The plural form of the present tense is *are*.

Students *are* usually very poor.

The singular form is *is*.

Leonard *is* very poor.

Exercise

Insert a verb, either *is* or *are,* in the blank in the sentence. Write *S* or *P* in the blank to the left of the sentence to tell whether the subject is singular or plural.

_____   **1.** Roses _____ beautiful.

_____   **2.** This pink rose _____ beautiful.

_____   **3.** Plastic records _____ nearly obsolete.

_____   **4.** Tapes and compact discs _____ more popular.

_____   **5.** My baby _____ the cutest child in the world.

_____   **6.** Babies _____ often very demanding.

_____   **7.** This town _____ very different from my hometown.

_____   **8.** It _____ larger and friendlier.

_____   **9.** Cigarettes _____ bad for our health.

_____ **10.** My dog _____ a loveable mutt.

Subject-Verb Agreement with Intervening Phrases

Frequently, a subject is separated from its verb by other words or phrases. The verb must agree with the true subject, not with a word in an intervening phrase. Prepositional phrases cause the most trouble.

The electrical **wiring** in old houses is often dangerous.
           s   **v**

Even though the noun *houses* is closer to the verb than the noun *wiring, wiring* is the true subject of the verb. It is specifically the wiring that is dangerous, not necessarily whole houses. *Wiring* is singular, so it takes the singular form of the verb.

To find the true subject of a verb, you must be able to recognize **prepositional phrases.** Prepositional phrases begin with a preposition and usually end with a noun. Here is a list of common prepositions.

about	before	down	like	past
above	behind	during	near	through
across	below	except	off	to
after	beneath	for	on	under
against	beside	from	onto	underneath

along	between	in	out	until
among	beyond	inside	out of	up
around	by	into	over	with
at				

Exercise A

It has been said that prepositions name anything a plane can do to a cloud. The sketch on page 218 illustrates what we mean. What prepositions can you add?

Below are sentences containing prepositional phrases. In each sentence, draw a line *through* the prepositional phrase(s).

Example

American sports have been enriched ~~by the talents of men and women from various ethnic backgrounds.~~

1. Minority athletes in America have confronted many obstacles on the path to success in sports.

2. Every major sport has blocked black athletes from participation at some time in its history.

3. Football has been the most open of all major sports.

4. However, even professional football prohibited blacks from participation from 1934 to 1945.

5. Arthur Ashe has recorded the names of several black football players during the early years of college football (the 1890s).

6. Amherst, the University of Michigan, MIT, and Beloit College are among the first white schools that included black players on their teams.

7. Black colleges did not participate in intercollegiate sports in the early years because sports were too expensive.

8. In 1892, William Henry Lewis was the first black football player named to an All-American team.

9. He first played for Amherst and then for Harvard.

10. He became an assistant district attorney in Boston after graduation from Harvard Law School.

Exercise B

In the following sentences, the subjects are separated from their verbs by prepositional phrases. First, cross out the prepositional phrase. Next, find the subject and label it. Then fill in the blank with the correct form of the verb.

1. People in trouble _____ (needs, need) more than good advice.

2. The sandwiches in my lunch _____ (is, are) soggy.

3. The first page in all books _____ (is, are) the title page.

4. Paul McCartney of the Beatles _____ (is, are) possibly the most talented musician of the rock era.

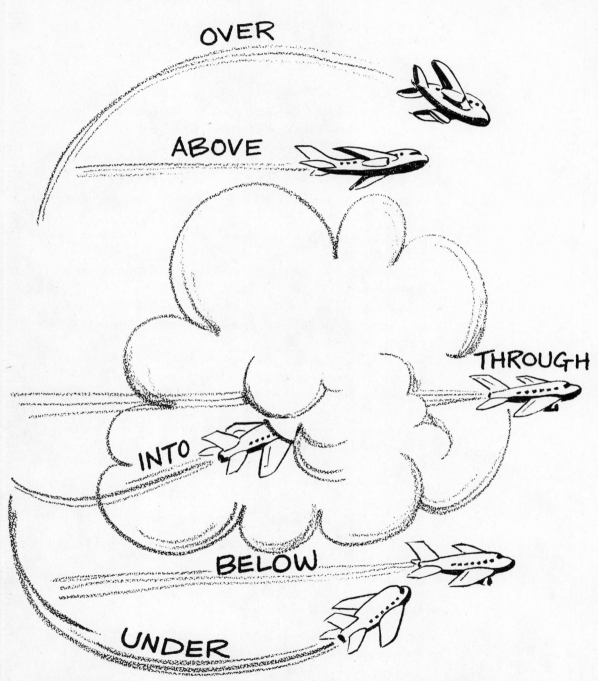

OVER

ABOVE

THROUGH

INTO

BELOW

UNDER

What other prepositions from the list on pages 216–217 could be added to the sketch?

5. The quality of the streets and water systems in many major cities _____ (is, are) declining.

6. The colors of the rainbow _____ (is, are) red, orange, yellow, green, blue, indigo, and violet.

7. The cost of four years of college education _____ (increases, increase) yearly.

8. The cats in my neighborhood _____ (kills, kill) all of the baby birds.

9. The sound of car security systems _____ (pierces, pierce) the stillness of the night.

10. My favorite color for cars _____ (is, are) deep red.

11. The safest color for cars _____ (is, are) bright yellow, because people can see it easily.

12. The cells of the bone marrow _____ (manufactures, manufacture) the red blood cells.

13. The course of most of the major rivers on the North American continent _____ (runs, run) from north to south.

14. The study of physics in the twentieth century _____ (has revolutionized, have revolutionized) peoples' thinking about the universe.

15. The best-known musician of the "outlaws" of country music _____ (is, are) Willy Nelson.

Indefinite Pronouns and Subject-Verb Agreement

Indefinite pronouns are another category of pronouns that cause trouble. Some indefinite pronouns take plural verbs and some take singular verbs. Some will not cause you any trouble when it comes to subject-verb agreement. This group includes words like

most   all   some   both

Here are some examples of these indefinite pronouns in use.

Most of the students at our college are commuters.
s   v

Most of the milk is sour.
s   v

The indefinite pronoun *most* is the subject of the verb in both sentences. Although *most* takes the plural in the first sentence and the singular in the second, you would never use the wrong verb ending because it just would not sound right.

Indefinite pronouns that end in *-one* or *-body* are a different story, however. They are grammatically singular even though they might clearly refer to more than one person. They take the singular form of the present tense verb.

Indefinite Pronouns Ending in -one	Indefinite Pronouns Ending in -body	Other Indefinite Pronouns
one		each
no one	nobody	either
anyone	anybody	neither
everyone	everybody	none
someone	somebody	

Each and *either* are singular because they do indicate just one. *Neither* and *none* mean zero, less than one, but we do not have a verb form to go with zero (fortunately), so we use the singular.

Here are two examples.

Everyone <u>likes</u> the food at Donny's.
   s   v

Anybody <u>is</u> capable of this job.
   s   v

The verbs are singular, so add the *-s* ending.

Indefinite Pronouns and Intervening Phrases

Indefinite pronouns cause even more trouble when they are separated from the verb by a prepositional phrase. Just remember the rule for subjects and verbs separated by prepositional phrases: *The subject of the verb is never located in a prepositional phrase.*

Everyone *except the employees* **likes** the food at Donny's.
   s   v

Except the employees is the prepositional phrase. The verb must still agree with its true subject, *everyone*.

Anybody *with any brains* **is** capable of this job.
   s   v

With any brains is the prepositional phrase. The verb must agree with its true subject, *anybody*.

Here are two more examples.

Neither *of us* **watches** TV anymore.
   s   v

One *of them* **talks** incessantly; the other is always silent.
   s   v

Exercise A

In each sentence cross out the prepositional phrase. Circle the true subject of the verb. Then write the correct form of the present tense of the verb in the blank.

   1. Most of my friends _____ (listens, listen) to heavy metal music.

2. Only one of my friends _____ (likes, like) country music.

3. One of my favorite groups _____ (is, are) Alabama.

4. Both of my pens _____ (is, are) out of ink.

5. Neither of my pencils _____ (is, are) sharpened.

6. One of us _____ (needs, need) a deodorant.

7. All of the players on the football team _____ (lifts, lift) weights for at least an hour a day.

8. Everybody from Minnesota _____ (loves, love) to brag about the cold.

9. Nobody in writing classes _____ (likes, like) grammar exercises.

10. None of the kindergarteners _____ (writes, write) yet.

Exercise B

Editing Your Own Essays: Subject-Verb Agreement: Review the essays you have written so far in this course. Has your instructor marked any errors in subject-verb agreement? If so, on a clean sheet of paper, copy over the sentences with the errors and correct them.

I.2   OBJECTS AND COMPLEMENTS OF VERBS

You are now familiar with the subject-verb sentence pattern and some of the grammatical problems that come with it. You need to learn about one more element that is often a part of this basic pattern. First, let us review a moment. In the typical subject-verb pattern, the subject always precedes the verb in the sentence.

Albert frowned.
  s   v

Sometimes, however, the subject and verb do not provide enough information by themselves to make the sentence sound like a complete thought.

My **dog** bit.
  s   v

We want to know whom or what the dog bit. The word that receives the action *bit* is called the **object** of the verb:

My **dog** bit the mailman.
  s   v

Here is another example.

That young **woman** is.
            s   v

In this example, we want to know who or what the young woman *is*. We call the word that supplies this information the **complement.** The complement is a word that comes *after* the verb and completes the meaning of the verb (notice the similarity between the words *complete* and *complement*). The complement either renames or describes the subject.

That young woman is a veterinarian.
     s   v   c

That young woman is smart.
     s   v   c

    You can think of subject, verb, and object or complement as the basic building blocks of the English sentence. In the next section of this text, you will be working with much more complicated sentences than the examples above, but you will see how they are all constructed around these four basic elements. For now, you will do some exercises to help get a good grasp of these basic elements.

Exercise A

In the sentences below, the subject, verb, object, and complement are all italicized. Label each italicized word by writing *s* beneath the subjects, *v* beneath the verbs, *o* beneath the objects, and *c* beneath the complements. The best way to figure out which is which is to find the verb first and then locate the subject (*before* the verb in the sentence) and the object or complement (*after* the verb). (*Hint:* None of these basic elements is ever found in a prepositional phrase. Your teacher might also have you cross out all of the prepositional phrases in the sentences below. If you do so, the basic elements of subject, verb, and object or complement will stand out more clearly.)

1. Acid *rain is* an international *problem*.
2. A *combination* of sulphur or nitrogen oxides with moisture in the air *makes* acid *rain*.
3. Acid *rain is* diluted *acid* falling from the sky.
4. *It kills forests* and *poisons lakes*.
5. *It* also *causes* lung *disease*.
6. Every *state* in the northeastern United States *produces tons* of sulfurous and nitrous pollutants every year.
7. The prevailing *winds carry* the *pollutants* straight to Canada.
8. The only *hope* for a solution to the problem *is* international *cooperation*.

Exercise B

The object or complement has been omitted from the following sentences. Make up an object or complement to complete the meaning of the sentence.

1. Benny licked _____ .
2. Ricky Henderson hit _____ .
3. My favorite rock group is _____ .
4. The very worst amusement park ride is _____ .

5. When I was downtown last night, I bought _____ .

6. You can pick out good apples at the store because they are _____ .

7. In his new outfit, Bao really looks _____ .

8. The post office sent _____ .

9. The boss gave _____ .

10. Letitia planted _____ .

I.3 MODIFIERS

Adjectives and Adverbs

When you add more words to the subject-verb-object or -complement sentence construction, you are adding **modifiers,** of which there are two types. **Adjectives** are modifiers that describe nouns and **adverbs** are words that primarily describe verbs. These modifiers restrict, increase, change, clarify, or refine the information in the basic subject-verb-object or -complement sentence. The rule for adding these modifiers is that both adjectives and adverbs should be placed next to the words they modify, but adverbs, unlike adjectives, can sometimes move around in a sentence. It is important to remember that English depends on word order to make sense. To be as graphic as possible about it, here is the framework upon which our language is ordered.

  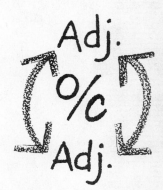

Note the relationships among sentence elements.

Single-Word Modifiers

Simple. Obvious. No problem. Well at least it seems so when we add single-word modifiers to a simple sentence.

The *noisy* kids are *quickly* eating *pepperoni* pizza.

Notice that we can move the adverb *quickly* around and the sentence still makes sense, but what about moving the adjectives *noisy* and *pepperoni*?

Exercise

First, read through the group of sentences below. Next, recopy the sentences on your own paper, adding single-word modifiers to each sentence in the group. Finally, circle the adjectives, and underline the adverbs.

Example

> The students left the courtyard.
> The students <u>unhappily</u> left the (sunny) courtyard.

Students and Teachers

1. The students walked into class.

2. They put their books down.

3. The teacher looked at the students.

4. The bell rang.

5. Harley sauntered to his desk.

6. Mr. Snodgrass pressed his lips together.

Notice that the less specific the subject and verb, the more adjectives and adverbs are needed to modify them.

Phrase Modifiers

We can also add more than single word modifiers to a sentence. Phrases, groups of words that lack either a subject or a verb, can also act as modifiers.

> The noisy kids **with poor table manners** are quickly eating pepperoni pizza **with their dirty fingers.**

Both of the highlighted phrases look alike in that each begins with a preposition and ends with a noun, but each acts differently in the sentence. The first acts as an adjective describing the kids (noun); the second acts as an adverb describing how the kids are eating (verb). We can add more modifying phrases to this sentence if we wish.

> **Screaming insults at each other,** the noisy kids with poor table manners are quickly eating pepperoni pizza.

This highlighted phrase, called a **present-participle phrase** or an **-ing phrase,** also describes *kids* (noun). In fact, *-ing* phrases always act as adjectives and thus describe nouns.

Notice also how this phrase is punctuated.

Comma Rule

When a long phrase begins a sentence, set it off with a comma. Whether or not to use commas when a phrase interrupts a sentence or comes at the end of a sentence varies. You will find an explanation of why this is so under Relative-Clause Modifiers later in this handbook.

Exercise

Return to the Students and Teachers sentences you wrote for the previous exercise and add modifying phrases to them. Put parentheses around the modifying phrases and label them as adjectives or adverbs.

Example

> The students left the courtyard.
> (Muttering to each other,) the students unhappily left the sunny courtyard.

You could continue to add modifying words and phrases to these sentences and the sentences would still be "correct," but after all, the point of using modifiers is to show more precisely the relationship between the basic parts (subject, verb, object or complement) of a sentence and not to overload the sentence with a confusion of modifiers.

Subordinate-Clause Modifiers

Besides adding modifying words and phrases to a sentence, also called a **main clause,** you may also add modifying clauses, known as **subordinate clauses.** Subordinate clauses explain or modify the action in the main clause and act as adverbs. They always begin with one of the following words, called **subordinating conjunctions,** which show the relationship between the subordinate and the main clause:

after	if, even if	when, whenever
although, even though	in order that	where, wherever
as	since	whether
because	so that	while
before	unless	until

After the subordinating conjunction come both a subject and verb and, perhaps, an object or complement.

> **Because they have played hard and missed their lunch,** the noisy kids with poor table manners are quickly eating pepperoni pizza with their dirty fingers.

or

> The noisy kids with poor table manners are quickly eating pepperoni pizza with their dirty fingers **because they have played hard and missed their lunch.**

This sentence with the highlighted subordinate clause and a main clause is called a **complex sentence** to distinguish it from a **simple sentence,** a sentence with just a main clause.

Notice that the subordinate clause can come before or after the main clause. Notice also the difference in punctuation between the two versions.

Comma Rule

When a subordinate clause comes before a main clause, set it off with a comma. When it comes after a main clause no comma is necessary.

Writers use complex sentences because they combine ideas to show their relationship more completely. This is important not only to writers, who must discover and communicate the relationship among their ideas, but also to readers, who must understand those relationships. For example, look at the extra dimension the subordinated clause adds to the main clause in our "pizza" sentence above: Readers seeing only the main clause,

> The noisy kids with the poor table manners are quickly eating pizza with their
> dirty fingers

would think poorly of the children and would probably assume that the writer had judged them unfavorably as well. With the addition of the subordinate clause,

> because they have played hard and missed their lunch

readers understand the reason behind the children's behavior in the main clause and also understand that the writer is not condemning the kids as much as explaining the circumstances behind, and thus the reasons for, their behavior. We understand all this because of the power of the subordinating conjunction *because!*
Combine the following simple sentences using subordinating conjunctions.

> John loves Marsha.
> Marsha loves Tom.

Explain the difference in emphasis and meaning each conjunction conveys. For example, what is the difference in emphasis between

> *Although* John loves Marsha, Marsha loves Tom.

and

> John loves Marsha *although* Marsha loves Tom.

What is the difference in *meaning* between

> *Because* John loves Marsha, Marsha loves Tom.

and

> John loves Marsha *because* Marsha loves Tom.

Now try using the subordinating conjunction *when.*

Complex Sentences in Your Own Writing

What we discover from this exercise is that combining sentences and subordinating one to another can yield a variety of meanings that simple sentences lined up like soldiers, one after the other, cannot possibly capture.

You can practice modifying your sentences throughout your whole writing process. For example, when you are trying to *invent* something to write, you might brainstorm, then look at your brainstorming list and begin adding modifying words and phrases to ideas on the list. Then you might combine one idea with another in a subordinated sentence, and so on. Many writers claim that this kind of "playing" can sometimes lead to new insights.

When you are trying to *revise* something you have already written, you might look at the places that seem incomplete to you, or where your instructor or group members have asked for more information or an explanation of unclear information. Then you might try to combine two ideas in your writing to show how one modifies or explains the other.

If you need to add more to what you have already written, you could pick sentences to expand by adding modifying words, phrases, and subordinate clauses.

Exercise

Go back to the two Students and Teachers exercises. To what you have already written, add subordinate clauses or combine the existing simple sentences into subordinate sentences. Circle the subordinating conjunction, and remember, punctuate your complex sentences correctly!

Example

Muttering to each other, the students unhappily left the sunny courtyard (when) the clock struck eight.

Relative-Clause Modifiers

Unlike a subordinate clause, which acts as an adverb and begins with a subordinating conjunction, a **relative clause** usually acts as an adjective and begins with one of the following **relative pronouns:**

who
whom
whose
which
that

Using relative clauses in your writing allows you to avoid unnecessary repetition as well as to combine closely related ideas.

Kids love to eat pizza. Pizza is a nutritionally good food for them also.

Since *pizza* occurs in both sentences, you can combine both by replacing the repeated word, a noun, with *which*.

Kids love to eat pizza, **which is also a nutritionally good food for them.**

Here is another example.

Politicians have a public relations problem with some voters. Politicians focus on their media images instead of issues.

Notice where the repeated word occurs in both sentences. Now note the revision.

Politicians, **who focus on their media images instead of issues,** have a public relations problem with some voters.

These sentences are now complex sentences, not because they contain a subordinate clause, but because they contain a *relative* clause.

Although you probably noticed that the relative clauses in the sample sentences were set off with commas, the comma rule for punctuating relative clauses is more complicated than that. Look at the relative clause, set off with commas, in the previous example again. Now look at what happens when the relative clause is *not* set off with commas.

Politicians **who focus on their media images instead of issues** have a public relations problem with some voters.

Do you see the difference in meaning? The sentence with commas implies that *all* politicians focus on their media images instead of issues. The sentence without commas implies that only *some* politicians focus on their media images instead of issues.

Comma Rule

Whether you use commas to set off relative clauses depends on the meaning of the information within your sentences.

This rule applies to phrases as well.

Exercises

1. Review and write down the comma rules for punctuating phrases and clauses.
2. In the essay you are now writing, find and label or compose and label two sentences illustrating each rule.

Editing Your Own Essays: Commas

Look through your essays. If your instructor has pointed out comma errors, find them and fix them. On a separate sheet of paper, write the sentence with the error and then write the corrected version. Attach this exercise to the original essay and turn them in.

I.4   ERRORS IN SENTENCE STRUCTURE

Even when writers have a good working knowledge of the framework of English sentence structure, they can sometimes make errors. Here is an abbreviated discussion of some commonly made errors.

Fragments

When writers forget that phrases and subordinate and relative clauses are modifiers and not independent sentences, they sometimes make errors called **fragments,** groups of words that cannot stand on their own as complete sentences.

Phrase Fragments

There are three major kinds of phrase fragments.

1. *-Ing* (or present-participle) fragments

   The lost child cried. **Not knowing how to get home.** She tried to find a police officer. (fragment)

   To fix the fragment, attach it to the appropriate word in the sentence before or after it.

   Not knowing how to get home, the lost child cried. She tried to find a police officer. (corrected)

   or

   The lost child cried. **Not knowing how to get home,** she tried to find a police officer. (corrected)

2. *-ed* (past-participle) fragment

   Exhausted from studying so hard. Roman slept for 14 hours. (fragment)

   Exhausted from studying so hard, Roman slept for 14 hours. (corrected)

3. *to* or *in order to* + verb (infinitive) fragment

   Toby baked more cookies for the party than he needed. **To (in order to) be on the safe side.** (fragment)

    Because *to* or *in order to* + verb (infinitive) phrases act as adverbs, they can move around in the sentence.

   To (in order to) be on the safe side, Toby baked more cookies for the party than he needed. (corrected)

   or

   Toby baked more cookies for the party than he needed **to (in order to) be on the safe side.** (corrected)

Exercise

Fix the following fragments.

1. Joe had not eaten all day. Feeling faint with hunger. He stumbled into the deli.

2. Priscilla tried to wake the household. She broke her knuckle. Banging on the door.

3. Spike hollered at his friend. Fighting his way out of the crowd. (*Hint:* How will your choice of where you attach this fragment determine the sentence's meaning?)

4. The dog ran after the sheep, Jumping over the fence.

5. Running to answer the phone, Grace stepped on the cat.

6. Frightened by the dog, The toddler cried for help.

7. Teresa turned pale. Stunned by the news of the accident.

8. The city looked beautiful. Blanketed with new-fallen snow.

9. Hanging onto the rope and scared to death, Josh balanced on the edge of the cliff.

10. Sonia fell asleep, Watching TV.

11. I don't care what she said. To tell you the truth.

12. Jaime stayed home today, To avoid the traffic problems caused by the snowstorm.

13. Karim has unreasonable expectations, **For example,*** assuming his new baby will walk and talk by nine months.

14. Gabriella likes many things about school. **Especially** having lunch, recess, and a free study period.

15. My car has its disadvantages. **Such as** starting only in warm weather.

Clause Fragments

There are two kinds of clause fragments.

1. subordinate-clause fragments

   Jan loved that dog. **Because he was so feisty.**

   To fix this fragment, you must first recognize subordinate conjunctions (review your list, page 225), and then know how to attach the subordinate clause to the main clause (review how to punctuate complex sentences, pages 226–228).

   Jan loved that dog **because he was so feisty.**

2. relative-clause fragments

   Angelo is always late. **Which makes me angry.**

   I always like cake. **That has double fudge frosting.**

   Of all the relative pronouns, *which* and less frequently *that* most often introduce a fragment. To fix the fragment, you must first recognize relative pronouns (review your list, page 227), and then how to attach the relative clause to the main clause (review the comma rule, page 228).

   Angelo is always late, **which makes me very angry.**

   I always like cake that has double-fudge frosting.

---

*Whenever you use these boldfaced words, *for example, especially, such as,* as well as the words *also, except, including,* make sure they are attached to a complete sentence because the information following them is often a fragment.

Exercise

Fix the following fragments:

1. I dream of staying in bed on cold winter mornings. When I know I have to get up.
2. Jackie works out after school and before work. Whenever she gets the chance.
3. Jeff can be loud and vulgar. After he has too much to drink. Which does not happen very often.
4. Wherever you are. That is where I want to be.
5. Since Andrea applied for the modeling job. Which everybody doubts that she will get. She spends all her time looking at herself in the mirror.
6. Although some people wear expensive clothes. They often cannot really afford them.
7. Until we stop illegally dumping toxic wastes into the ocean. Our beaches will be hazardous to our health.
8. If the baby goes to sleep. His mother will get to do some writing. Which will keep her from failing her writing class.
9. Unless Gus eats six small meals a day. He gets sick.
10. We have our money spent. Before we even get our paychecks. Which are too small in the first place.

Editing Your Own Essays: Fragments

Look through the essays you have written for this class. If your instructor has indicated that you have written fragments, find them and fix them. On a separate sheet of paper, write down the fragment. Then write down the corrected sentence. Finally, turn in this exercise attached to the essay(s).

Misplaced Modifiers

When writers forget that adjectives and adverbs, whether words or phrases, should be placed next to the word they modify, they make errors called **misplaced modifiers.**

Quietly, I heard the baby crying for ten minutes before he began to scream.

To fix this sentence, ask whether the adverb *quietly* should modify *heard* or *crying*. The most logical version seems to be

I heard the baby **quietly** crying for ten minutes before he began to scream.

Here is another example.

The toddlers played, ignoring their mothers **in the sandpile.**

To fix this sentence, ask what word, if not *mothers*, this prepositional phrase should really modify.

The toddlers played in the sandpile, **ignoring their mothers.**

Now what? Is the sandpile ignoring their mothers? No.

Ignoring their mothers, the toddlers played in the sandpile.

Remember, place the modifying phrase as close as possible to the word it modifies.

Exercise

Fix the misplaced modifiers in the following sentences:

1. Cheerfully, I heard my husband talk about his wonderful day while I lay miserable and sick in bed.
2. Softly, Jill heard Bill walking up the stairs.
3. I spent $100 on the shirt that I bought yesterday with the rhinestone buttons.
4. Flooding over the bridge, Dan saw the water from the dam.
5. Lilly bought the dress displayed in the store window with the plunging neckline and the slit skirt.
6. Scurrying over his salad, Kevin saw a cockroach.
7. The guest speaker will talk about Satanism at the Catholic Church.
8. Rolling down the hill, Steve dodged the massive boulder.
9. The murderer was a fat man with long red hair, weighing 300 pounds.
10. As a little boy, Julia talked about knowing her husband.

Editing Your Own Essays: Misplaced Modifiers

Go through the essays you have written for this class. If your instructor has noted that you have written misplaced modifiers, find them and fix them. On a separate sheet of paper write down your original sentence followed by your corrected sentence. Attach this exercise to the essay and turn in both.

I.5   FUSED SENTENCES AND COMMA SPLICES

The Need for Conjunctions

When writers forget that they can use certain words called **conjunctions** to combine sentences, they make errors called **fused sentences** or **comma splices:**

Autumn is here the leaves are changing color.   (fused)
Autumn is here, the leaves are changing color.   (comma splice)

There are a number of ways to fix fused sentences and comma splices.

1. Make separate sentences out of the clauses. (This method is the least effective. If the writer had wanted the ideas separated, she or he would not have put them together in the first place.)

2. Make one clause a subordinated clause. This is a very effective way of fixing the error.

3. Combine the clauses with a comma and a **coordinating conjunction** (and, but, or, nor, for, so, yet). Unlike subordinating conjunctions, which combine clauses that have an unequal relationship, coordinating conjunctions combine, or coordinate, clauses of equal importance. Depending upon how much emphasis you wish to give to each clause, this is an effective way of fixing the error.

4. Combine the clauses with a semicolon (;). A semicolon takes the place of a comma plus a coordinating conjunction. This is an effective way of fixing the error if the relationship between the clauses is so close that a period would be too strong a break and so clear that a coordinating conjunction is not necessary to clarify that relationship.

5. Combine the clause with a semicolon and a **conjunctive adverb,** followed by a comma, to show a relationship between sentences that remain two separate clauses. Conjunctive adverbs are connective words other than conjunctions.

Here is a list of the most common conjunctive adverbs.

therefore	however
nevertheless	consequently
furthermore	then
afterward	thus

Here are examples of their use.

Ricky often stays up late; **nevertheless,** he is always on time for his early morning class.
Laura often babysits for their family; **however,** she does not babysit for the neighbors.

Not all of these strategies are equally effective in every sentence. Which words you choose will vary according to the logic of the sentence. Which of the following is the most logical revision of the comma splice below and why?

Autumn is here, the leaves are changing color.

1. Autumn is here because the leaves are changing color.

2. Autumn is here, so the leaves are changing color.

3. Autumn is here; the leaves are changing color.

4. Autumn is here; therefore, the leaves are changing color.

Exercise

Fix the following fused sentences and comma splices using the methods outlined above. Feel free to change the order of the clauses in each sentence if you wish, and be sure to pick the most appropriate method of fixing the errors.

1. We are a nation of consumers; *consequently,* we do not always have the money to pay for what we buy.

2. Many people are more concerned about keeping up appearances than saving their money they spend money to look outwardly prosperous.

3. Young couples from middle-class families cannot afford to buy homes, *because* they will probably never have the money their parents had.

4. Those with houses might not be able to afford to fix their plumbing; they will paint and wallpaper their bathrooms and kitchens instead.

5. The plight of the poor is much worse; nobody wants to think about that, especially those who have enough money to live comfortably.

6. Some of the newly poor sink into despair; *however,* others learn to live gracefully with only the bare necessities. Some, who have lost jobs, enjoy having free time, but only if they have enough money for food and shelter.

7. Maybe we should all learn to trade service for service; *therefore* de-emphasizing the importance of money might be a good idea, *thus* having friends is a good way to make this idea work.

8. Unlikely as it may sound, *nevertheless,* having friends to depend on may be better than having family, for some families having children means becoming poorer and poorer.

9. Single mothers and their children suffer the most from poverty; some mothers who work can afford day care, *but* then they must worry about the safety and psychological well-being of their children.

10. The number of children living in poverty is rising; *consequently* it is already higher than for any other group. Some people blame irresponsible parents, *which* that does not help the situation.

Editing Your Own Essays: Fused Sentences and Comma Splices

Look through the essays you have written for this class. If your instructor has noted that you have written fused sentences or comma splices, find the errors and fix them. On a separate sheet of paper write down the incorrect sentence and then the corrected version. Turn in this exercise attached to the original essay.

Fused Sentences and Comma Splices with Pronouns

Sometimes fused or spliced sentences occur because writers do not recognize that pronouns, specifically personal and demonstrative pronouns (see the list on page 212), can be the subject of a sentence.

Erin likes to play volleyball it is one of her favorite sports.   (fused)
Erin likes to play volleyball; it is one of her favorite sports.   (corrected)

Exercise

Fix the fused sentences and comma splices below. Circle the pronoun that is a subject in each of the sentences.

1. Andrew's football team lost the game; it was a heartbreaker to lose.

2. Carmen wants to go to Disneyland, that is her only wish in the world she constantly begs her parents to take her.

3. Looking for a parking space close to his classroom, James circles the parking lot for 45 minutes everyday, this has been going on for weeks he is frequently late for class.

4. Becky just spent $150 dollars on a pair of dress shoes, *therefore* those are the only new shoes she can have for five years, according to her mother.

5. Writers should be prepared to repeat stages of their writing process many times and write at least two drafts of their papers, these are the steps that will yield well-written essays. *therefore*

Other errors occurring with pronoun use are problems with reference and agreement.

I.6 PRONOUN ERRORS

Pronoun Reference

Pronouns present special problems in writing. They can cause straightforward errors (as in the exercise above), or they can cause problems that interfere with the reader's understanding. Because they are so important, we will spend some time studying the conventions of pronoun usage.

The two kinds of pronouns that cause most problems for students are **personal pronouns** and **demonstrative pronouns.**

Here is a list of some important personal pronouns in English.

I, me
you
he, she, it, him, her
we, us
they, them

Here, again, are the demonstrative pronouns.

this, that
these, those

You will remember that pronouns *replace* nouns in sentences. Here is an example of what this means.

Although Alicia was very worried about her drivers' test, *she* passed *it.*

Imagine this sentence if the English language did not have such a category of words as pronouns.

Although Alicia was very worried about Alicia's drivers' test, *Alicia* passed the *test.*

Do you see that *she* in the first instance replaced the noun *Alicia?* In the same way, *it,* a pronoun, replaced the noun *test.*

You can also see that pronouns can prevent a lot of boring repetition. However, there is a catch. Readers must be able to figure out which noun a pronoun has replaced. If they cannot, they will be confused.

Read the following sentence:

> Martin stared at the painting for a long time. *It* reminded *him* of the small mid-
> western town where *he* grew up.

What noun in the first sentence does each of the italicized pronouns in the second sentence replace? In this sentence, you have no trouble figuring out which noun each pronoun replaces. The noun that the pronoun replaces is called its **antecedent.** The antecedent should be stated explicitly in the previous sentence or in the same sentence as the pronoun to prevent confusion for the reader.

> The car knocked over the fence. *He* was very angry.

What noun does *he* replace? We are not sure, because there is no antecedent stated anywhere in the previous sentence. The writer probably means the owner of the fence but might mean the driver of the car. Confusion like this is corrected by removing the pronoun and writing the noun back in.

> The car knocked over the fence. The farmer was very angry.

Here is a slightly different example.

> Joy told Ellen that the boss was angry with her.

This time, the antecedent appears in the sentence. It is either Joy or Ellen. But the reader is still confused, because it is not clear which of the two women is the recipient of the anger. In this case, the entire sentence needs to be rewritten to make the reference clear.

> Joy, still pale and trembling, told Ellen that the boss had just yelled at her.

Details have been added to make it clear that Joy was the person with whom the boss was angry.

Here is one more example.

> My favorite TV channel is MTV. *This* makes my dad very mad.

What is the antecedent of *this?* MTV? The fact that I watch MTV? The fact that it is my favorite channel? The demonstrative pronouns, *this, that, these,* and *those,* do the same job as other pronouns: they replace a noun. If the noun they have replaced is not explicitly stated, the reader will be confused. The specific antecedent of a demonstrative pronoun is a particularly difficult problem to deal with. Usually when the antecedent of a demonstrative pronoun has been omitted, the entire sentence must be rewritten to avoid using the pronoun:

> My favorite TV channel is MTV, but my dad gets mad when I watch it because
> he hates rock music.

Exercise

The following sentences are first printed as a paragraph so that you can see how the sentences are supposed to fit together, but they do not really fit very well because of the errors in pronoun reference. Then the paragraph is broken up into individual sentences with the pronouns underlined. If you can locate the antecedent of the underlined pronoun, write the antecedent in the blank following the sentence. (*Hint:* The antecedent may be in the previous sentence.) If the antecedent is not clear, rewrite the sentence containing the pronoun to clear up the confusion.

Commuter students face very different problems from students who live on campus. For one thing, they have to spend extra time finding parking on or near campus. This is often very difficult. They may spend as much as two or three hours of their precious time traveling from home to school. If their car breaks down, they may have to miss class while they fix it. This can be very expensive. Those who ride public transporation are at the mercy of transit schedules. It is often unreliable. They have breakdowns, too. It may also mean that they do not have time to meet with professors after class or to study in the library. Commuter students usually think that they have a tougher life than students who live on campus.

1. Commuter students face very different problems from students who live on campus. For one thing, <u>they</u> have to spend extra time finding parking on or near campus. Antecedent: *Commuter students*. Or, rewrite: _____
_____

2. <u>This</u> is often very difficult. Antecedent: *parking*. Or, rewrite: _____
_____

3. <u>They</u> may spend as much as two or three hours of their precious time traveling from home to school. Antecedent: _____ . Or, rewrite: _____
Commuter students

4. If their car breaks down, <u>they</u> may have to miss class while <u>they</u> fix it. Antecedents: _____ , _____ . Or, rewrite: _____

5. <u>This</u> can be very expensive. Antecedent: _____ . Or, rewrite: _____
which can be very expensive.

6. <u>Those</u> who ride the public transportation are at the mercy of transit schedules. Antecedent: _____ . Or, rewrite: *The commuter students who ride the public transportation are at the* ...

7. <u>It</u> is often unreliable. Antecedent: _____ . Or, rewrite: _____
which are often unreliable

8. <u>They</u> have breakdowns, too. Antecedent: *public* . Or, rewrite: _____
_____

9. <u>It</u> may also mean that <u>they</u> do not have time to meet with professors after class or to study in the library. Antecedent: _____ . Or, rewrite: _____

_____

10. Commuter students usually think that <u>they</u> have a tougher life than students who live on campus. Antecedent: ~~students~~ Or, rewrite: _____

_____

Editing Your Own Essays: Pronoun Reference

Review the essays you have written so far. Has your teacher marked any errors in pronoun reference? If so, on a clean sheet of paper, copy over the sentence preceding the error and the sentence with the error. Then revise so that the pronoun reference is clear.

Pronoun Agreement

As subjects must agree with their verbs, so pronouns must agree with their antecedents. Recall that in grammar there are three persons, first, second, and third; and two numbers, singular and plural.

First Person

I, me (singular)
we, us (plural)

Second Person

you (singular and plural)

Third Person

he, him, she, her, it (singular)
they (plural)
any noun (singular or plural)
any indefinite pronoun (singular or plural, see page 220 to review the list)

Writers who have mastered subject-verb agreement will have very little trouble with pronoun-antecedent agreement. We need to review only a couple of errors with pronoun-antecedent agreement that commonly occur in practice. The first is unnecessary shifts in number.

Unnecessary Shifts in Number

Shifts from third-person singular to third-person plural are very common errors. Although nouns such as *person, teacher, doctor,* are grammatically third-person singular, they are often understood to be plural in context (in their sentence) when they refer to any, and not a specific, person, teacher, or doctor. Look at the following example:

A **teacher** (third-person singular, but in context it refers to any and all teachers) is often blamed for students' failures, but **they** (third-person plural, consistent with the sense of the sentence, but grammatically incorrect) are not always praised for students' successes.

We can revise this sentence in two ways.

A **teacher** is often blamed for students' failures, but **she or he is** (note the change in verb to agree with a singular subject!) not always praised for students' successes.

or

Teachers are often blamed for students' failures, but **they** are not always praised for students' successes.

Many writers prefer the second revision of this sentence because it does not focus on gender. In the first revision, to avoid gender bias writers should use *she or he*.

Unnecessary Shifts in Person

Another pronoun-reference error is unnecessary shifts in person. Shifts between second-person and third-person are very common errors because we can talk about people in general in either the second or third person:

You (second person) should never be late, but sometimes **you** cannot help it.

or

One (third person) should never be late, but sometimes **one** cannot help it.

Both these sentences mean exactly the same thing, so sometimes as we write, we unconsciously shift back and forth between the second and third person and make this common error.

One should never be late, but sometimes **you** cannot help it.

Remember, use either *one* or *you* but not both in the same sentence.

Exercise A

Circle the pronouns in each sentence. Then correct the faulty pronoun shifts in number or person.

1. When a person is late for class, they miss important information that you really cannot make up.

2. One should not impose on others, but you can always borrow a classmate's notes if you are late for class.

3. One should take their studying seriously.

4. Nobody should have to spend their time doing meaningless work.

5. Everyone has a right to their privacy.

6. You can find many bargains at sales, but one usually has to spend a lot of time looking for them.

7. When a lawyer loses a case, they do not always receive prompt payment from their client.

8. One of the basketball players broke their arm. (*Hint:* Identify the prepositional phrase first.)

9. Everyone should participate in class unless you plan to avoid learning and want to earn a poor grade.

10. Anybody with any patience can learn to write if they practice at it as they would if they were trying to learn a new sport or a new dance.

Exercise B

Use all you have reviewed in this section about pronoun usage to fix any problems with faulty pronoun reference and agreement that you can find in the following paragraph from Joshua's expository essay draft in Chapter 8. Begin by first circling all the pronouns and their antecedents. Write the correct pronoun in the margin next to the appropriate line.

Alcohol commercials use a variety of ways to influence the viewer. We view comedians, pro-athletes, movie stars, and even in the case of the Bartyle and James commercial, we see older men who represent ordinary and simple people. For example in the Budweiser commercial they use a dog, called spuds (the party animal), to illustrate fun times and partying; there are people gathered around a pool, laughing, dancing, and singing. People are socializing and being accepted. The viewer sees this as inticing and fun, sending messages to our mind that if you drink you will have fun and be accepted also, however this is not the case if you have ever gone to a party, they usually turn out quite differently. There are other commercials that display masculinity. Joe Piscipo plays the part of a muscle man, who shakes a guys hand so hard that his arm rips out of socket. This also sends a message to our subconscious minds, that it is funny and you wish you were strong and rough as him. In the Bartyle and James commercials as stated before, appeal to us because they are viewed as being ordinary and common older men that are selling a great product. So you see that all these commercials have alot of things in common they are funny, full of excitement, and showing that drinking is all fun and games, what they don't show is the thousands of people killed in accidents related to alcohol.

Editing Your Own Essays: Pronoun Errors

Look through your own essays. If your instructor has marked any pronoun errors in your papers, find them and fix them. First, on a separate sheet of paper write the incorrect sentence, then the corrected sentence. Attach the exercise to the original essay(s) and turn them in.

II Beyond Grammar: Strategies for Coherence

As you have worked your way through this text, you have learned that on the largest scale, an essay is unified if it makes a point to a particular audience and has subpoints supporting that major point. You have also learned that an essay is well developed if it has appropriate and adequate evidence supporting its subpoints. Additionally, you have learned that an essay is coherent if readers can follow the connection between your ideas from sentence to sentence and paragraph to paragraph throughout the essay. As you recall, you created coherence in your narrative essay by organizing your material chronologically, and you created coherence in your advertisement analysis by organizing your material spatially, that is describing and analyzing the logical sequence of what you saw first, second, and so on. Also, you created coherence in your product names essay by classifying specific information into broader and related categories.

You have practiced these strategies of coherence, and more, within the context of the specific writing assignment of each chapter. While it is true that effective coherence must grow out of the demands of each paper's subject, it is also true that identifying, separating, and defining particular writing techniques creates a common vocabulary among writers that can help you to recognize, talk about, and direct your writing and editing processes.

This section of the Handbook reinforces what you have already practiced by identifying, defining, and giving further examples of five common techniques for coherence.

1. using parallel structures within sentences
2. repeating words or replacing them with pronouns
3. using transitional words and phrases
4. using synonyms for, or a different grammatical structure of, the same word
5. using a general categorizing word to encompass a number of specifics

We will begin with sentence coherence.

II.1 SENTENCE COHERENCE: PARALLEL STRUCTURE

You are already familiar with some techniques for achieving sentence coherence. When you studied phrases and clauses as modifiers earlier in the handbook (pp. 224–228), you were working on making the *relationships* among ideas in the sentence clear to your reader. This is what we mean by **sentence coherence.** In this section, we will deal with another technique for achieving sentence coherence, **parallel structure.** Parallel structure comes into play when we need to put two or more equally important ideas into a single sentence. We call the resulting list a **series,** and we separate the items in it by commas.

My favorite cities are *Quebec, New York, Boston, and New Orleans.*
My dog *chewed up my best shoes, ate my only houseplant, and knocked over
    the floor lamp.*

Now look at the following famous sentences:

To be or not to be, that is the question.
Friends, Romans, countrymen, lend me your ears.
I came, I saw, I conquered.

One of the reasons that these quotations are so well remembered is, believe it or not,
their grammatical structure. In each sentence, two or more ideas in a series are conveyed by the same grammatical structure: in the first sentence by the *to* verbs, in the
second by a series of nouns, and in the third by a repeated subject and verb. Repetition
of the same grammatical structure to indicate that the ideas are equally important is
called parallel structure. Using parallel structure is another way to achieve coherence
in writing.

Famous speakers and writers are not the only ones to use parallel structure in
their sentences. We should all use parallel structure when we are naming a series of
ideas of equal importance.

Exercise

Rewrite the sentences below, making the ideas in the series parallel.

Example

I woke up with *a sore throat, feeling sick to my stomach, and muscles that ached.*
I woke up with a sore throat, sick stomach, and aching muscles.

1. The restaurant where I work serves *low-fat main dishes, vegetables that are
   fresh, and uses little salt.*

2. When I first started checking at the grocery store, I thought I would never
   learn *the difference between a rutabaga and a turnip, how to tell a casaba
   from a persian melon, or different green apples like Granny Smith and golden
   delicious.*

3. This weekend I *have to study for my physics exam, my essay for writing class
   has to get written, and I work all day Sunday.*

4. People always told me my mother was beautiful. She had *dark brown eyes,
   hair that was long, black, and shiny, and her skin was glowing.*

5. The most important things in the world to me are *my children and getting
   my degree.*

6. As we near the end of the twentieth century, I find myself *looking back on
   major historical events in this country, the most important things that were
   invented, and how international relations have changed.*

7. The major events of the twentieth century will probably be *World War I, the*

Great Depression, fighting World War II, the Cold War, and how Eastern Europe changed beginning in 1989.

8. Major inventions include the *rocket, television, penicillin, the birth control pill, and dropping the atomic bomb.*

9. I often wonder whether the twentieth century has been *one of progress, or whether we really became more barbaric, or if we came out even.*

10. I also wonder whether the countries of *South America, Central America, and Mexico, the United States, and Canada* will ever learn to cooperate with each other.

Editing Your Own Essays: Parallel Structure

Review your own essays. Has your teacher marked errors in parallel construction? If so, on a clean sheet of paper, copy the sentences with errors. Then rewrite each sentence, correcting the errors in parallel structure.

II.2   PARAGRAPH COHERENCE

To get from a coherent sentence to a coherent essay, you must be aware of some characteristics that give paragraphs coherence. Of course, you have already learned ways to develop coherent paragraphs within the context of your essay assignments, but here we will review and generalize about strategies writers can use to ensure coherence within and among their paragraphs.

Transitional Words and Phrases for Coherence

Among the many devices that writers can use to contribute to coherence within and among paragraphs are transitional words and phrases, including conjunctive adverbs and conjunctions. This way of providing coherence is the most obvious and easily used. To review, here is a list of the most commonly used transitions.

Causal Connections: I went to bed [because] it was late.

because	hence	necessarily
since	consequently	for
whenever	accordingly	meanwhile
therefore	as a result	if . . . then
thus		

Time Connections: You should talk to me [before] the paper is due.

when	since	as soon as
before	whenever	afterward
until	after	at last
while	till	meanwhile

Transitions That Erase Whatever Has Come Before Them: I love you, [but] I cannot stay.

but	and yet	nonetheless
yet	even so	nevertheless
however	still	

Transitions That Erase What Comes After Them: [Although] I love you, I cannot stay.

although	even if	notwithstanding that
even though	supposing that	in spite of the fact that

Comparisons by Analogy

similarly	as though	as
likewise	like	in the same way that
such as		

Comparisons by Contrast

in contrast	on the contrary	on the other hand

Example Markers

:	for instance	in fact
for example	to illustrate	for one thing
such as	in other words	

Sequence Markers by Numbers

one, two . . .   first, second, third . . .

Sequence Markers by Sections

a problem	in summary	in short
another problem	finally	in conclusion

Additive Sequence Markers

and	in addition	furthermore
also	further	

Sequence Markers for Emphasis

indeed	certainly	in any event
above all	in fact	moreover
especially	most important	

Other Methods for Achieving Coherence

There are other ways of providing coherence. Some of the more common are

1. repeating words, or emphasizing a subject with repeated pronoun reference
2. using synonyms for *(brilliant = extraordinarily intelligent)* or different grammatical forms *(brilliant, brilliantly, brilliance)* of the same word
3. using a general categorizing word to encompass a number of specifics (The numbers of elephants, rhinoceroses, and tigers have plummeted in the past 20

years. Many environmental groups are attempting to protect these *endangered species*.)

There are other elements of coherence as well, but keep in mind that you will not necessarily find all of them working within a single paragraph.

Exercises

1. Let us look at how some of these elements work in the following paragraph:

Except for math, few (1) *subjects* create as much (2) *anxiety* for (3) *students* as does (4) *writing*. (5) *Many factors* combine to create this (6) *dread* of the (7) *discipline*, (8) *but* we will discuss only the (9) *most devastating*. (10) *First,* and most (11) *discouraging*, is that (12) *beginning writers,* including some of their instructors, believe that (13) *being able to write well is an inborn talent* when, in fact, it is a (14) *skill* that (15) *anybody,* especially (16) *college students,* has the tools to master. (17) *Next,* and perhaps every bit as debilitating, is the (18) *low self-esteem* many (19) *fledgling authors* have. This (20) *lack of positive self-image* creates self-conscious, lifeless (21) *writing* because (22) *insecure writers* overwhelm any idea (23) *they* may have with harsh self-criticism until they completely block any (24) *flow of words* onto the page. (25) *These factors,* which war against any impulse to (26) *write,* are the most difficult for (27) *would-be writers* to overcome (28) *because they* are rooted in (29) *concepts* that may be emphasized by the (30) *writing situation* but are not caused by (31) *it.*

On your paper, write down each number and italicized word or phrase. Identify the technique for coherence it illustrates by writing either *transitional word* or *transitional phrase, repeated word* or *pronoun* taking the place of a noun, *synonym,* or *categorizing word* next to it.

2. Underline and label all the elements of coherence you can find working in the following paragraphs.

Animals have allergies, but hypersensitivity to Homo sapiens is not thought to be among them. Allergies occur with the same frequency in the human and dog populations, afflicting about one creature out of six, and human beings and dogs are allergic to many of the same things, including pollen and dust. Unlike human beings, however, dogs rarely sneeze or get a runny nose (they do get itchy skin), and don't ever become allergic to one another.

From *The Atlantic Monthly,* September 1989, p. 16.

By 1952, the community of biologists was rapidly becoming aware that DNA was the essential hereditary substance. Most of this awareness was created by the many experiments of the preceding decade, culminating in the work of Hershey and Chase. But the first work on the nucleic acids dated back almost a century before this. Nucleic acids were discovered and first characterized by a German chemist, Friedrich Miescher (1844–1895). Miescher was interested in the chemical composition of cells obtained from discarded bandages; after he changed to a somwehat pleasanter source, salmon sperm. He found that he could obtain nuclei in a high degree of purity by treating cells with proteolytic enzymes—which fact by itself should make one doubt if nuclei are

predominantly protein. From these nuclei Miescher isolated, and characterized in chemical terms, what we now call the class of nucleic acids.*
From Garrett Hardin, *Biology: Its Human Implications*, p. 100.

The failure of Mr. Fit [a ten-year clinical trial designed to prove that coronary heart disease could be prevented] did not end the scientific drive to demonstrate that coronary heart disease could be prevented. From the start many researchers had believed that the long-sought evidence would emerge not from new behavior-modification efforts but from the classic medical intervention of drugs. However, three important requirements had to be met. First, it had to be shown to be possible to lower blood-cholesterol levels significantly for long enough to measure the benefits, something no one had done. Second, the cholesterol reductions, once achieved, had to be shown to reduce the incidence of coronary heart disease. The investigators were searching for a risk factor that could be modified, not just a more accurate method of identifying those most likely to die. Third, the treatment used to lower blool-cholesterol levels could not harm more people than it helped. The clearest and simplest proof of that would be showing that lowering blood-cholesterol levels prolongs life. Not only is a lower total mortality the main object but it is an important check against the possibility that intervention creates unanticipated health hazards—reducing heart attacks but causing other, unexpected problems. These were the challenges for the heart institute as its investigators drew up plans for its second large effort, known officially as the Coronary Primary Prevention Trial, or CPPT. It was launched at the same time as Mr. Fit but would take longer to complete.
From *the Atlantic Monthly*, September 1989, p. 48.

Editing Your Own Essays: Paragraph Coherence

Look through your expository essays. At random or according to your instructor's comments, pick a paragraph from each essay and identify, by underlining and labeling, all the coherence strategies you used. If necessary, revise these paragraph according to what you have learned in this section.

---

*Did you notice that you do not have to understand all the information in this paragraph to be able to pick out some of the coherence strategies this author used?

III Mechanics: Common Concerns

III.1 CAPITALS AND PERIODS

You all know the most common uses of capital letters and periods: they mark the beginning and end of a sentence. To illustrate, here are a couple of extreme examples.

> The dog bit the mailman.
> We the people of the United States, in order to form a more perfect union, establish justice, insure domestic tranquility, provide for the common defense, promote the general welfare, and secure the blessings of liberty to ourselves and our posterity, do ordain and establish this Constitution of the United States of America.

Both of the above are complete sentences. Both begin with a capital letter and end with a period. (Note the parallel structure in the Preamble to the Constitution.)

However, capital letters and periods have many more uses. We will review capital letters first.

Capitalization

Here are the remaining basic rules for using capital letters.

1. Capitalize the pronoun *I*.

When I am under stress, I can't eat.

2. Capitalize the first word and all the important words in titles.[*]

The Brothers Karamazov

The Rise and Fall of the Third Reich

Rain Man

3. Capitalize all proper names.

Frank Campanella and Alice Jackson were the top students in the class.

Winnipeg is the capital of Manitoba.

The Navajo reservation is in three different states, Utah, New Mexico, and Arizona.

4. Capitalize a person's title when it precedes the name.

I had to wait 45 minutes to see Dr. Gonzales.

---

*Note that the titles of full-length works are also italicized.

5. Capitalize the title of the head of the nation but not other titles unless used with the person's name.

The President held a news conference.

The Premier returned home to deal with the emergency.

6. Capitalize terms that refer to family members when they are being used in place of the person's name but not when you put *my, your, his, her, our,* or *their* (personal pronouns) before them.

For their anniversary Father gave Mother a rosebud. (It's the same idea as if you had used their proper names: For their anniversary David gave Martha a rosebud.)

but

For their anniversary *my* father gave *my* mother a rosebud.

7. Capitalize the names of specific courses, but not of areas of study (except languages.)

Psychology 101

History 210

but

I am taking history, psychology, biology, and French.

Editing Your Own Essays: Capitalization

Review the essays you have written so far. If your teacher has marked any capitalization errors, copy the sentence with the error on a clean sheet of paper and correct it.

Periods

Here are two more basic rules for using periods.

1. Use periods after abbreviations.*

Mr. Garcia

Ms. Young

Dr. Yang

2. Use periods with expressions of time.

a.m.

p.m.

Editing Your Own Essays: Periods

Review your essays. If your teacher has marked any errors with periods, copy the sentence on a clean sheet of paper and correct the error.

*For the most part, in formal writing like college assignments you should avoid abbreviations and spell out the entire name instead (e.g., Birmingham, Alabama, not Birmingham, Ala.).

III.2   APOSTROPHES

Apostrophes have two completely different uses.

1. They are used to show where the letter has been omitted in a contraction.

do not

don't

cannot

can't

In formal writing like college assignments, you should avoid using contractions and write out the entire words instead, so this use of apostrophes should not be much of a problem.

2. They are used to show possession, that someone or something owns something else. This is the use of apostrophes that causes most trouble for college writers.

Here are three rules for where to put the apostrophe.

1. When the name of the owner does not end in *-s*, add *-'s*.

Bob	Bob's
father	father's
children	children's
someone	someone's

2. When the noun is singular but ends in *-s*, add *-'s*.

Jess's sister is 32 years old.

3. When the noun is plural and ends in *-s*, add an apostrophe only.

The teachers' strike lasted five weeks.

Many people think doctors' rates are too high.

Exercise

Write the possessive form (add an *-'s*) in the blank on the right.

Examples

The car belongs to Bob.	=	Bob's car
The decision made by the judge	=	The judge's decision
George has a problem	=	George's problem
1. The shirt belongs to Marge.	=	_____ shirt.
2. Mr. Munoz asked a question.	=	_____ question.
3. Our coach gave us helpful instructions.	=	_____ instructions.
4. His father had a car.	=	His _____ car.
5. My mother has a cold.	=	My _____ cold is better.

6. The baby has a new toy.   =   The _____ toy is broken.
7. The pictures were painted by Picasso.   =   _____ pictures are valuable.
8. These picture books are for children.   =   They are _____ books.
9. The tailback made the extra effort.   =   The _____ effort won the game.
10. Jason has a car.   =   _____ car needs new tires.

Editing Your Own Essays: Apostrophes

Review the essays you have written so far. If your teacher has marked any errors with apostrophes, copy over the sentence on a clean sheet of paper and correct the error.

III.3   SPELLING

We will mention only the most common spelling errors that cannot be corrected with a computer spell check.

To, Too, and Two

Though the words *to, too,* and *two* sound alike, they have distinctly different meanings.

> **to:** toward
>> My father claims he walked ten miles **to** school.
> **too:** more than enough, also
>> My shoes are **too** small.
>> My brother was **too** tall for submarine duty.
>> I want some ice cream, **too.**
> **two:** 2
>> It took me about **two** minutes to get into deep trouble.

Its and It's

The word *its* is a possessive.

The dog licked **its** leg.*

The word *it's* is a contraction for *it is*. This *it's* follows the contraction rule—the apostrophe marks the omitted letter.

It's nearly midnight.

As noted above, you should avoid contractions in college writing. That means you should always write out *it is,* and the only *its* you should use is the possessive—the one without the apostrophe.

---

*This *its* is a possessive pronoun just like *his* or *her*. Note the similarity: "My dog Daisy licked **her** leg."

GLOSSARY

A

Abstract
A very brief summary of an article or essay.

Action verb
A word that indicates movement or process and can indicate tense.

Adjective
A word that describes or modifies a noun.

Adverb
A word that describes or modifies a verb, an adjective, or another adverb.

Agreement
See Pronoun agreement and Subject–verb agreement

Analogy
An explanation of an unfamiliar object or idea by comparing it to a more familiar one.

Analysis
Narrowly, an identification of the parts of a whole in order to explain how they contribute to the function of the whole. *More broadly,* applying explanatory strategies to a specific problem.

Anecdote
A very short true story told to illustrate a point.

Antecedent
The noun to which a pronoun refers.

C

Classification
A systematic grouping of items into categories.

Clustering
A prewriting technique in which writers use a visual scheme to group related ideas.

Coherence
In essay writing, the logical integration of ideas from sentence to sentence and paragraph to paragraph.

Comma splice
The incorrect connection of two or more main clauses with a comma.

Complement
A noun or adjective following a verb that renames or modifies the subject.

Complex sentence
A sentence consisting of a main clause and one or more subordinate or relative clauses.

Conflict
In a narrative, the struggle between two or more opposing forces.

Conjunction
A word used to connect or combine other words, phrases, and clauses.

Context
The background or environment in which particular ideas can be understood.

Coordinating conjunction
A connecting word (*and, but, or, . . .*) that shows equal weight among the connected ideas.

D

Demonstrative pronoun
A pronoun (*this, that, these, those*) that is used as an adjective to point out something.

Denotative meaning
   The explicit meaning of a word, as opposed to its implied meaning.

Development
   In essay writing, the gathering and elaboration of evidence to support an opinion or generalization.

Diction
   Word choice.

Direct quotation
   The reproduction of a speaker's or writer's exact words put in quotation marks.

Document
   As a verb, to provide references to source material.

Draft
   As a verb, to write a preliminary version of an essay. *As a noun*, a preliminary version of an essay.

E

Evidence
   Information that supports an opinion or point of view.

Expository writing
   Writing that explains, informs, or analyzes.

F

Focus
   In essay writing, as a verb, the process of narrowing a topic. *As a noun*, the specific topic.

Fragment
   A group of words punctuated as a sentence that lacks a subject or verb (or both).

Freewriting
   Writing without regard to the formal conventions of writing to generate ideas.

Fused sentence
   Two or more clauses combined without conjunctions or punctuation.

G

Genre
A kind or type of writing.

H

Helping verb
A word combined with the main verb to indicate tense or mode in a verb phrase.

Hierarchical structure
The ranking of importance among ideas.

I

Indirect quotation
Approximate reproduction of a speaker's or writer's words not enclosed by quotation marks.

Infinitive
The base form of a verb, usually preceded by *to*.

-ing phrase
A phrase that begins with an *-ing* form of the verb and acts as an adjective or noun.

Irregular verb
A verb that forms the past tense in some way other than adding *-d* or *-ed*.

L

List of References
The American Psychological Association's term for a bibliography.

List of Works Cited
The Modern Language Association's term for a bibliography.

M

Main clause
A group of words with a subject and verb that can stand on its own as a sentence.

Main verb
In a verb phrase, the verb that carries the meaning (central action, process, or condition).

Misplaced modifier
A sentence error in which a modifier describes the wrong word.

Modifier
A word or group of words that describes or qualifies another word or group of words.

N

Narrative
A story or account.

Noun
The name of a person, place, thing, or idea.

O

Object
A noun following the verb and receiving its action.

P

Parallel structure
A structure in which ideas of equal weight are conveyed by the same grammatical form.

Paraphrase
A restatement of another's ideas in one's own words.

Past tense
The verb form indicating that the action happened in the past.

Periodical
A publication appearing at regular intervals.

Periodical index
A listing of articles that have appeared in periodicals.

Personal pronouns
A pronoun that stands for a person or persons (*I, me, we, us, you, he, she, it, him, her, they, them*).

Phrase
 A group of words lacking either a subject or verb and acting as a single part of speech—adjective, adverb, noun, or verb.

Point
 A statement of position, opinion, point of view, or essential idea.

Popular periodical
 A periodical intended for a general audience.

Preposition
 A word that introduces a modifying phrase.

Prepositional phrase
 A phrase that begins with a preposition, ends with a noun or pronoun, and acts as an adjective or adverb in a sentence.

Present tense
 A verb form indicating that the action is happening in the present.

Professional periodical
 A periodical intended for members of a particular profession.

Pronoun
 A word that is used in place of a noun.

Pronoun agreement
 The correspondence in number, person, and gender of a pronoun with its antecedent.

R

Regular verb
 A verb that forms its past tense by adding *-d* or *-ed*.

Relative clause
 (A clause that acts as an adjective and begins with one of these pronouns: *who, whose, whom, which, that.*

Relative pronoun
 One of the pronouns (*who, whose, whom, which, that*) that introduce an adjectival clause.

S

Scholarly periodical
A periodical intended for scholars in a particular academic field.

Sentence coherence
The logical relation of ideas within a sentence.

Series
A list of three or more items in a sentence.

Setting
In a narrative, the place where the events occur.

Standard English
A dialect of English generally accepted as approporate for use in education, business, government, the media, and other public spheres.

Subject
The person or thing that performs the action of the verb.

Subject pronoun
A pronoun that can serve as the subject of a verb (*I, we, you, he, she, it, they*)

Subject-verb agreement
The correspondence in number between a present tense verb and its subject.

Subordinate clause
A clause that is introduced by a subordinating conjunction and that acts as an adverb.

Subordinate conjunction
A word such as *because, although, when, since,* and *if* that introduces an adverbial clause.

Subpoint
A subordinate point supporting the main point of an essay.

T

Tense
The time a verb expresses: past (*looked*), present (*look*), future (*will look*).

Thesis
   See Point.

Topic sentence
   A sentence that introduces the topic and central idea of a paragraph (*see* Subpoint).

Turning point
   In a narrative, the pivotal point or climax of the action or conflict.

U

Unity
   In essays, the relevance of all of the parts to the same central topic and point.

V

Verb
   A word that names a mental or physical action or states a condition.

Verb phrase
   A verb consisting of more than one word.

Credits

Index